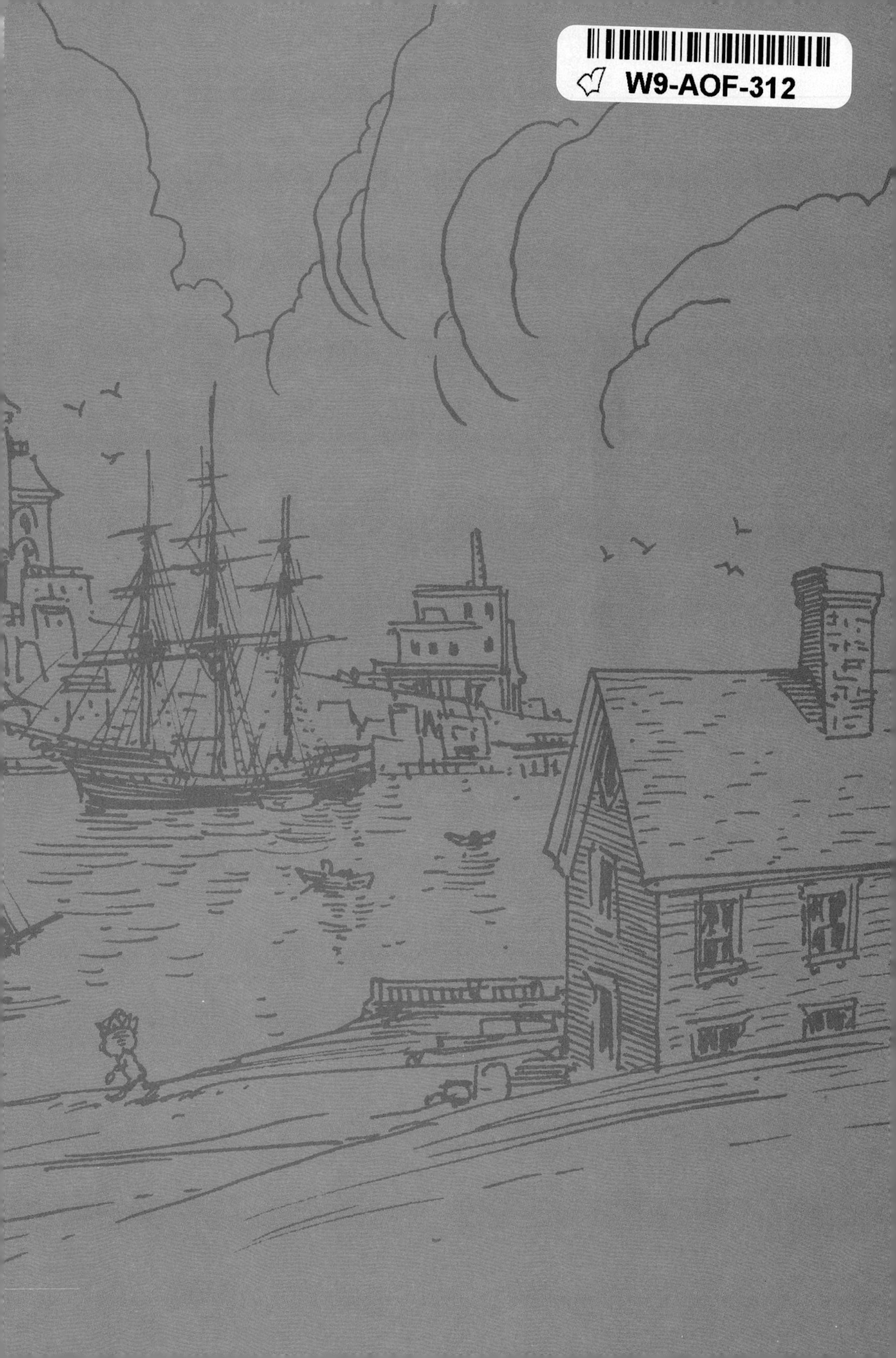

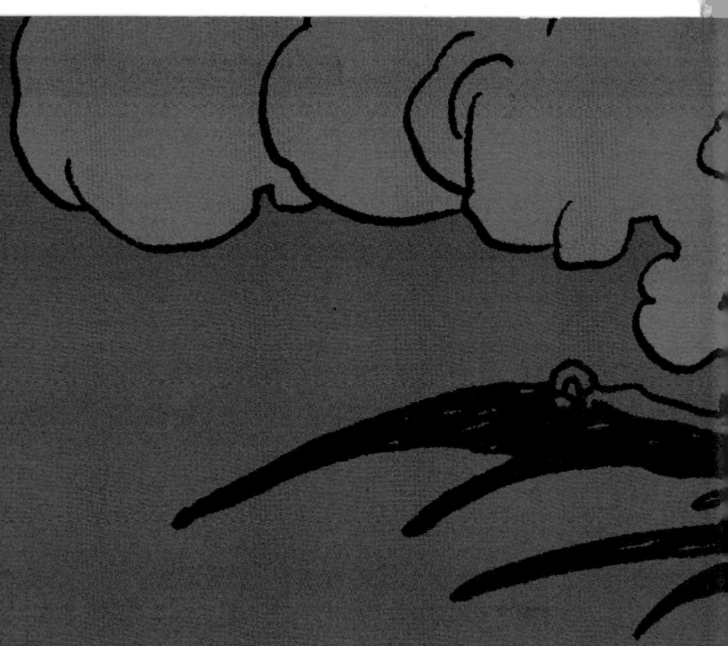

FANTAGRAPHICS BOOKS
7563 Lake City Way
Seattle, WA 98115

Editorial Liaison:
GARY GROTH

Book Design:
JACOB COVEY

Promotion:
ERIC REYNOLDS

Published:
GARY GROTH &
KIM THOMPSON

 For a free full-color catalogue of comics and cartooning, including more books by MR. MILLIONAIRE, call 1-800-657-1100. Our many books may be viewed and also purchased on our worldwide web site at www.fantagraphics.com.

First Fantagraphics Books edition: February 2006.

ISBN 1-56097-701-9

Printed in Singapore

Go soon to www.tonymillionaire.com.

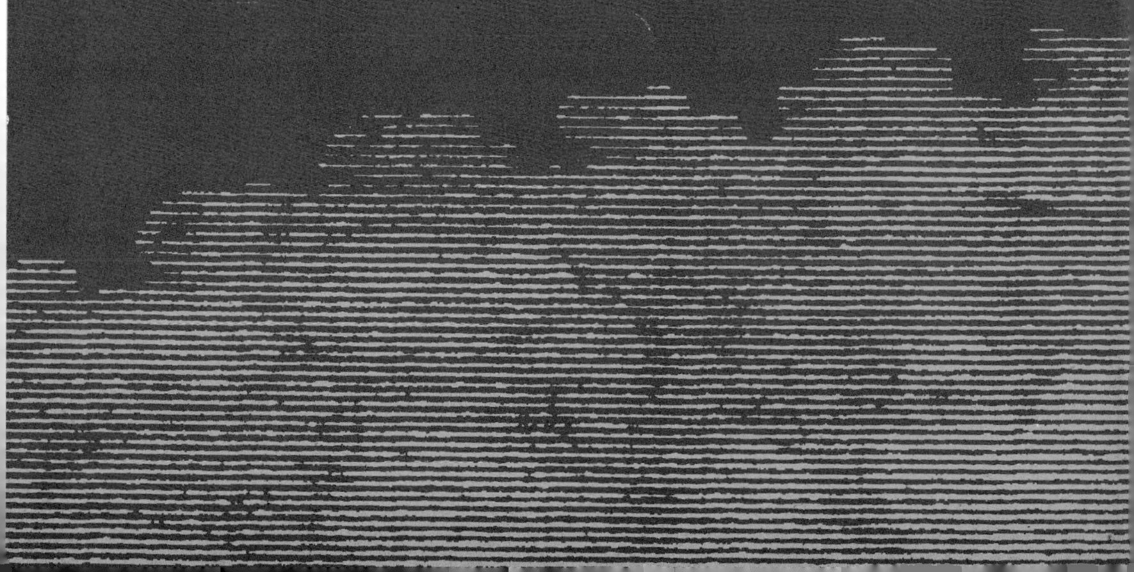

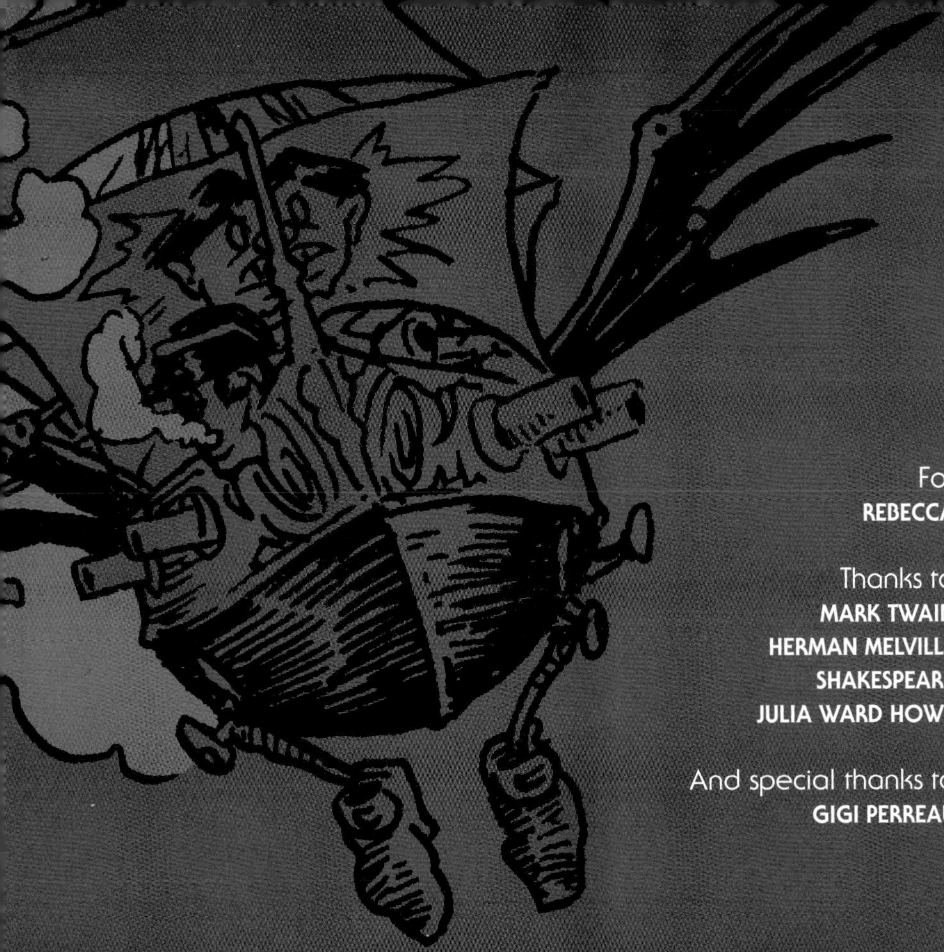

For
REBECCA

Thanks to
MARK TWAIN
HERMAN MELVILLE
SHAKESPEARE
JULIA WARD HOWE

And special thanks to
GIGI PERREAU

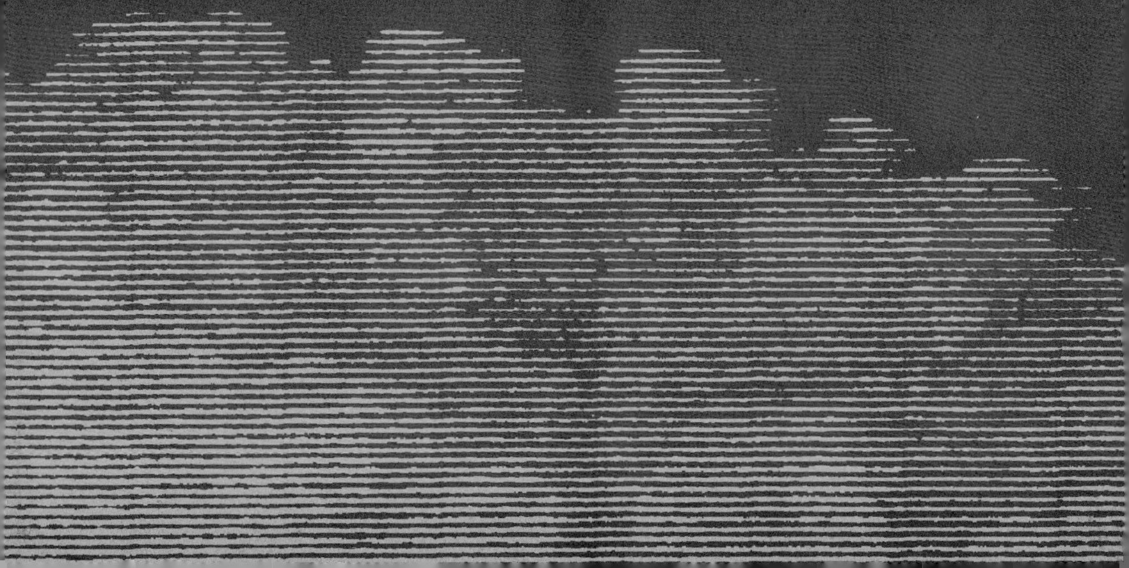

◖ Chapter One ◗

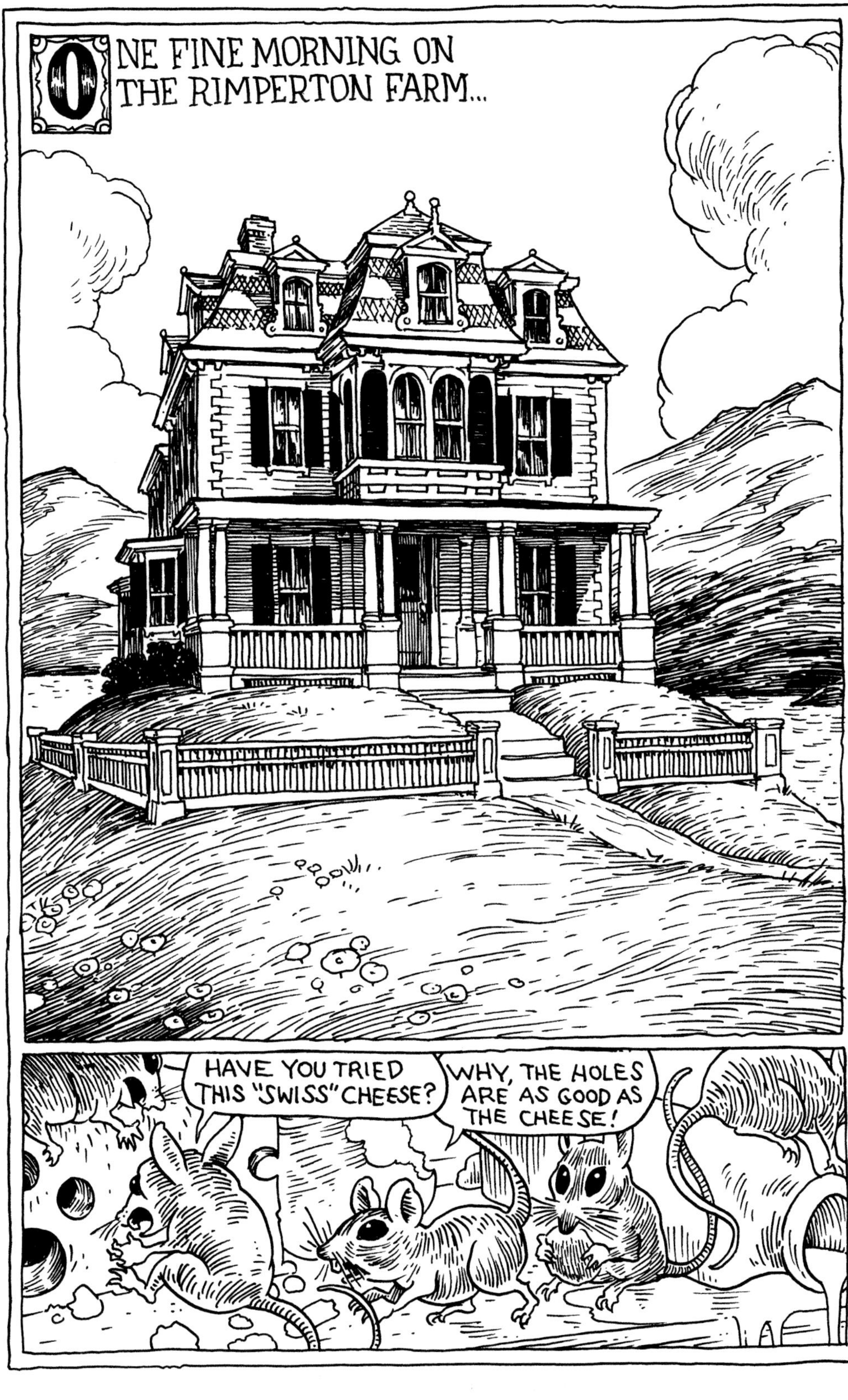
ONE FINE MORNING ON THE RIMPERTON FARM...
HAVE YOU TRIED THIS "SWISS" CHEESE?
WHY, THE HOLES ARE AS GOOD AS THE CHEESE!

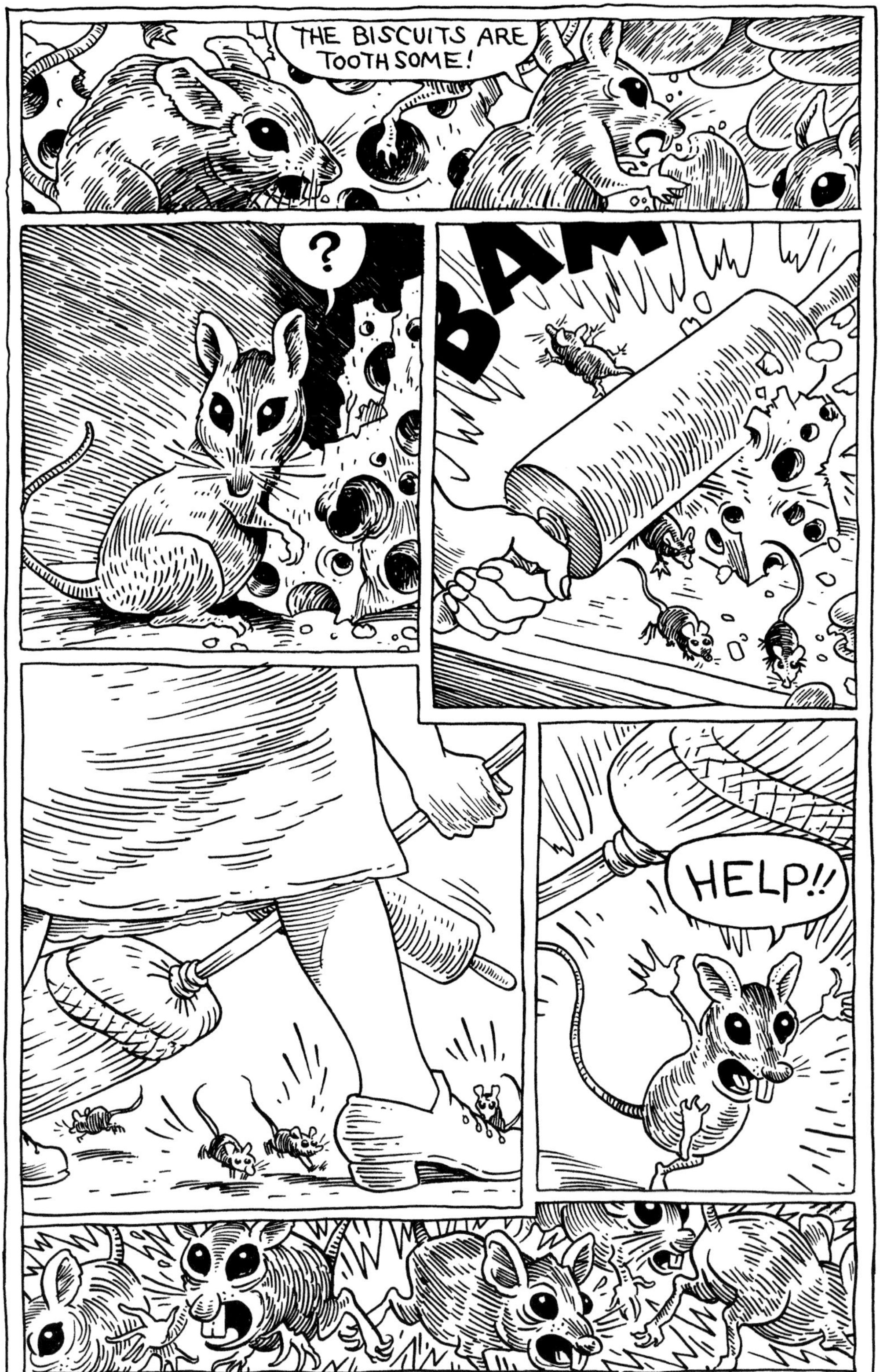
THE BISCUITS ARE TOOTHSOME!
?
BAM
HELP!!

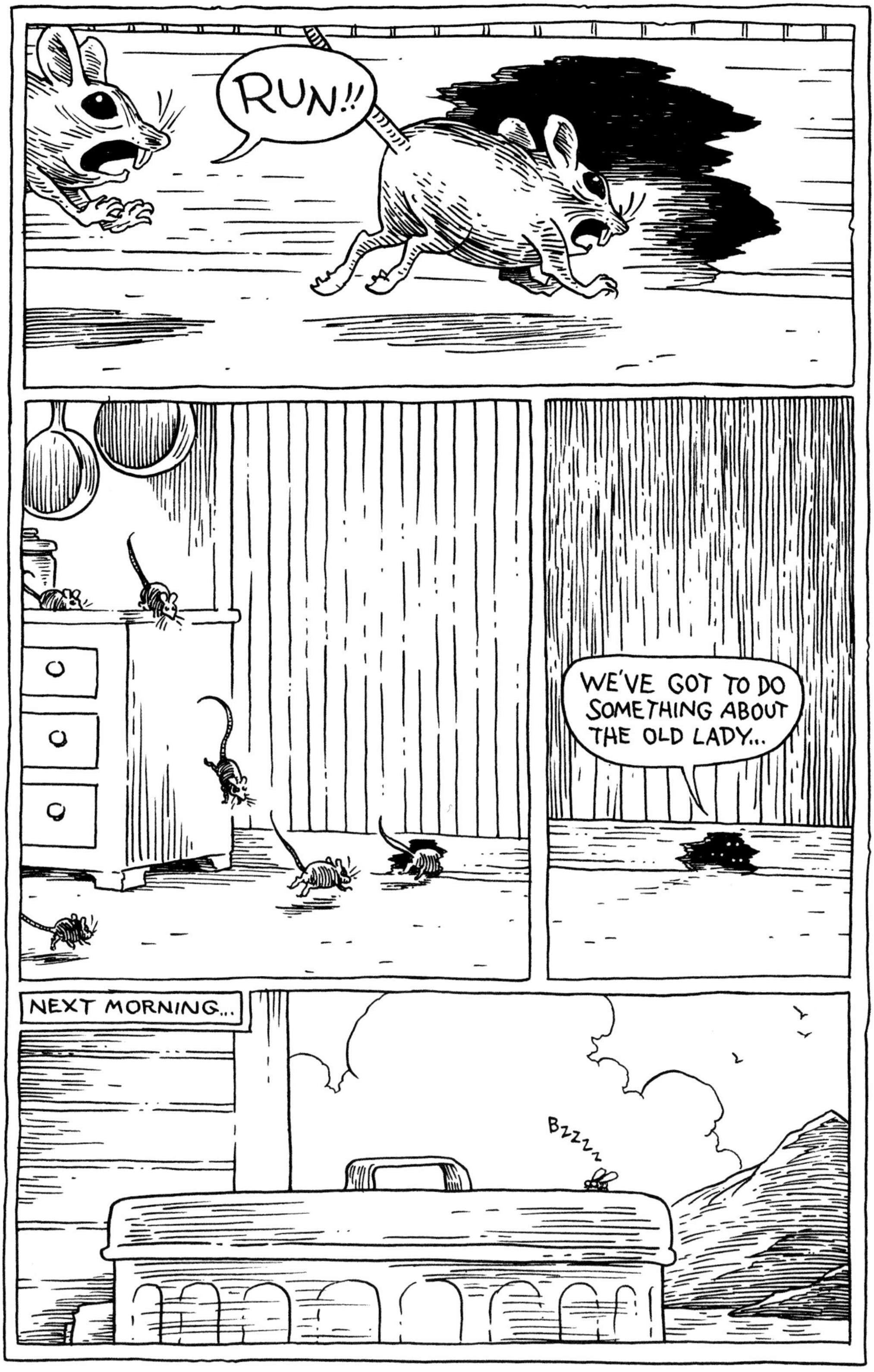
RUN!!
WE'VE GOT TO DO SOMETHING ABOUT THE OLD LADY...
NEXT MORNING...
BZZZZZ

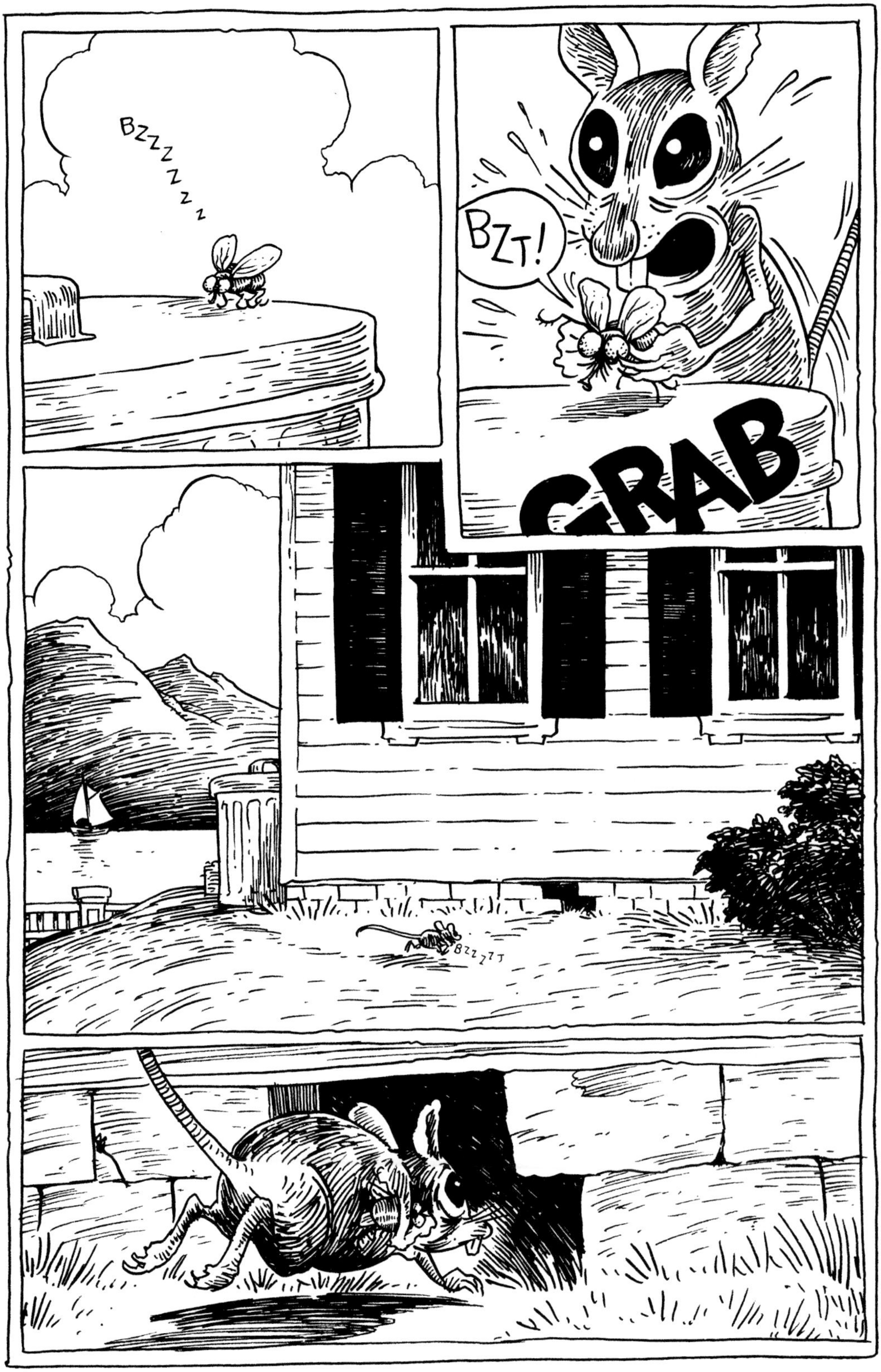
BZZZZZZZ
BZT!
GRAB
BZZZZT

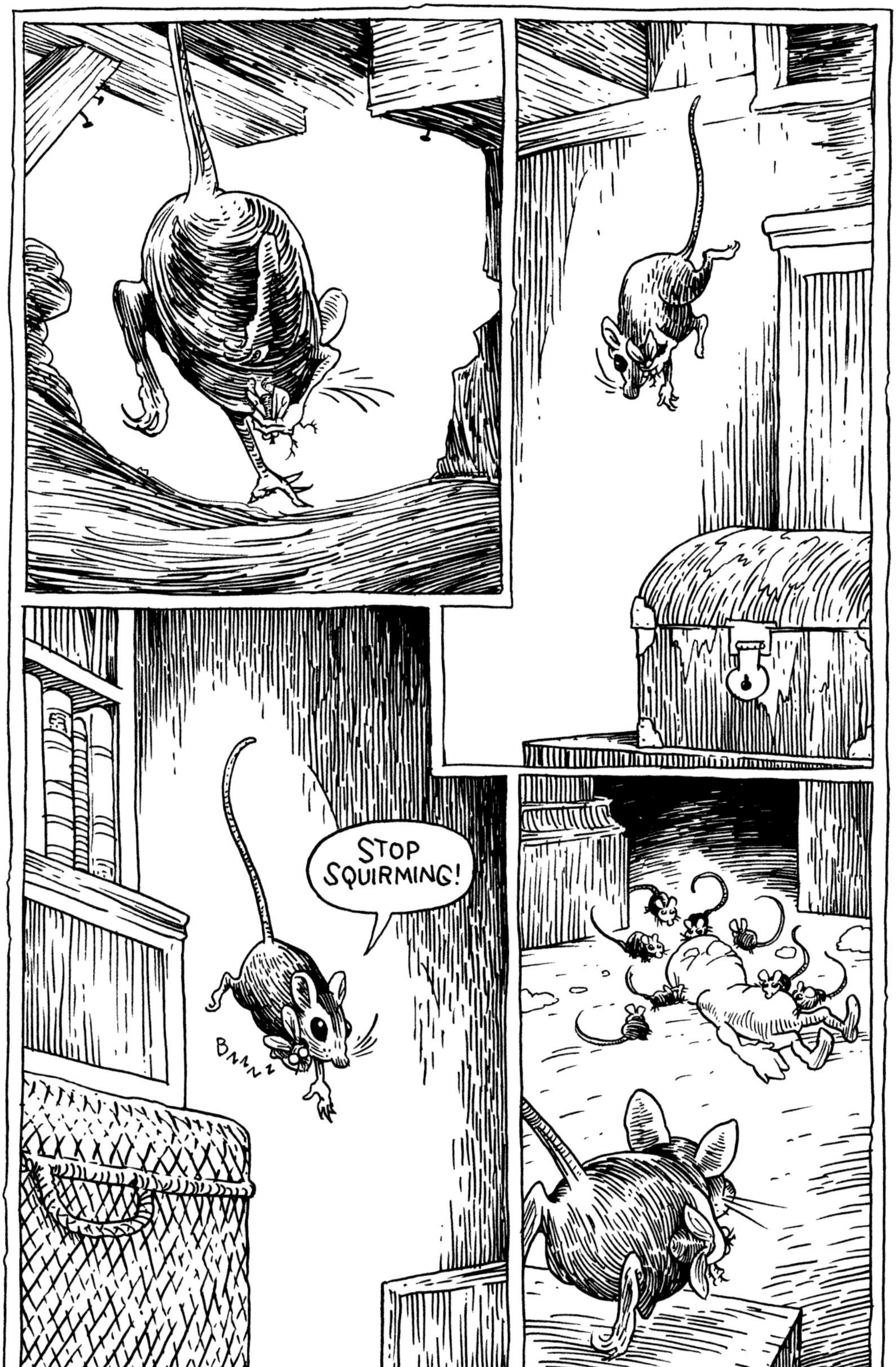
STOP SQUIRMING!
BNNNZ

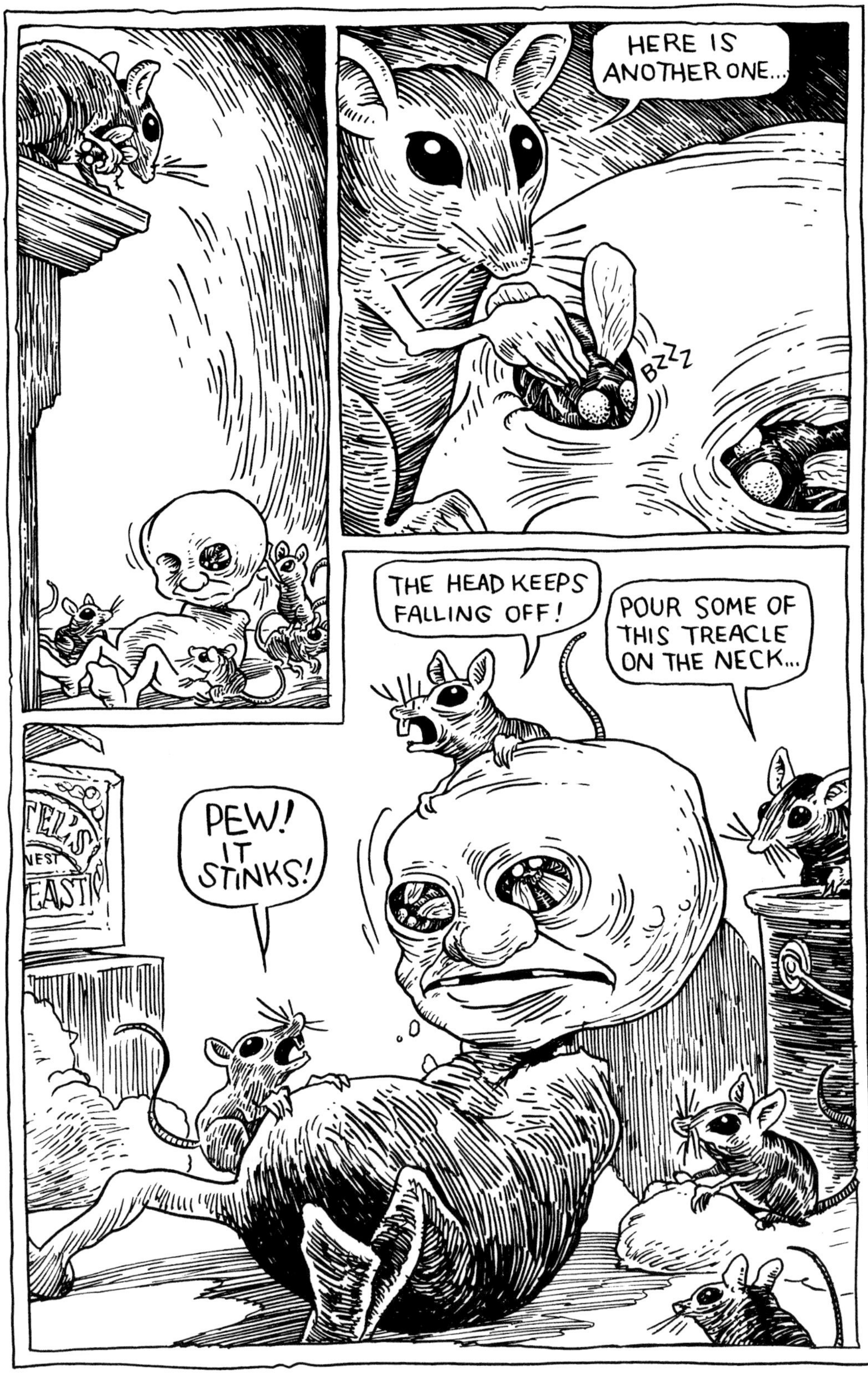
HERE IS ANOTHER ONE...
BZZZ
THE HEAD KEEPS FALLING OFF!
POUR SOME OF THIS TREACLE ON THE NECK...
PEW! IT STINKS!

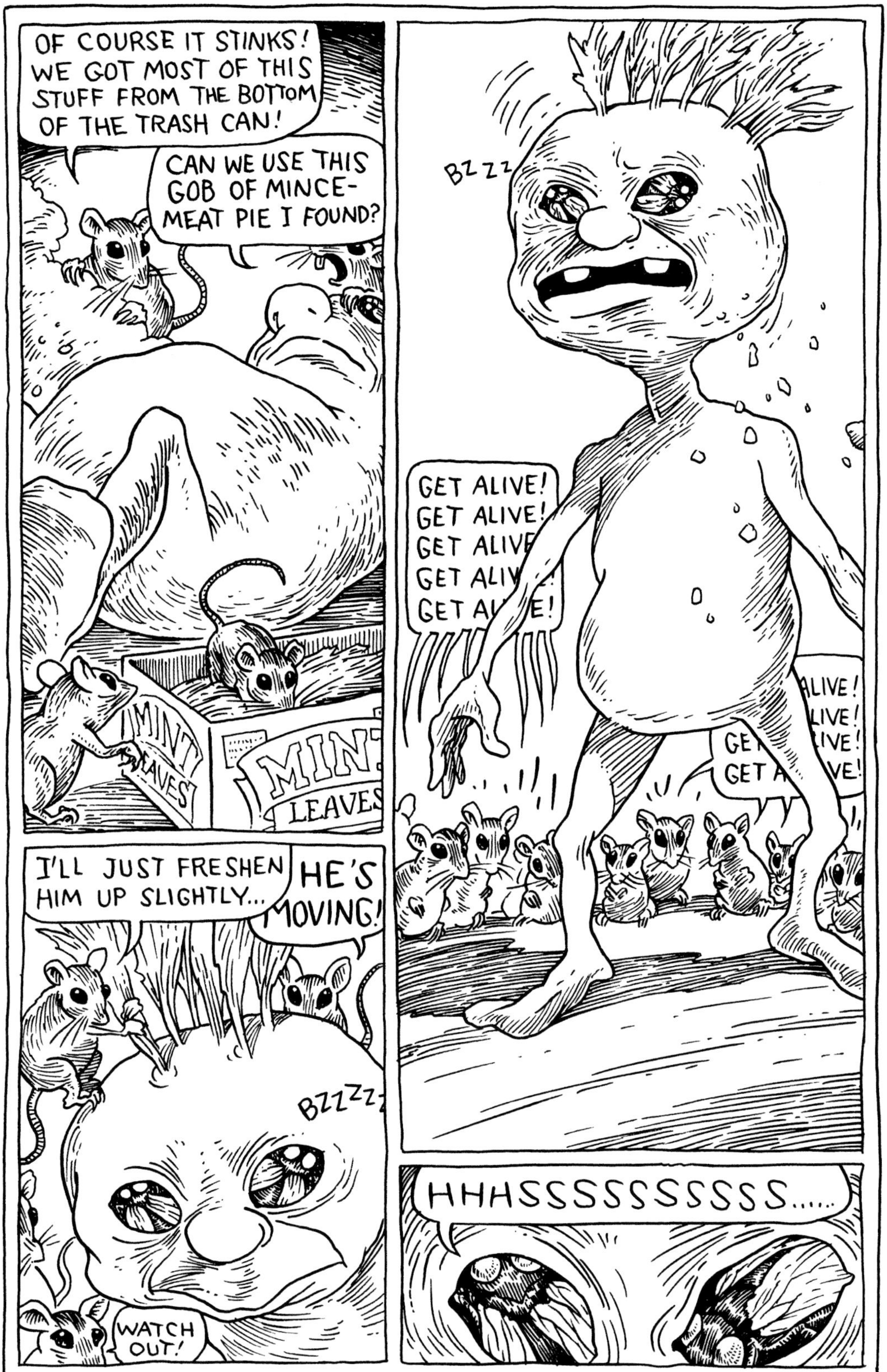
OF COURSE IT STINKS! WE GOT MOST OF THIS STUFF FROM THE BOTTOM OF THE TRASH CAN!
CAN WE USE THIS GOB OF MINCE-MEAT PIE I FOUND?
MINT LEAVES
MINT LEAVES
I'LL JUST FRESHEN HIM UP SLIGHTLY...
HE'S MOVING!
BZZZZZ
WATCH OUT!
BZZZ
GET ALIVE! GET ALIVE! GET ALIVE! GET ALIVE! GET ALIVE!
HHHSSSSSSSSSS.....

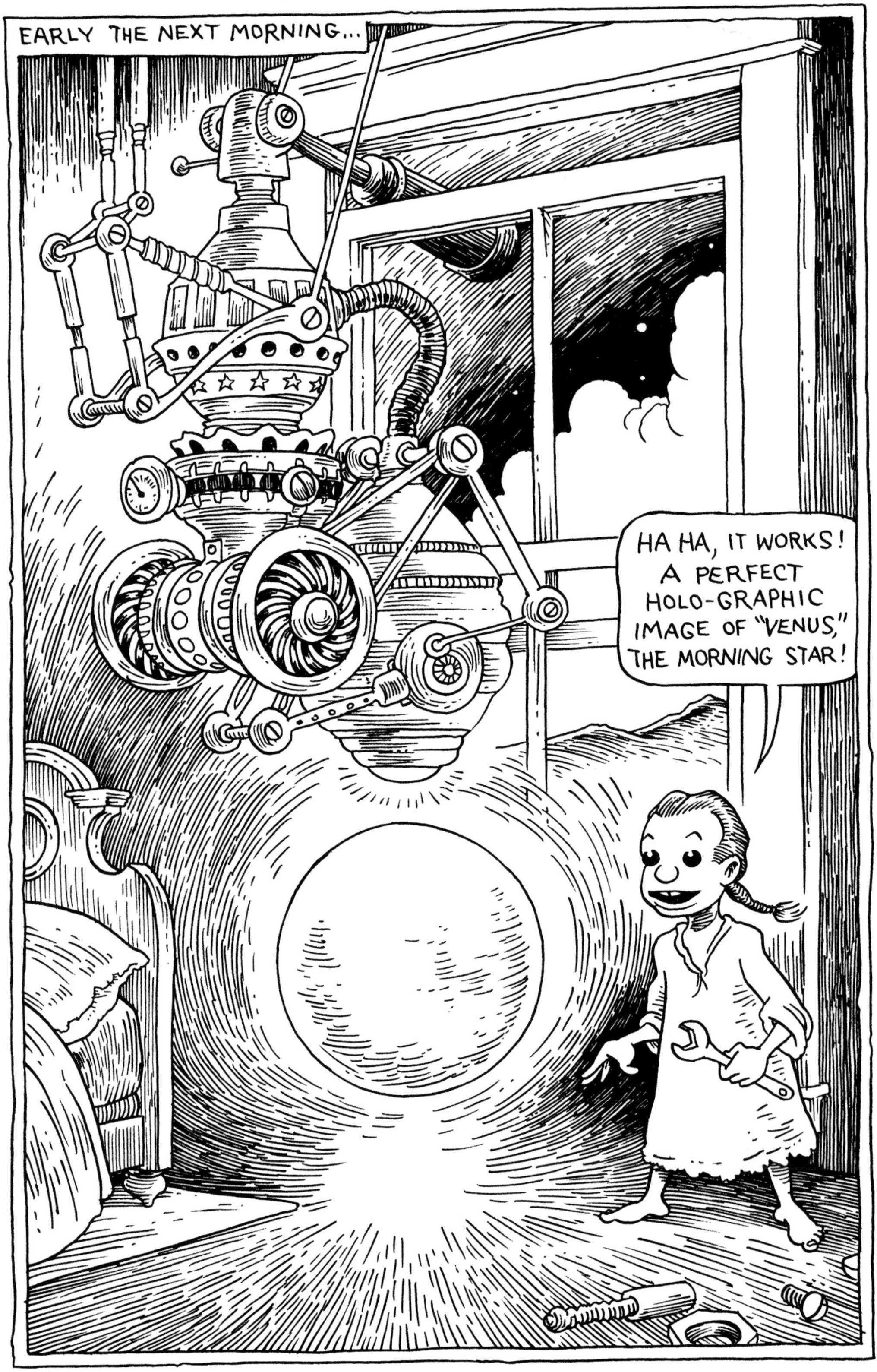
EARLY THE NEXT MORNING...
HA HA, IT WORKS! A PERFECT HOLO-GRAPHIC IMAGE OF "VENUS," THE MORNING STAR!

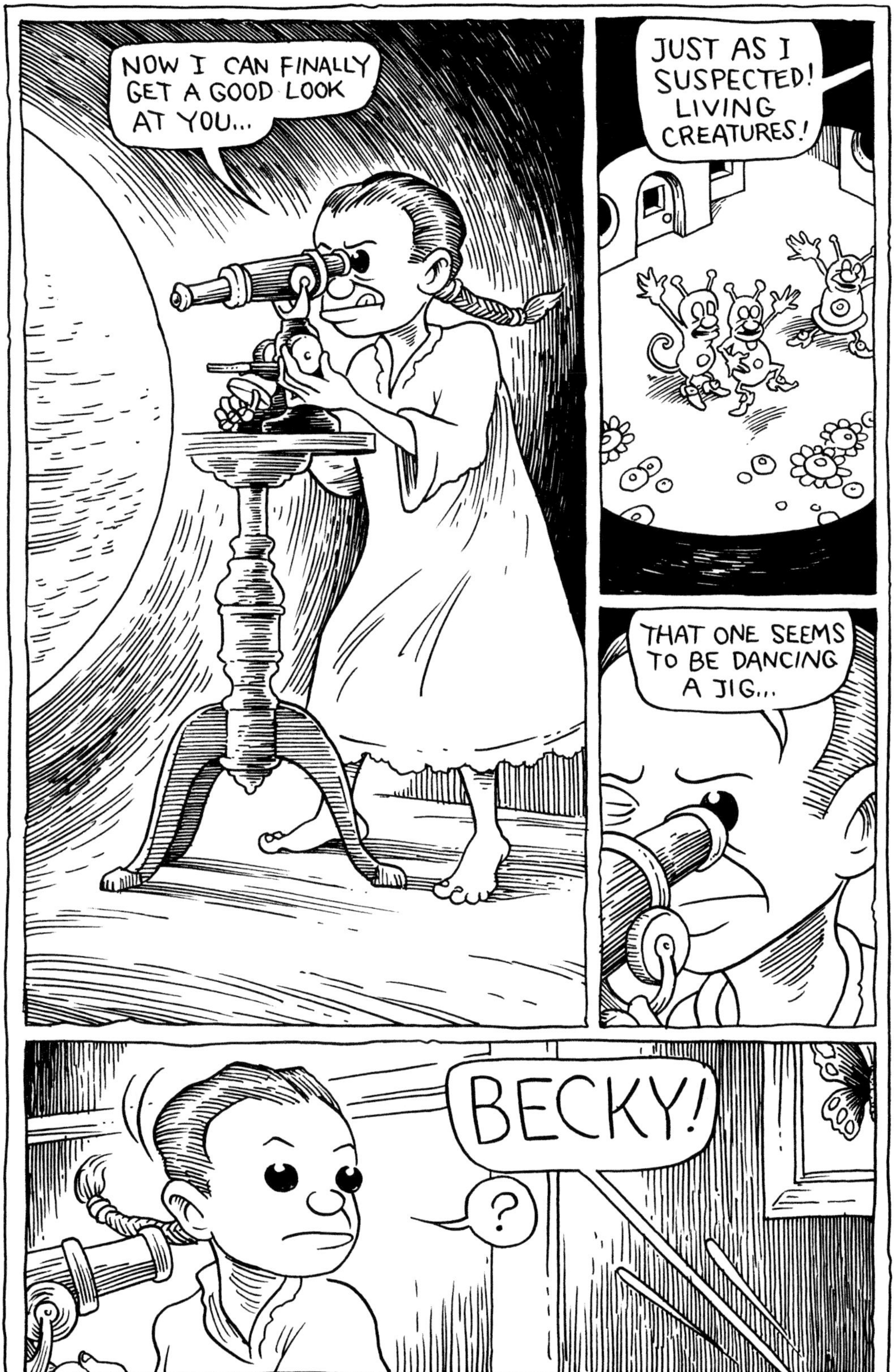
NOW I CAN FINALLY GET A GOOD LOOK AT YOU...
JUST AS I SUSPECTED! LIVING CREATURES!
THAT ONE SEEMS TO BE DANCING A JIG...
BECKY!
?

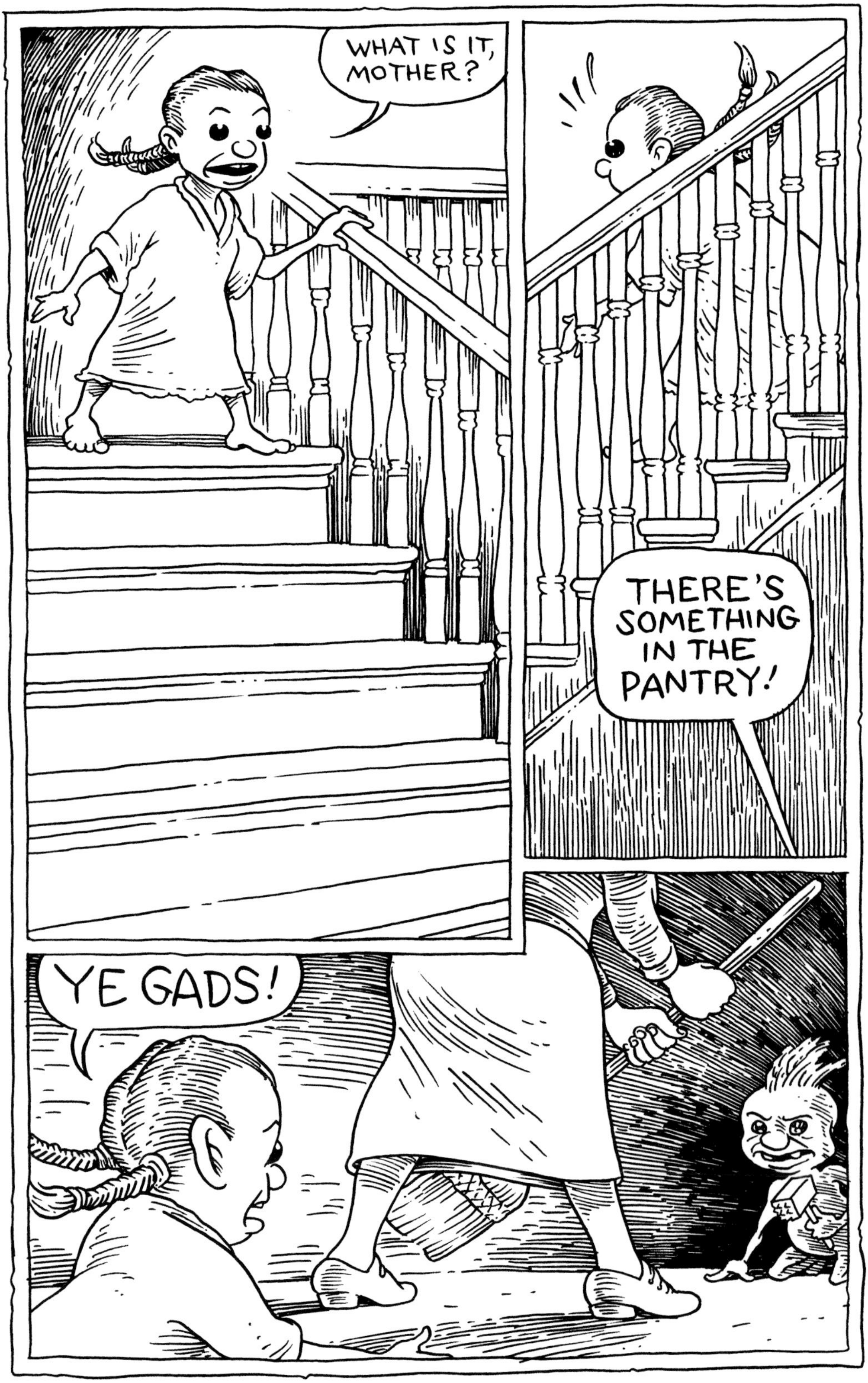
WHAT IS IT, MOTHER?
THERE'S SOMETHING IN THE PANTRY!
YE GADS!

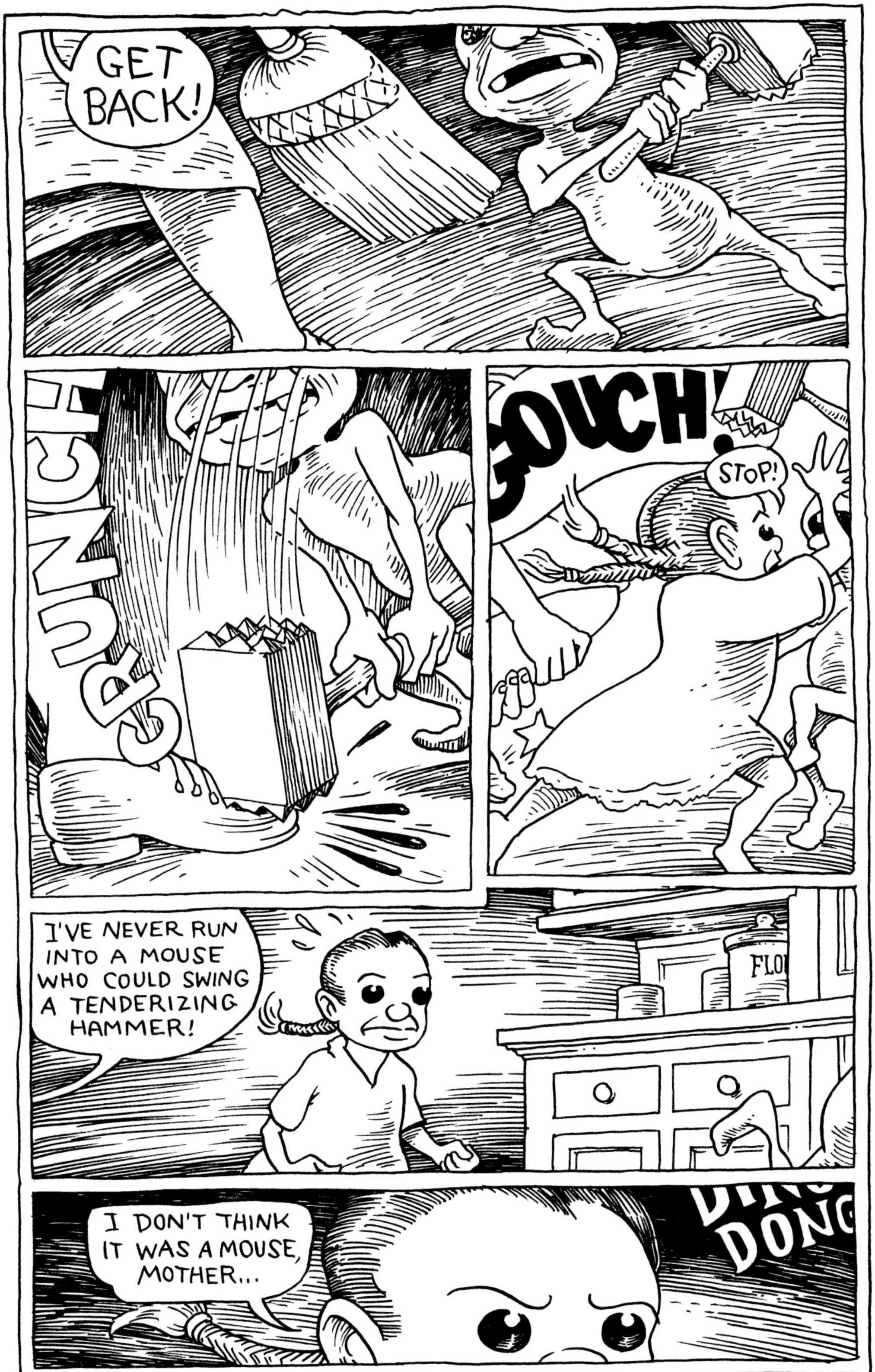
GET BACK!
CRUNCH
OUCH!
STOP!
I'VE NEVER RUN INTO A MOUSE WHO COULD SWING A TENDERIZING HAMMER!
I DON'T THINK IT WAS A MOUSE, MOTHER...
DONG

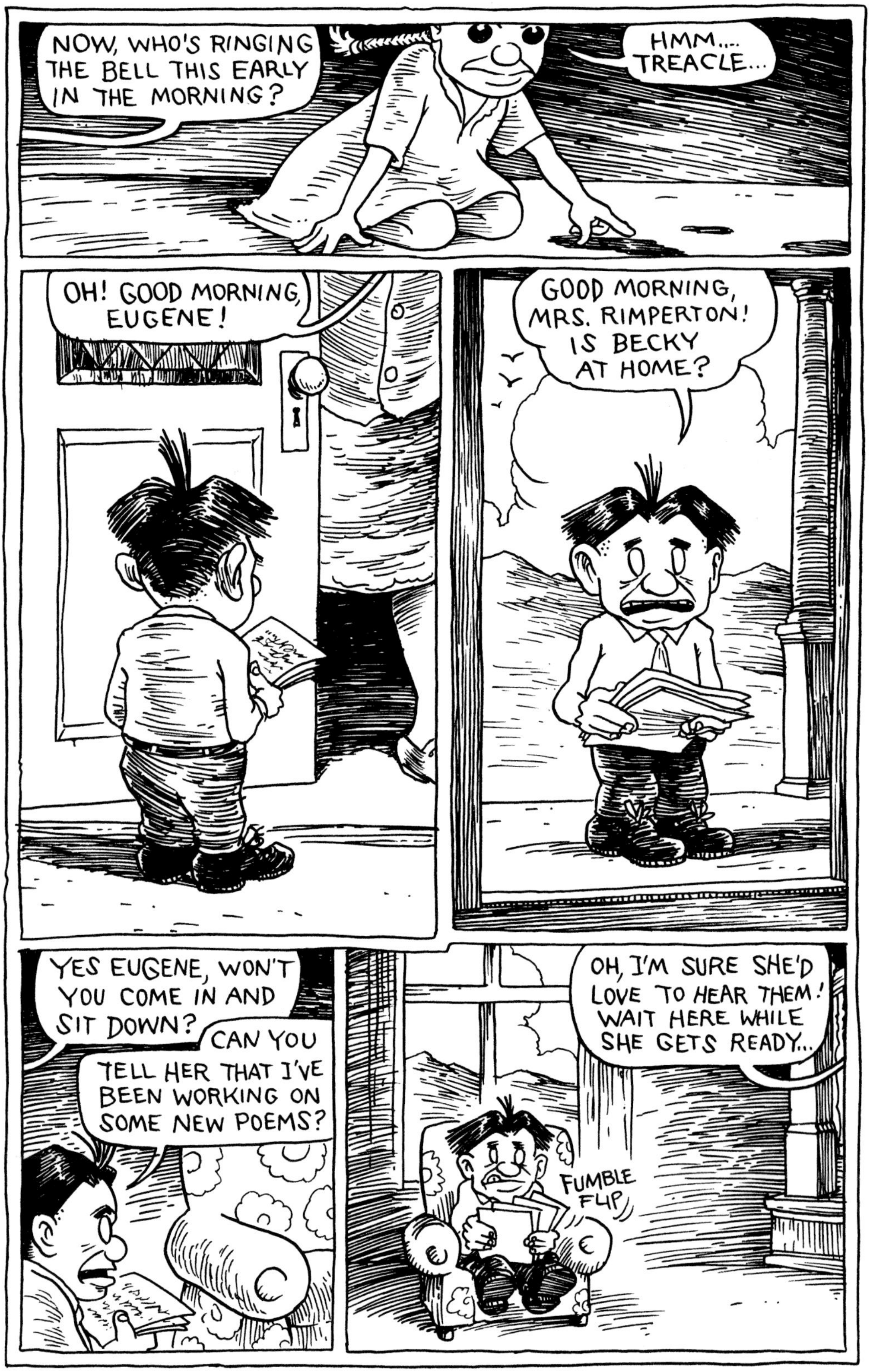
NOW, WHO'S RINGING THE BELL THIS EARLY IN THE MORNING?
HMM.... TREACLE...
OH! GOOD MORNING, EUGENE!
GOOD MORNING, MRS. RIMPERTON! IS BECKY AT HOME?
YES EUGENE, WON'T YOU COME IN AND SIT DOWN?
CAN YOU TELL HER THAT I'VE BEEN WORKING ON SOME NEW POEMS?
OH, I'M SURE SHE'D LOVE TO HEAR THEM! WAIT HERE WHILE SHE GETS READY...
FUMBLE FLIP

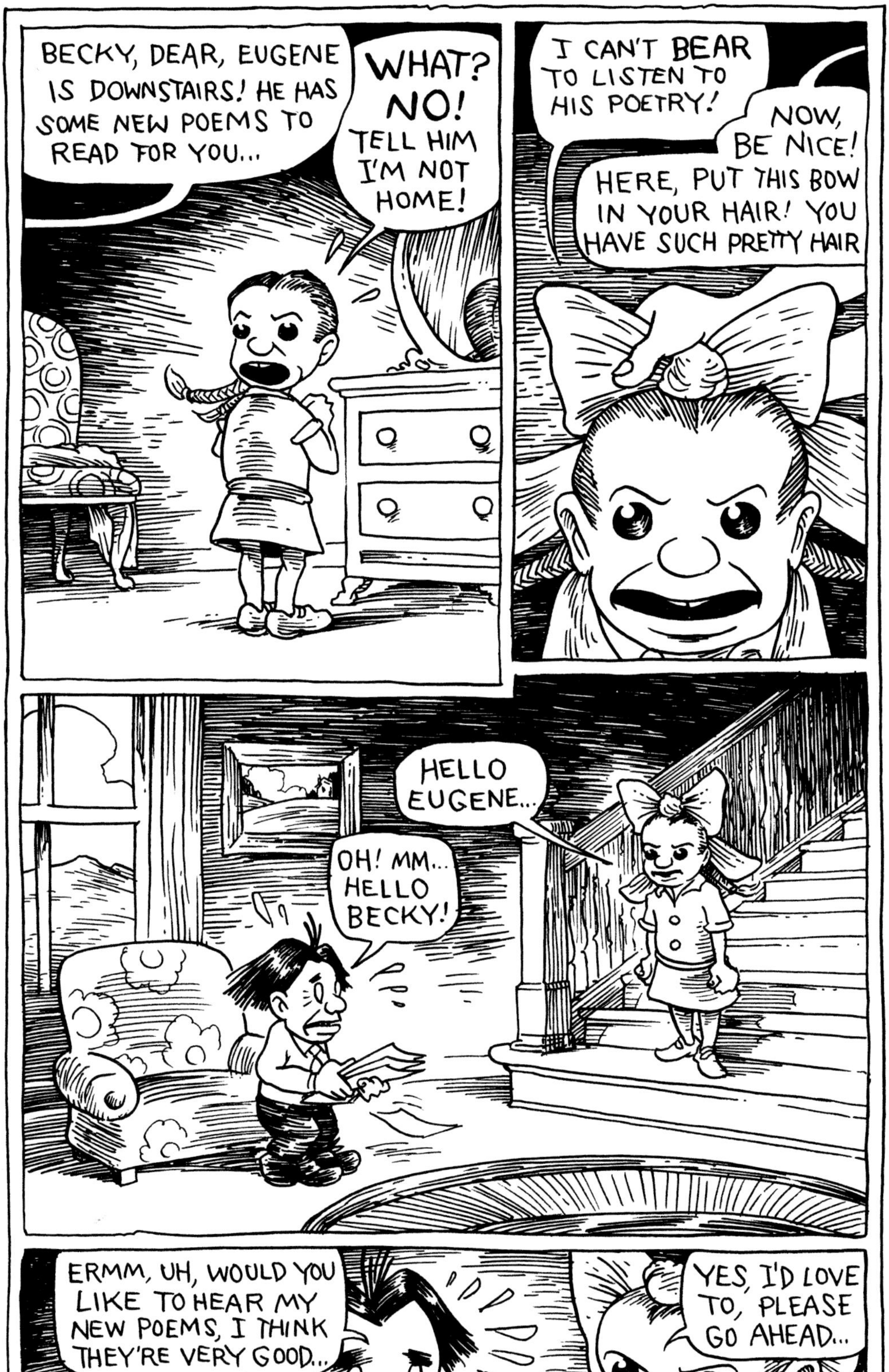

BECKY, DEAR, EUGENE IS DOWNSTAIRS! HE HAS SOME NEW POEMS TO READ FOR YOU...
WHAT? NO! TELL HIM I'M NOT HOME!
I CAN'T BEAR TO LISTEN TO HIS POETRY!
NOW, BE NICE! HERE, PUT THIS BOW IN YOUR HAIR! YOU HAVE SUCH PRETTY HAIR
HELLO EUGENE...
OH! MM... HELLO BECKY!
ERMM, UH, WOULD YOU LIKE TO HEAR MY NEW POEMS, I THINK THEY'RE VERY GOOD...
YES, I'D LOVE TO, PLEASE GO AHEAD...

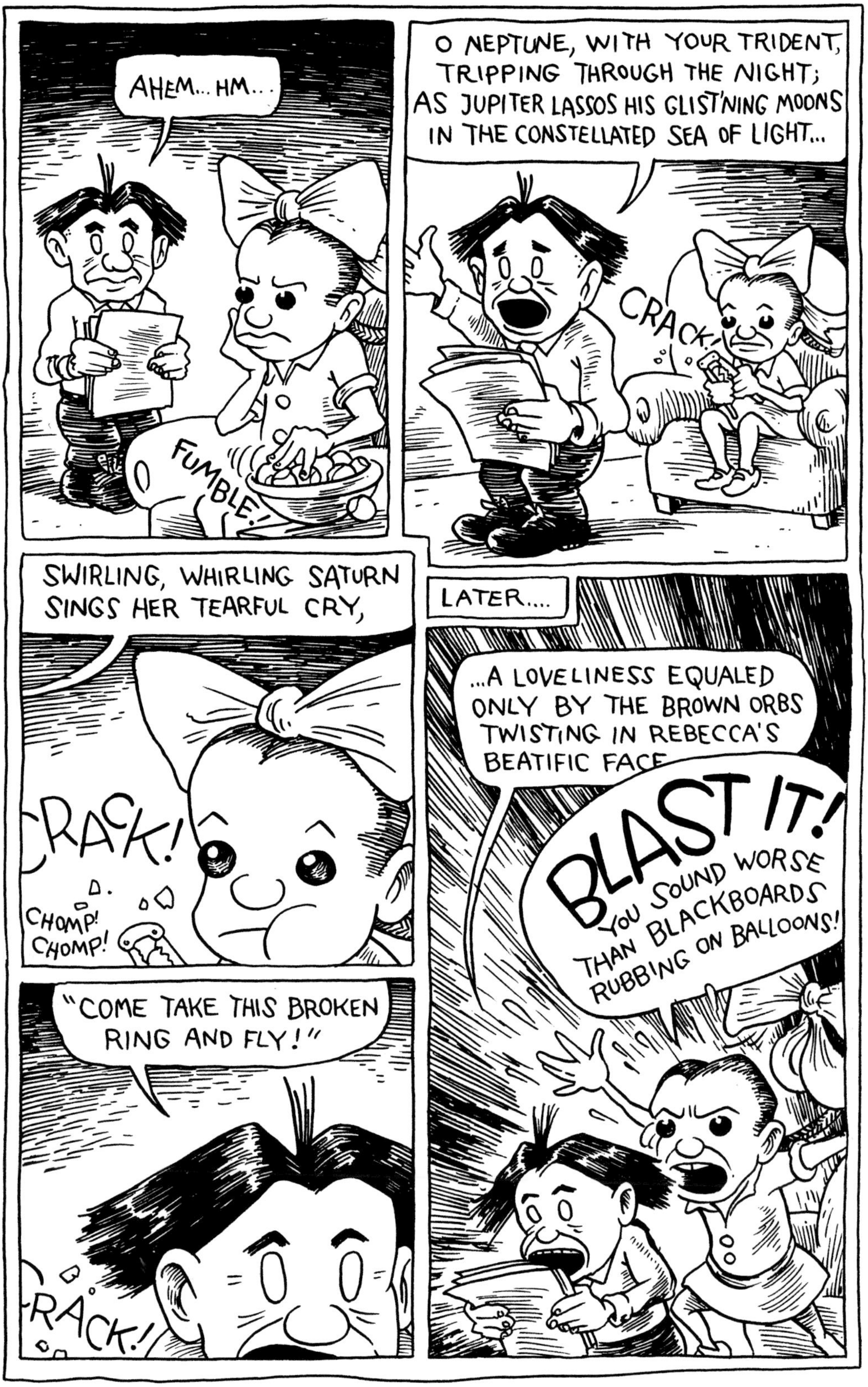
AHEM... HM...
FUMBLE!
O NEPTUNE, WITH YOUR TRIDENT, TRIPPING THROUGH THE NIGHT; AS JUPITER LASSOS HIS GLIST'NING MOONS IN THE CONSTELLATED SEA OF LIGHT...
CRACK!
SWIRLING, WHIRLING SATURN SINGS HER TEARFUL CRY,
CRACK!
CHOMP! CHOMP!
"COME TAKE THIS BROKEN RING AND FLY!"
CRACK!
LATER....
...A LOVELINESS EQUALED ONLY BY THE BROWN ORBS TWISTING IN REBECCA'S BEATIFIC FACE
BLAST IT! YOU SOUND WORSE THAN BLACKBOARDS RUBBING ON BALLOONS!

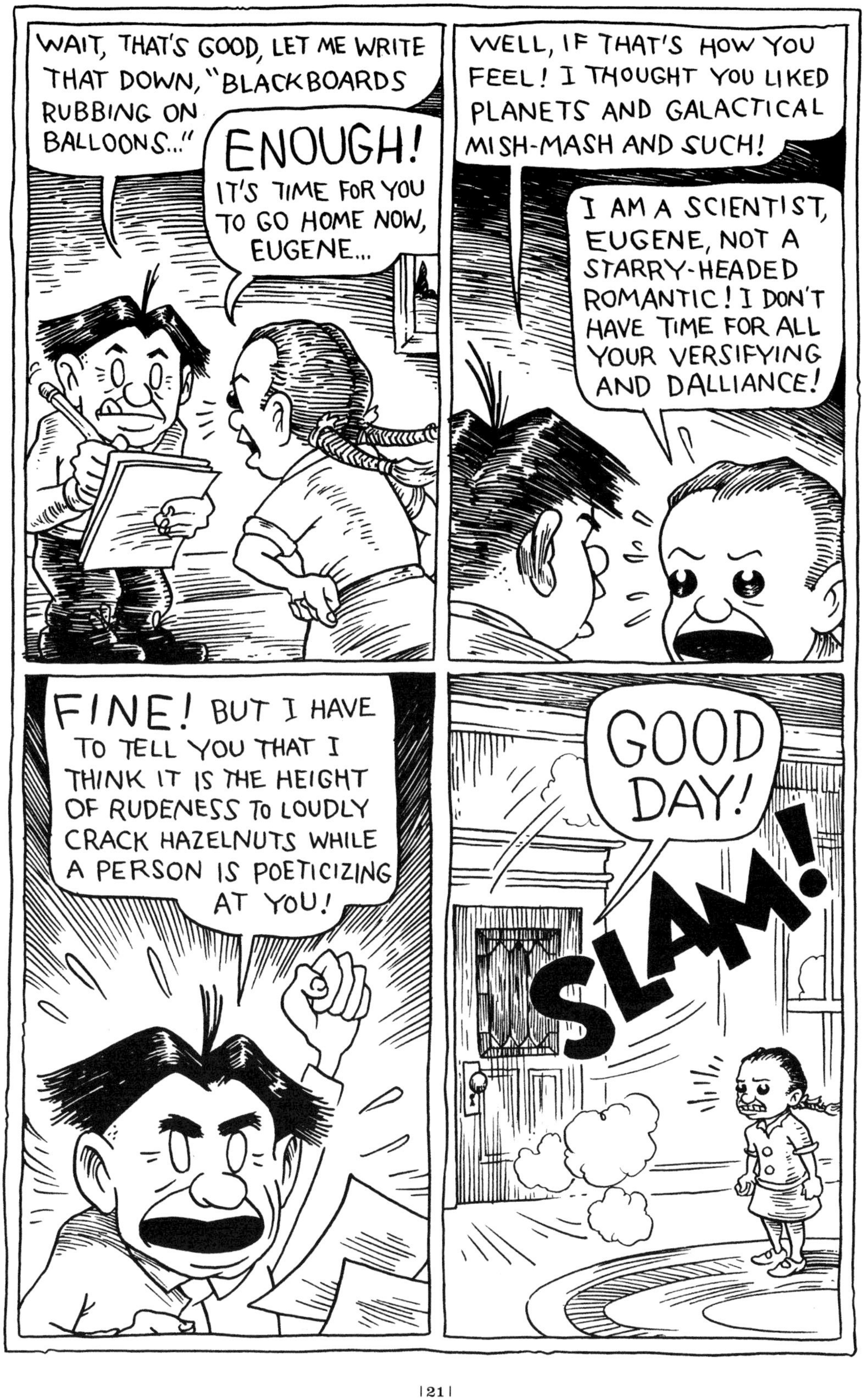

WAIT, THAT'S GOOD, LET ME WRITE THAT DOWN, "BLACKBOARDS RUBBING ON BALLOONS..."
ENOUGH! IT'S TIME FOR YOU TO GO HOME NOW, EUGENE...
WELL, IF THAT'S HOW YOU FEEL! I THOUGHT YOU LIKED PLANETS AND GALACTICAL MISH-MASH AND SUCH!
I AM A SCIENTIST, EUGENE, NOT A STARRY-HEADED ROMANTIC! I DON'T HAVE TIME FOR ALL YOUR VERSIFYING AND DALLIANCE!
FINE! BUT I HAVE TO TELL YOU THAT I THINK IT IS THE HEIGHT OF RUDENESS TO LOUDLY CRACK HAZELNUTS WHILE A PERSON IS POETICIZING AT YOU!
GOOD DAY!
SLAM!

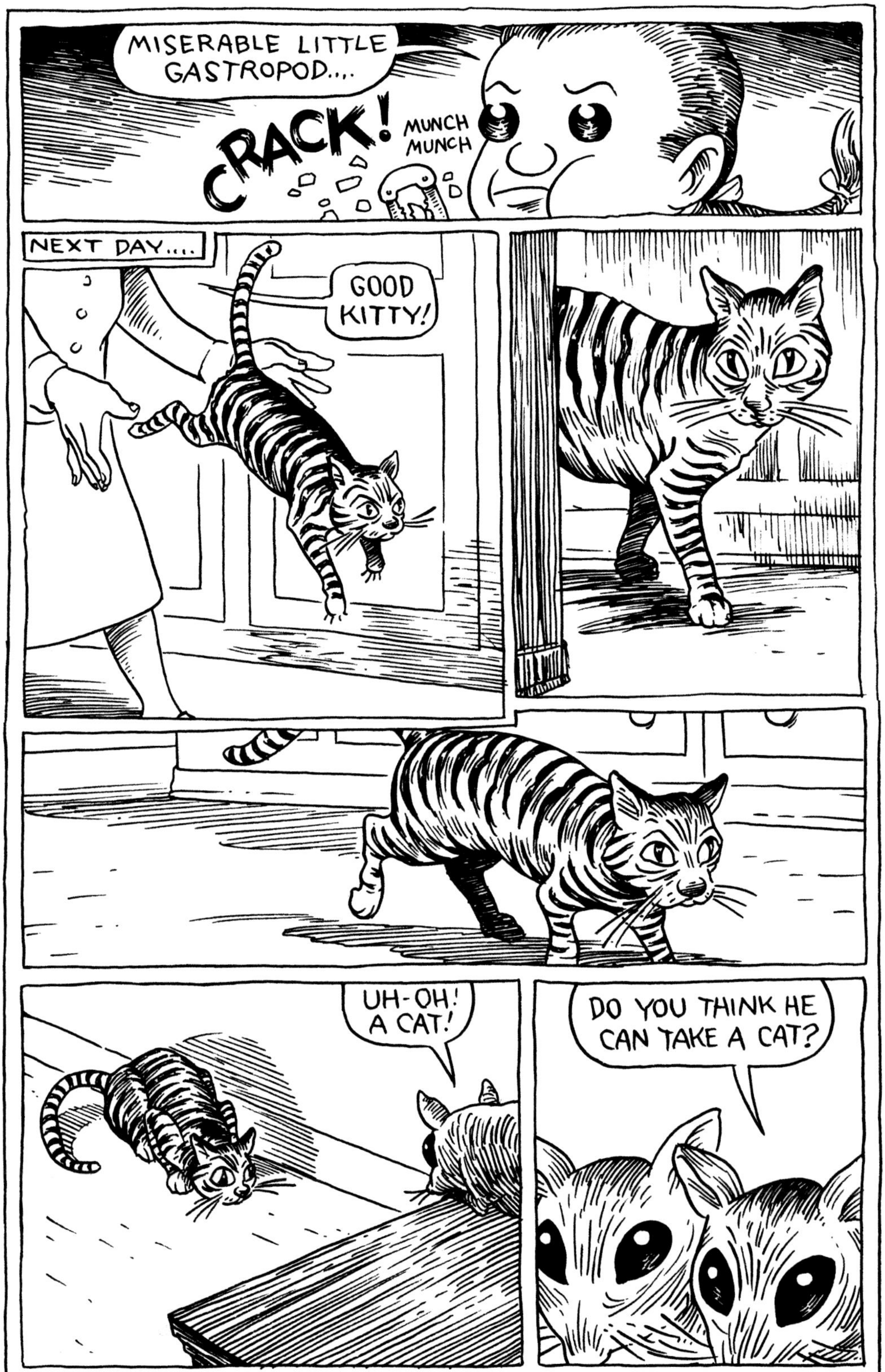
MISERABLE LITTLE GASTROPOD....
CRACK!
MUNCH MUNCH
NEXT DAY....
GOOD KITTY!
UH-OH! A CAT!
DO YOU THINK HE CAN TAKE A CAT?

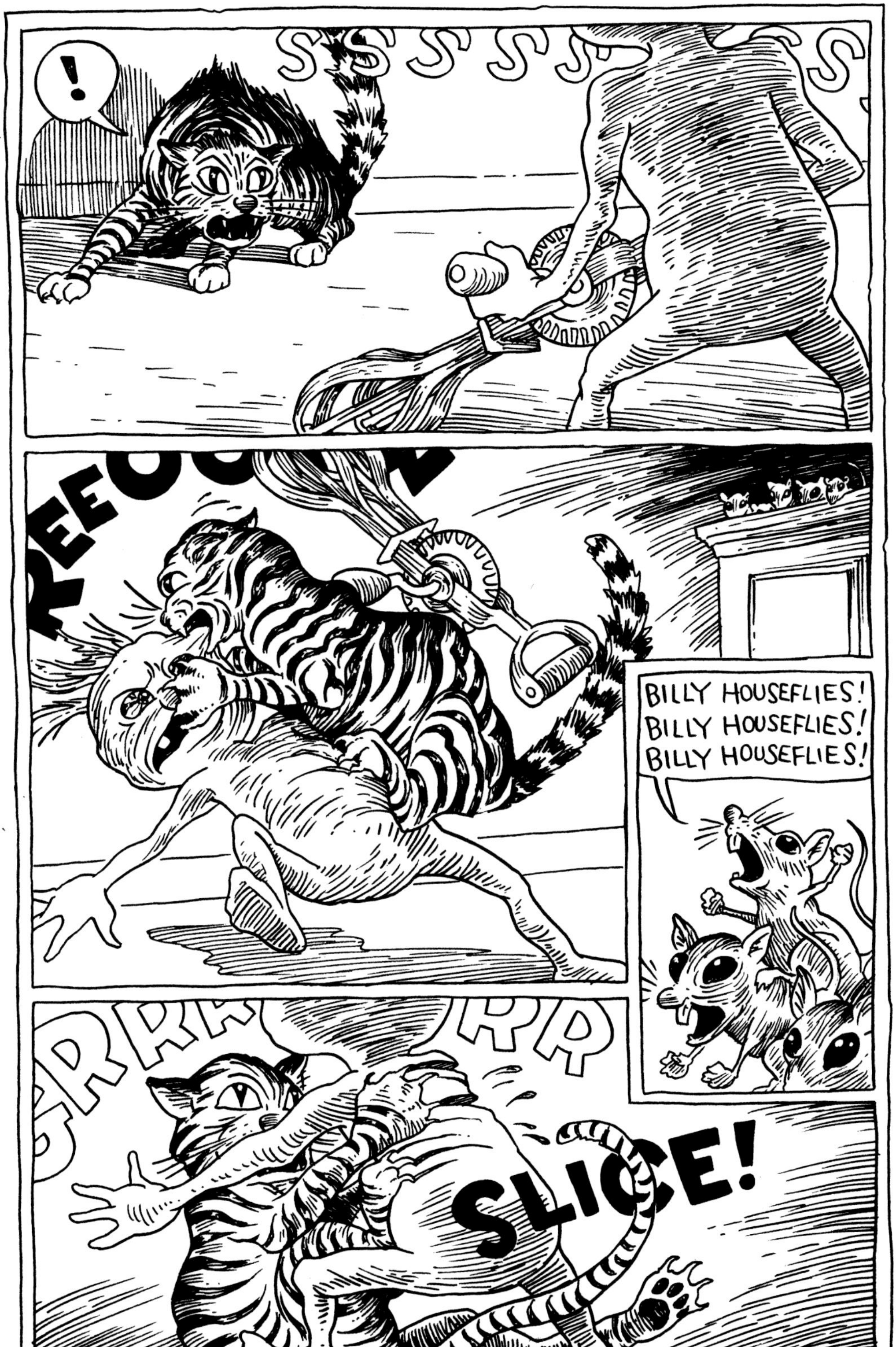
!
SSSSSSSSS
REEOOO
BILLY HOUSEFLIES!
BILLY HOUSEFLIES!
BILLY HOUSEFLIES!
GRRA
RR
SLICE!

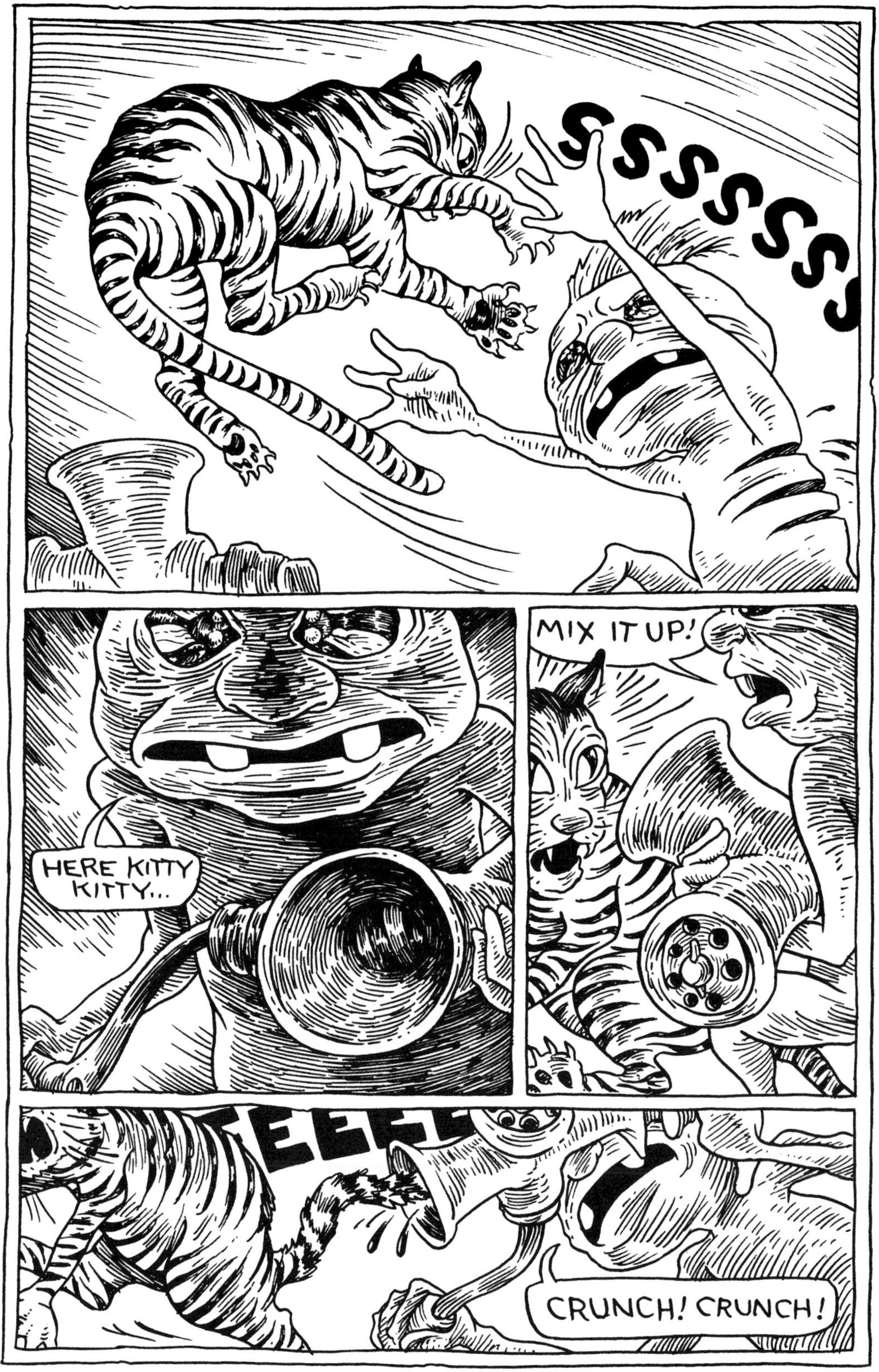
SSSSSS
HERE KITTY KITTY...
MIX IT UP!
EEEE
CRUNCH! CRUNCH!

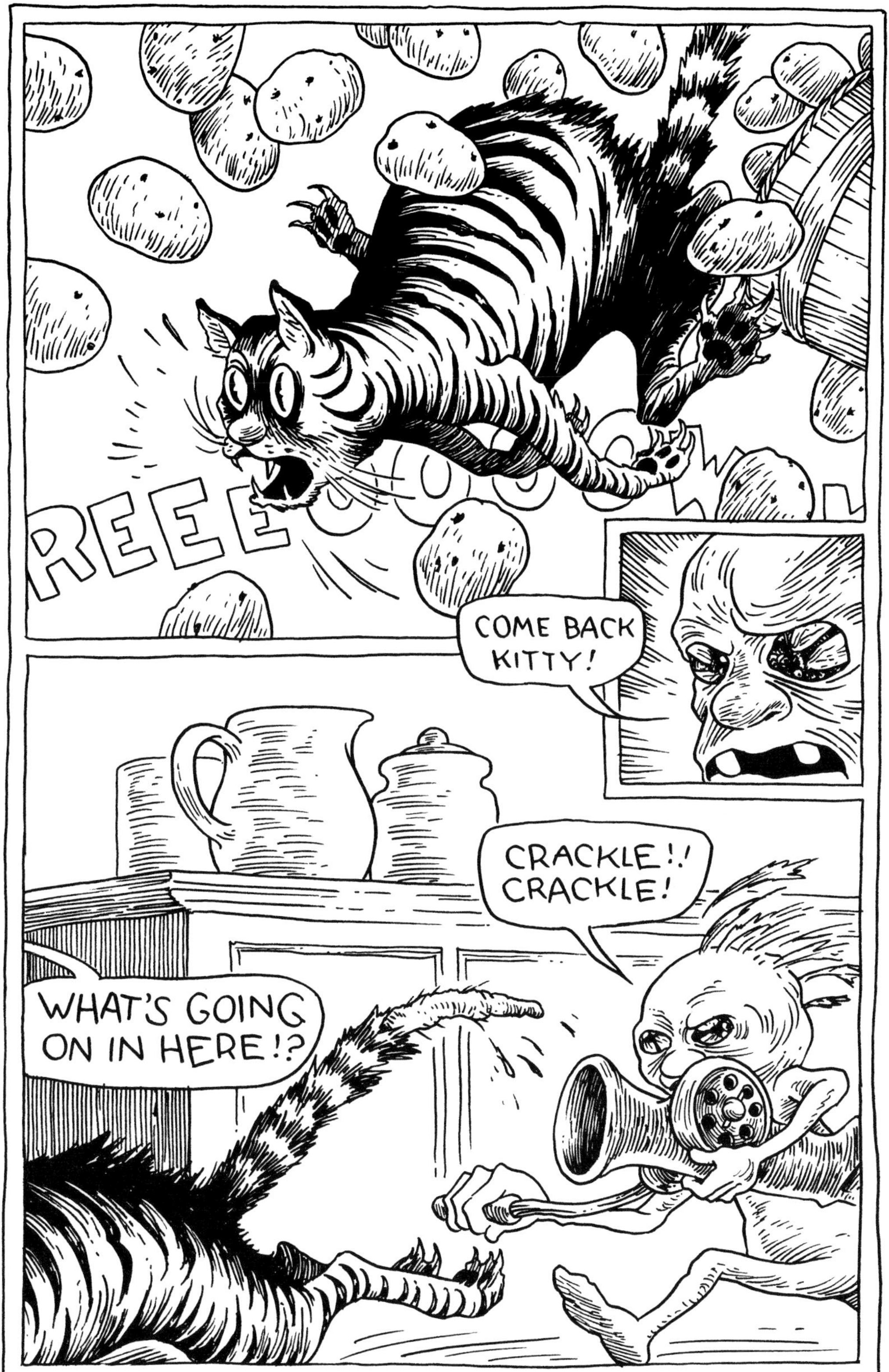
REEEOOOOWW
COME BACK KITTY!
CRACKLE!! CRACKLE!
WHAT'S GOING ON IN HERE!?

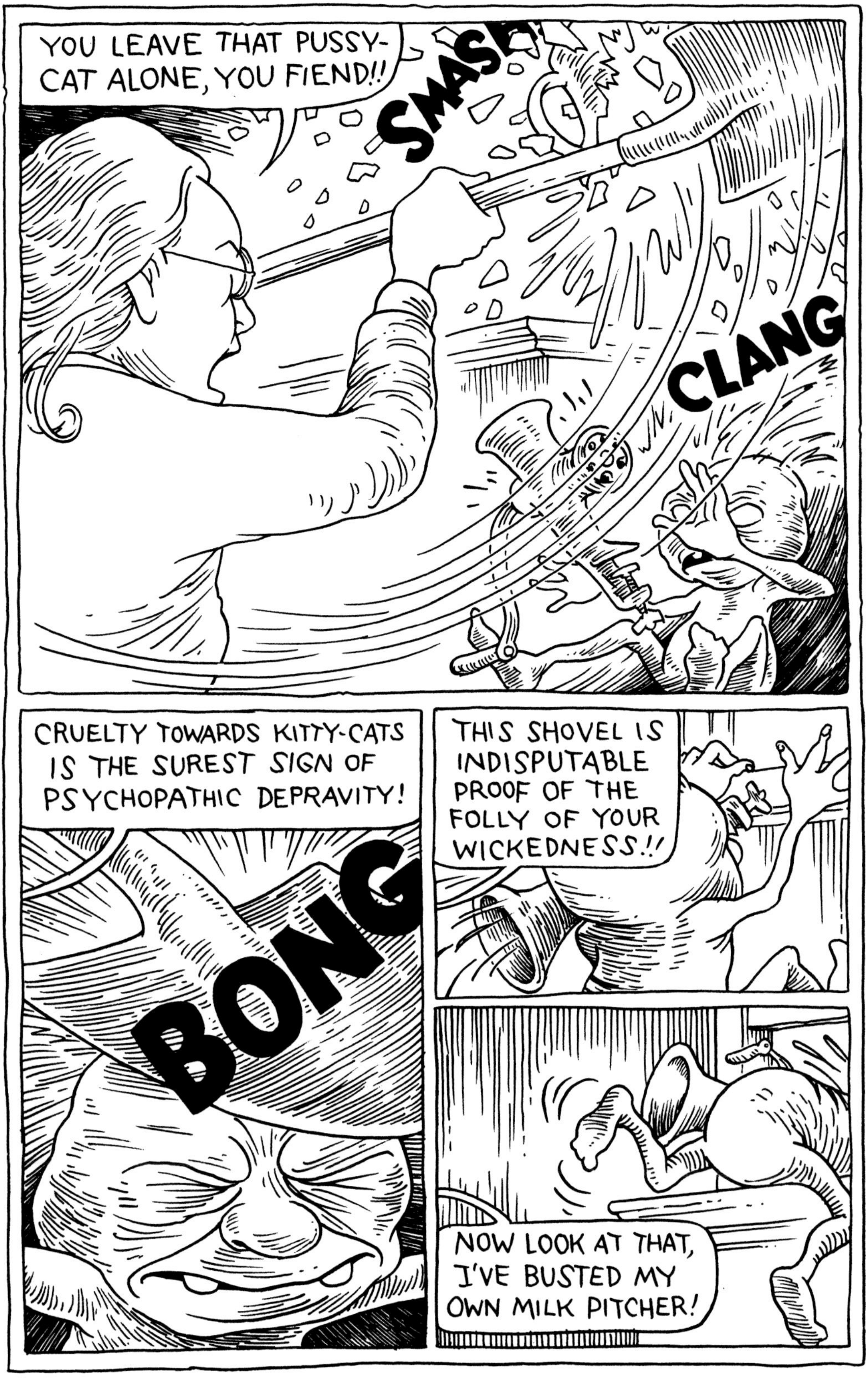
YOU LEAVE THAT PUSSY-CAT ALONE, YOU FIEND!!
SMASH
CLANG
CRUELTY TOWARDS KITTY-CATS IS THE SUREST SIGN OF PSYCHOPATHIC DEPRAVITY!
BONG
THIS SHOVEL IS INDISPUTABLE PROOF OF THE FOLLY OF YOUR WICKEDNESS!!
NOW LOOK AT THAT, I'VE BUSTED MY OWN MILK PITCHER!

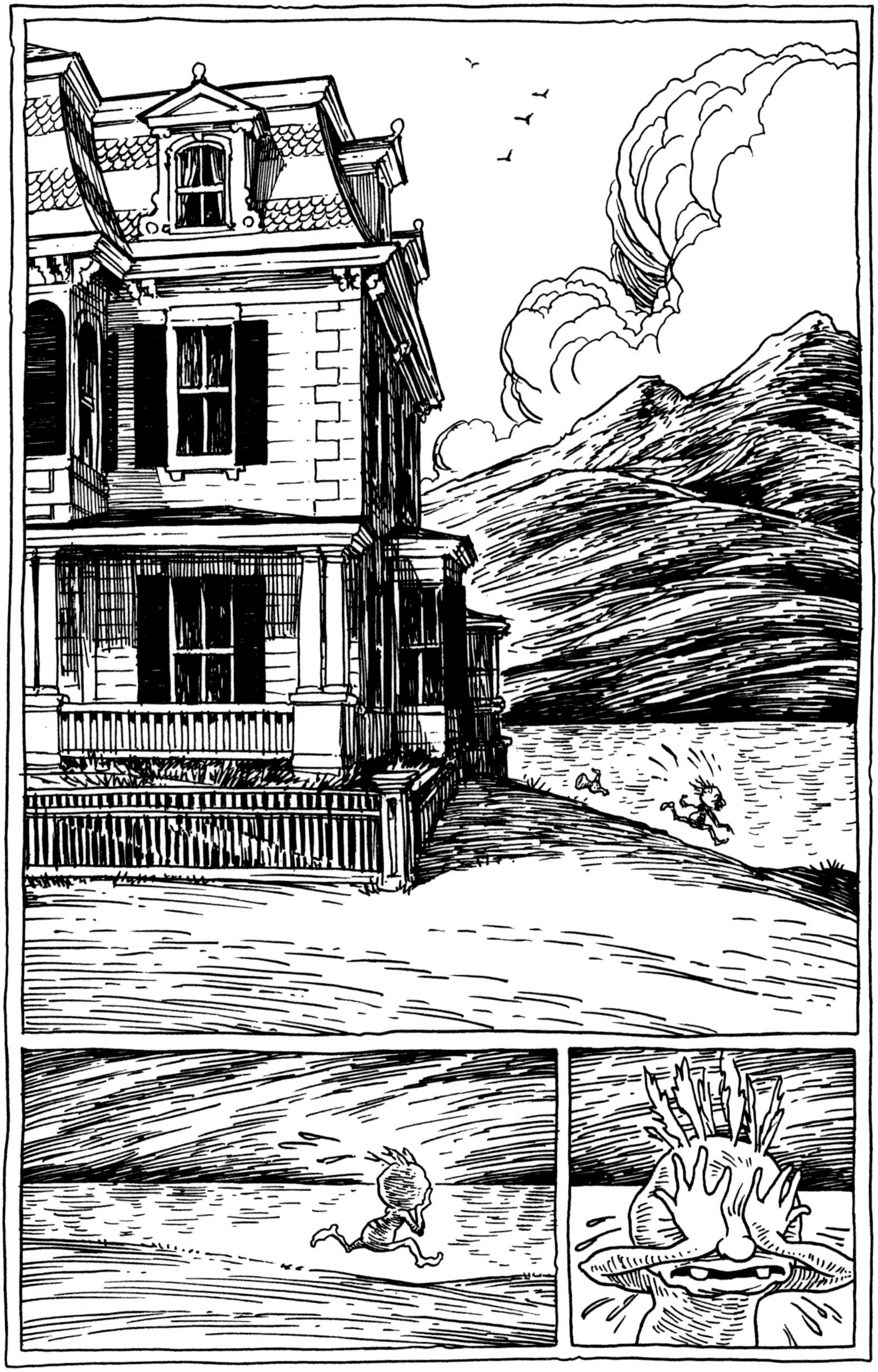

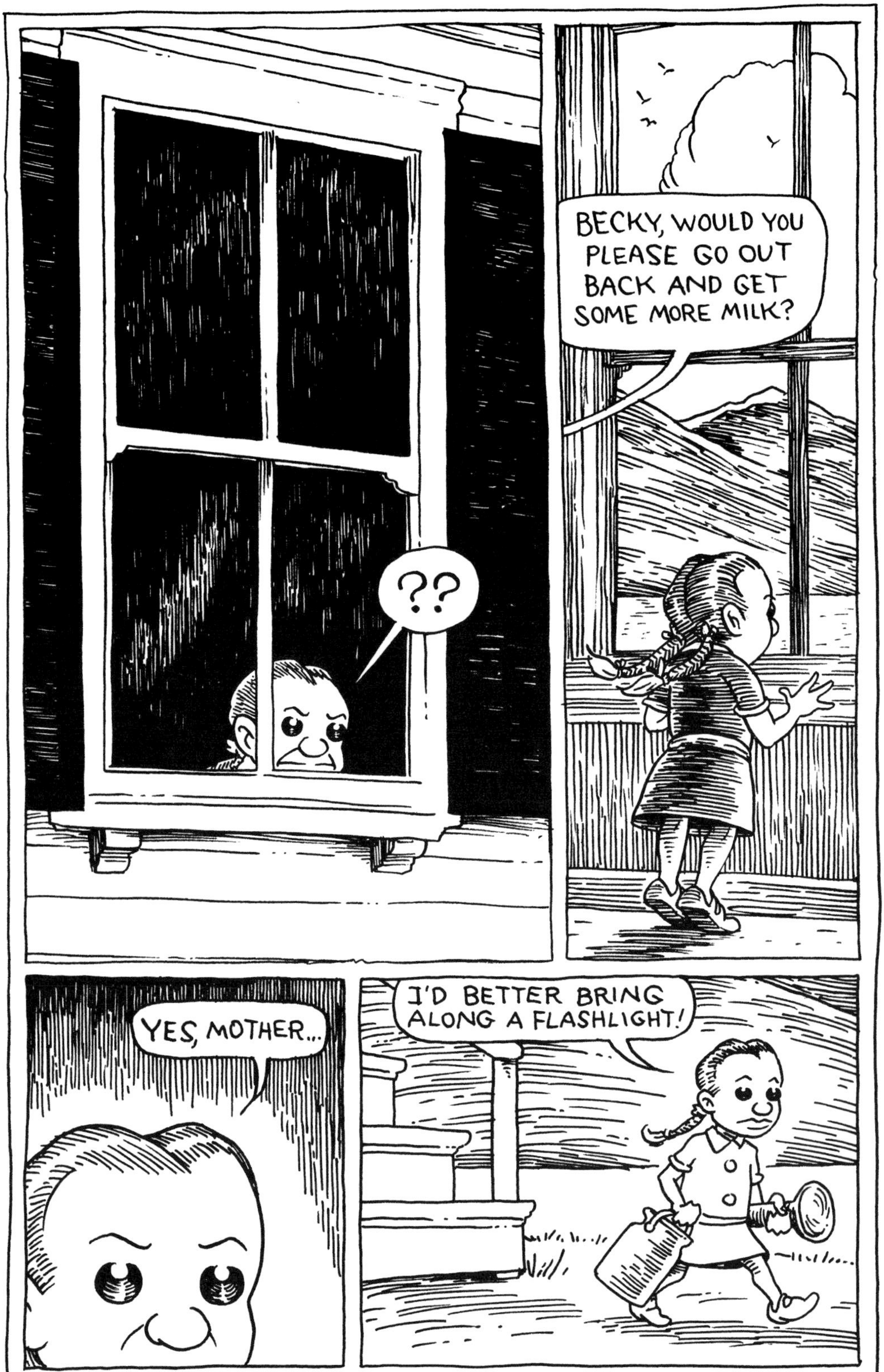
??
BECKY, WOULD YOU PLEASE GO OUT BACK AND GET SOME MORE MILK?
YES, MOTHER...
I'D BETTER BRING ALONG A FLASHLIGHT!

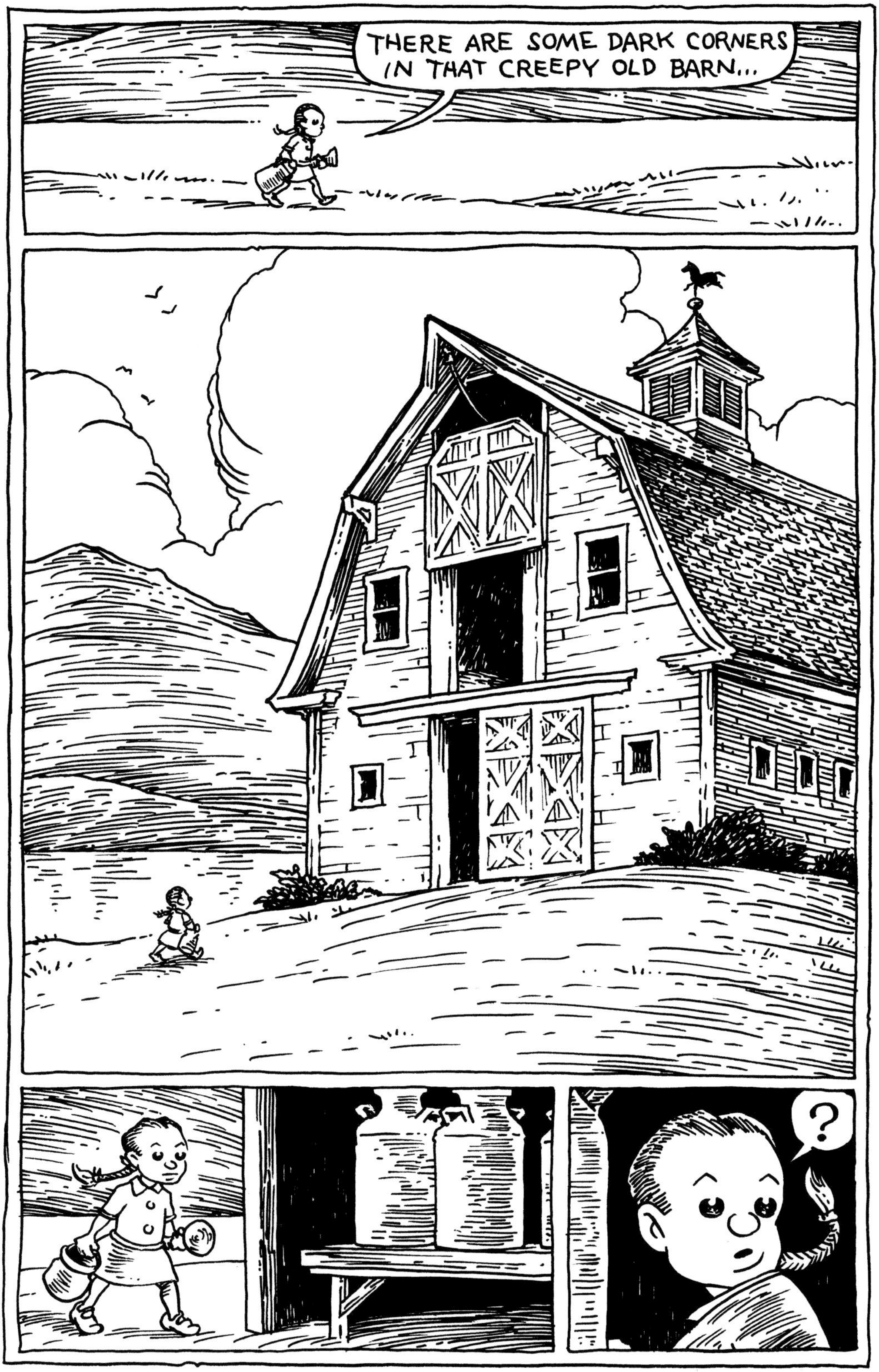
THERE ARE SOME DARK CORNERS IN THAT CREEPY OLD BARN...
?

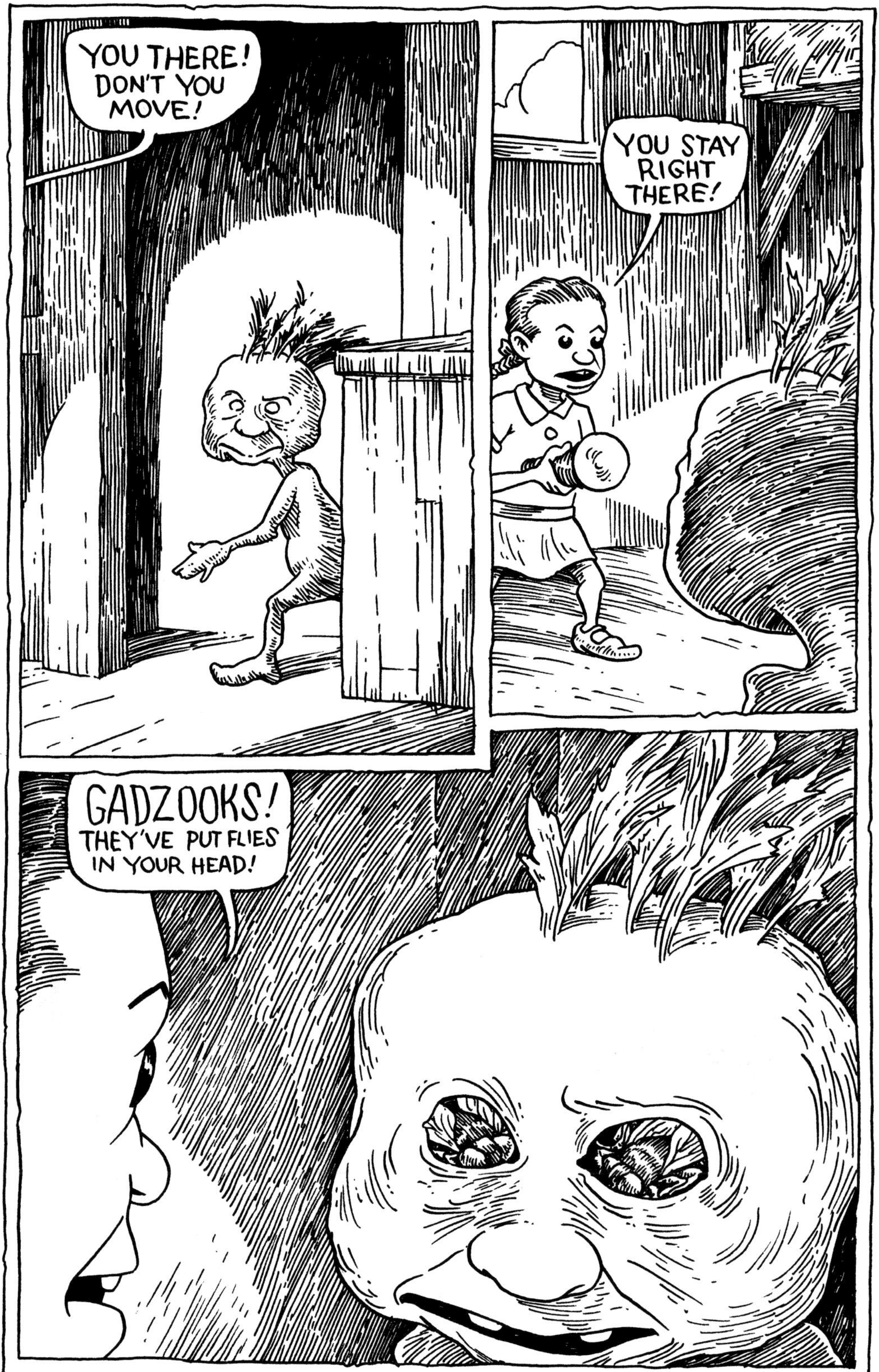
YOU THERE! DON'T YOU MOVE!
YOU STAY RIGHT THERE!
GADZOOKS! THEY'VE PUT FLIES IN YOUR HEAD!

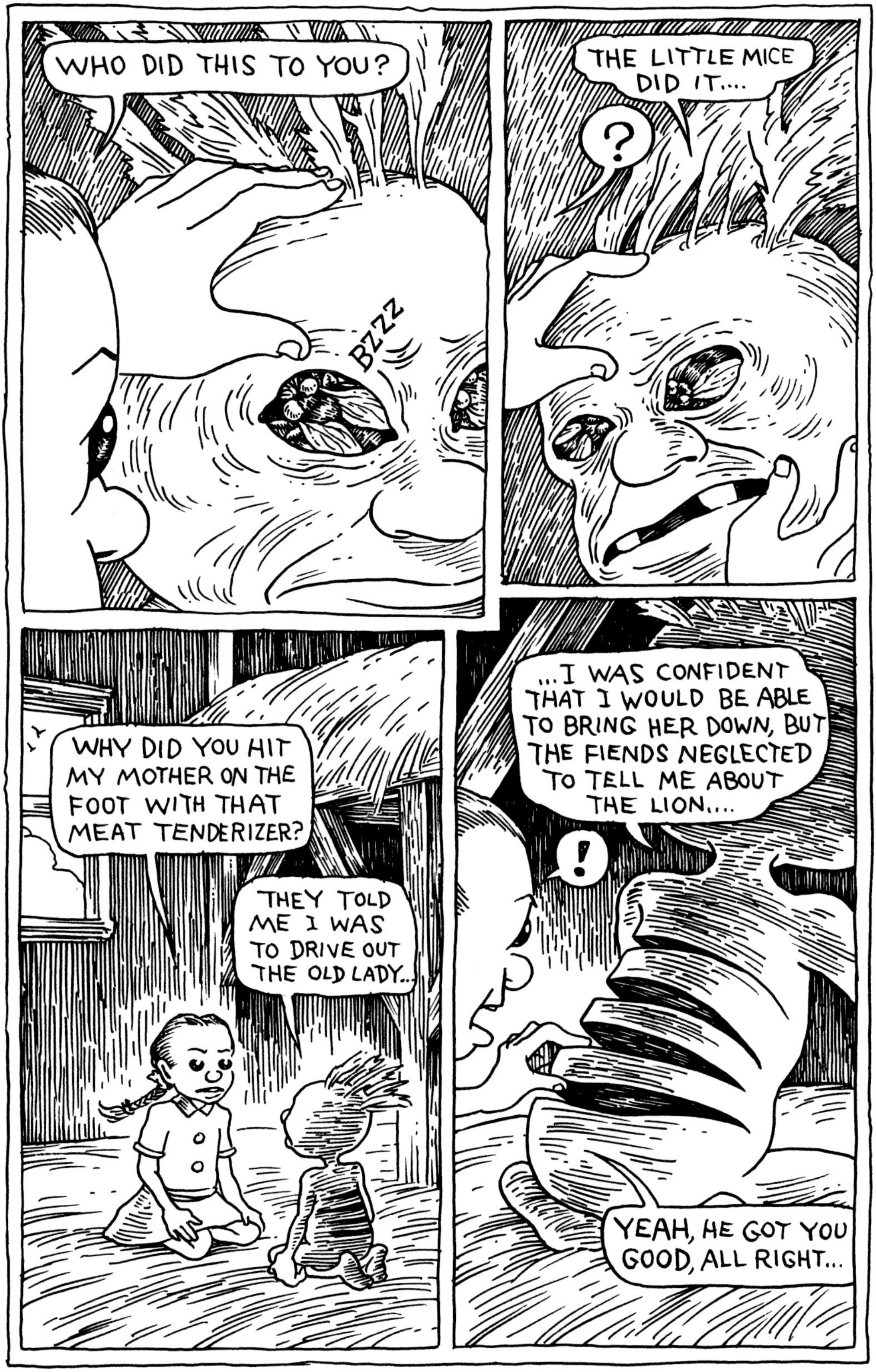
WHO DID THIS TO YOU?
BZZZ
THE LITTLE MICE DID IT....
?
WHY DID YOU HIT MY MOTHER ON THE FOOT WITH THAT MEAT TENDERIZER?
THEY TOLD ME I WAS TO DRIVE OUT THE OLD LADY...
...I WAS CONFIDENT THAT I WOULD BE ABLE TO BRING HER DOWN, BUT THE FIENDS NEGLECTED TO TELL ME ABOUT THE LION....
!
YEAH, HE GOT YOU GOOD, ALL RIGHT...

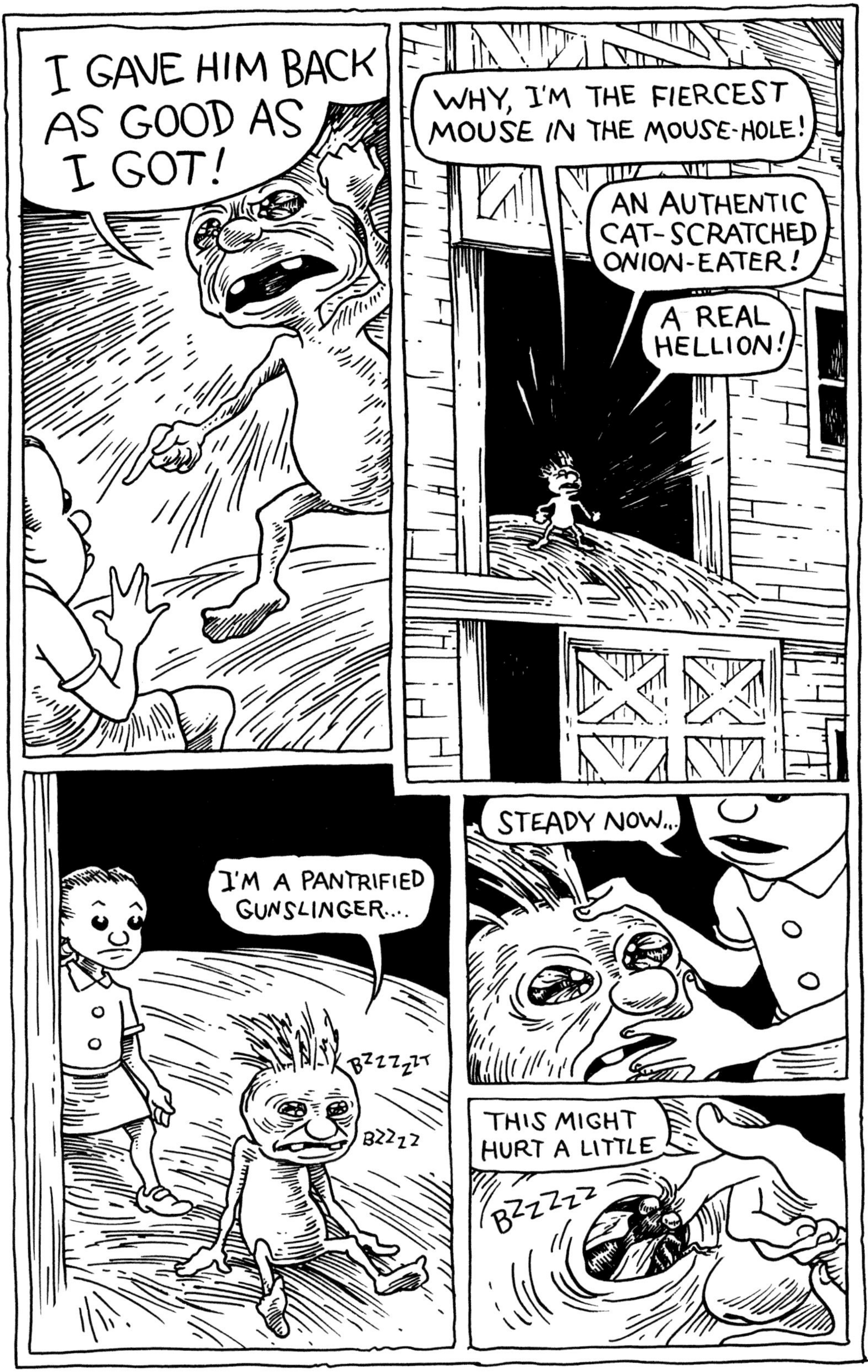
I GAVE HIM BACK AS GOOD AS I GOT!
WHY, I'M THE FIERCEST MOUSE IN THE MOUSE-HOLE!
AN AUTHENTIC CAT-SCRATCHED ONION-EATER!
A REAL HELLION!
I'M A PANTRIFIED GUNSLINGER...
BZZZZZT
BZZZZ
STEADY NOW...
THIS MIGHT HURT A LITTLE
BZZZZZ

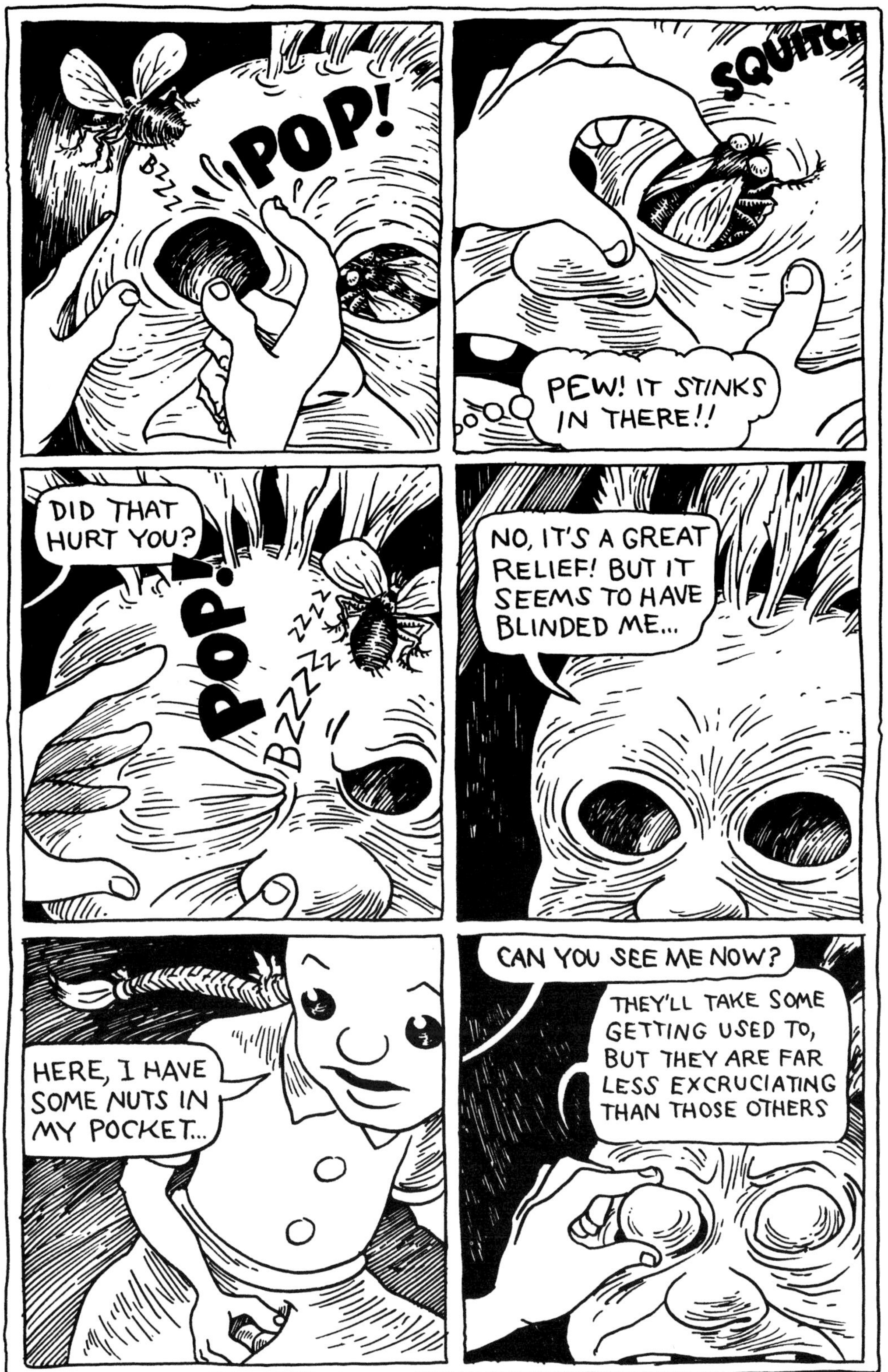
BZZZ
POP!
SQUITCH
PEW! IT STINKS IN THERE!!
DID THAT HURT YOU?
POP!
ZZZZ
BZZZZZ
NO, IT'S A GREAT RELIEF! BUT IT SEEMS TO HAVE BLINDED ME...
HERE, I HAVE SOME NUTS IN MY POCKET...
CAN YOU SEE ME NOW?
THEY'LL TAKE SOME GETTING USED TO, BUT THEY ARE FAR LESS EXCRUCIATING THAN THOSE OTHERS

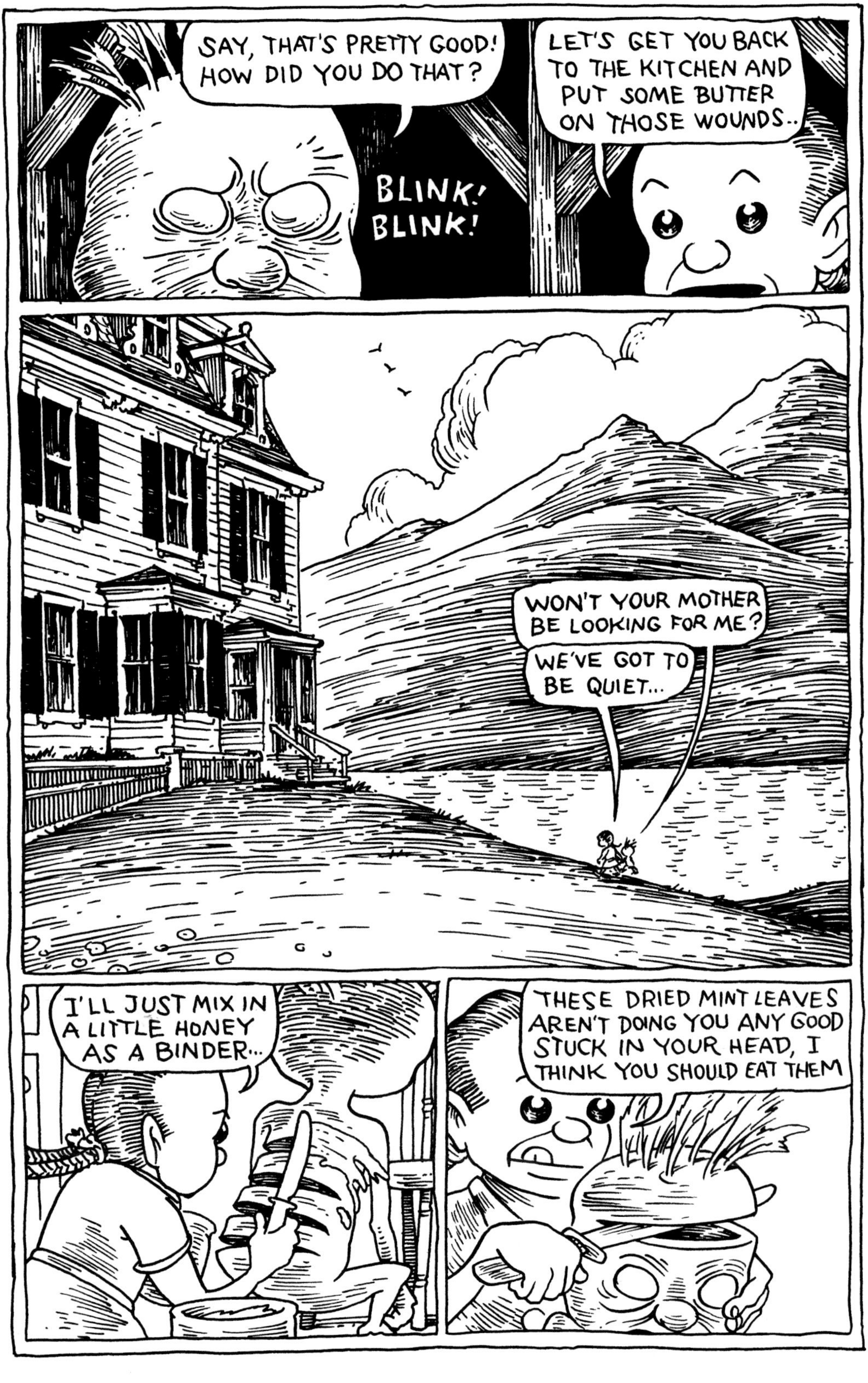
SAY, THAT'S PRETTY GOOD! HOW DID YOU DO THAT?
BLINK! BLINK!
LET'S GET YOU BACK TO THE KITCHEN AND PUT SOME BUTTER ON THOSE WOUNDS..
WON'T YOUR MOTHER BE LOOKING FOR ME?
WE'VE GOT TO BE QUIET...
I'LL JUST MIX IN A LITTLE HONEY AS A BINDER...
THESE DRIED MINT LEAVES AREN'T DOING YOU ANY GOOD STUCK IN YOUR HEAD, I THINK YOU SHOULD EAT THEM

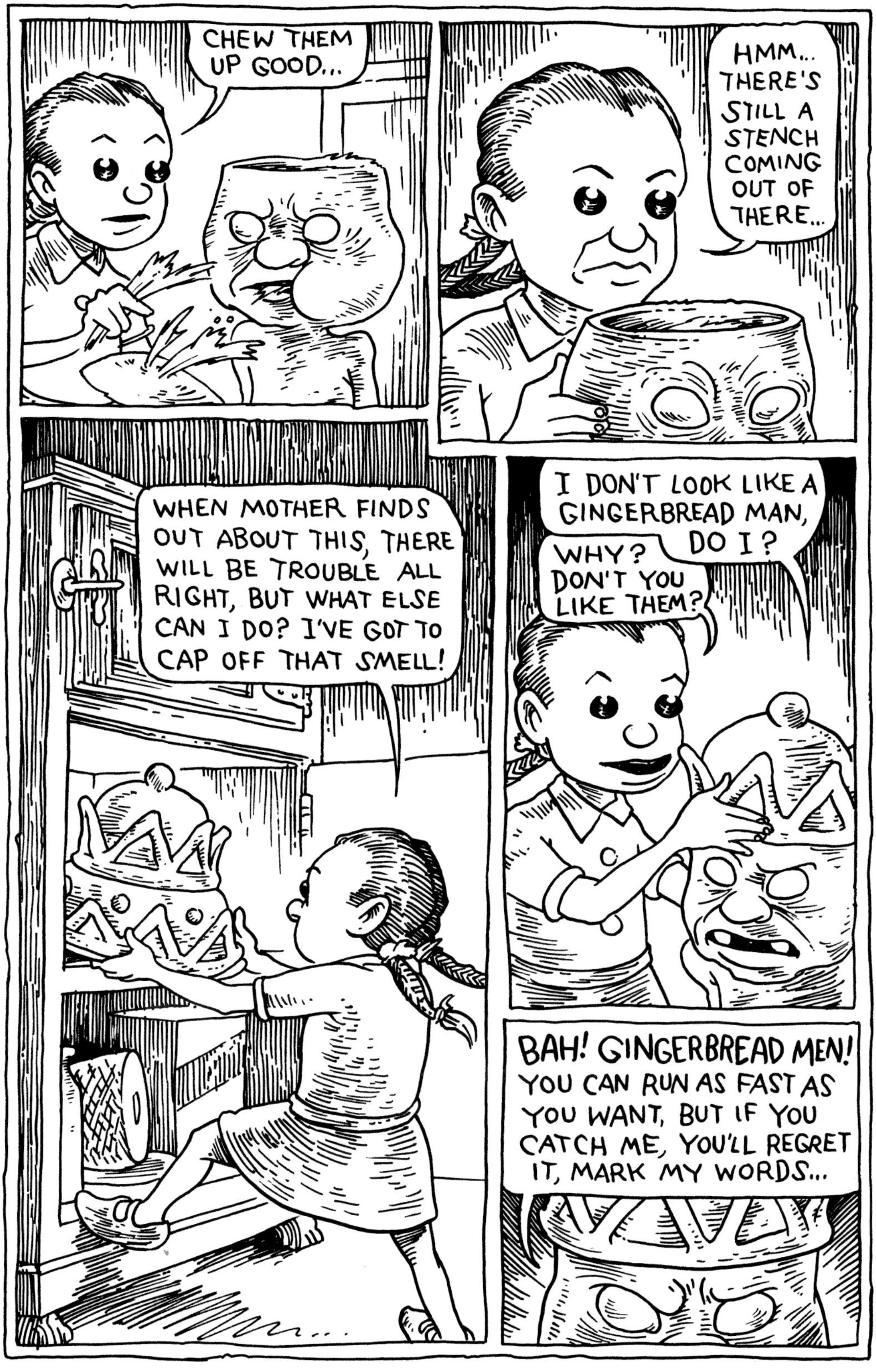
CHEW THEM UP GOOD...
HMM... THERE'S STILL A STENCH COMING OUT OF THERE...
WHEN MOTHER FINDS OUT ABOUT THIS, THERE WILL BE TROUBLE ALL RIGHT, BUT WHAT ELSE CAN I DO? I'VE GOT TO CAP OFF THAT SMELL!
I DON'T LOOK LIKE A GINGERBREAD MAN, DO I?
WHY? DON'T YOU LIKE THEM?
BAH! GINGERBREAD MEN! YOU CAN RUN AS FAST AS YOU WANT, BUT IF YOU CATCH ME, YOU'LL REGRET IT, MARK MY WORDS...

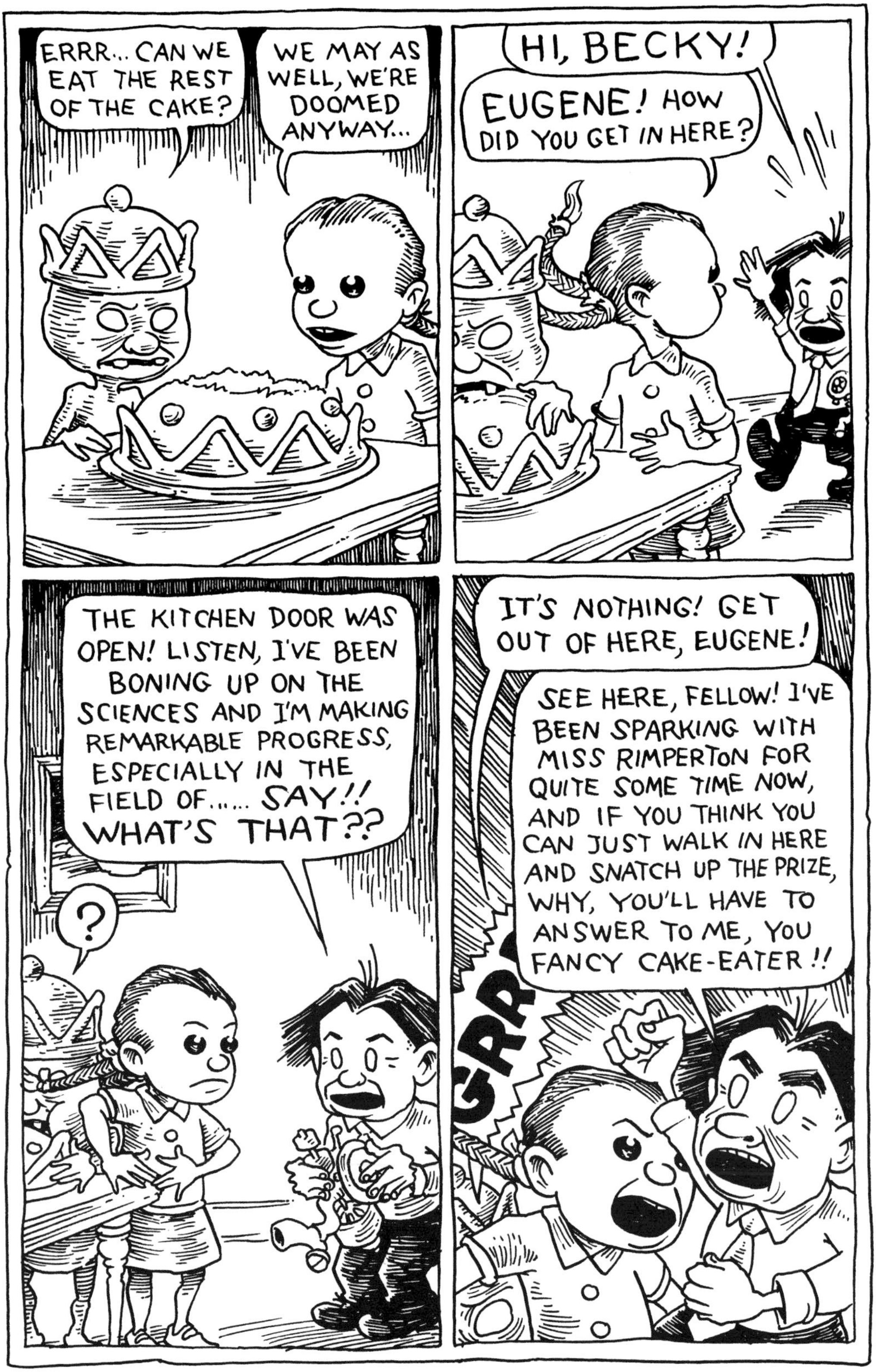
ERRR... CAN WE EAT THE REST OF THE CAKE?
WE MAY AS WELL, WE'RE DOOMED ANYWAY...
HI, BECKY!
EUGENE! HOW DID YOU GET IN HERE?
THE KITCHEN DOOR WAS OPEN! LISTEN, I'VE BEEN BONING UP ON THE SCIENCES AND I'M MAKING REMARKABLE PROGRESS, ESPECIALLY IN THE FIELD OF...... SAY!! WHAT'S THAT??
?
IT'S NOTHING! GET OUT OF HERE, EUGENE!
SEE HERE, FELLOW! I'VE BEEN SPARKING WITH MISS RIMPERTON FOR QUITE SOME TIME NOW, AND IF YOU THINK YOU CAN JUST WALK IN HERE AND SNATCH UP THE PRIZE, WHY, YOU'LL HAVE TO ANSWER TO ME, YOU FANCY CAKE-EATER!!

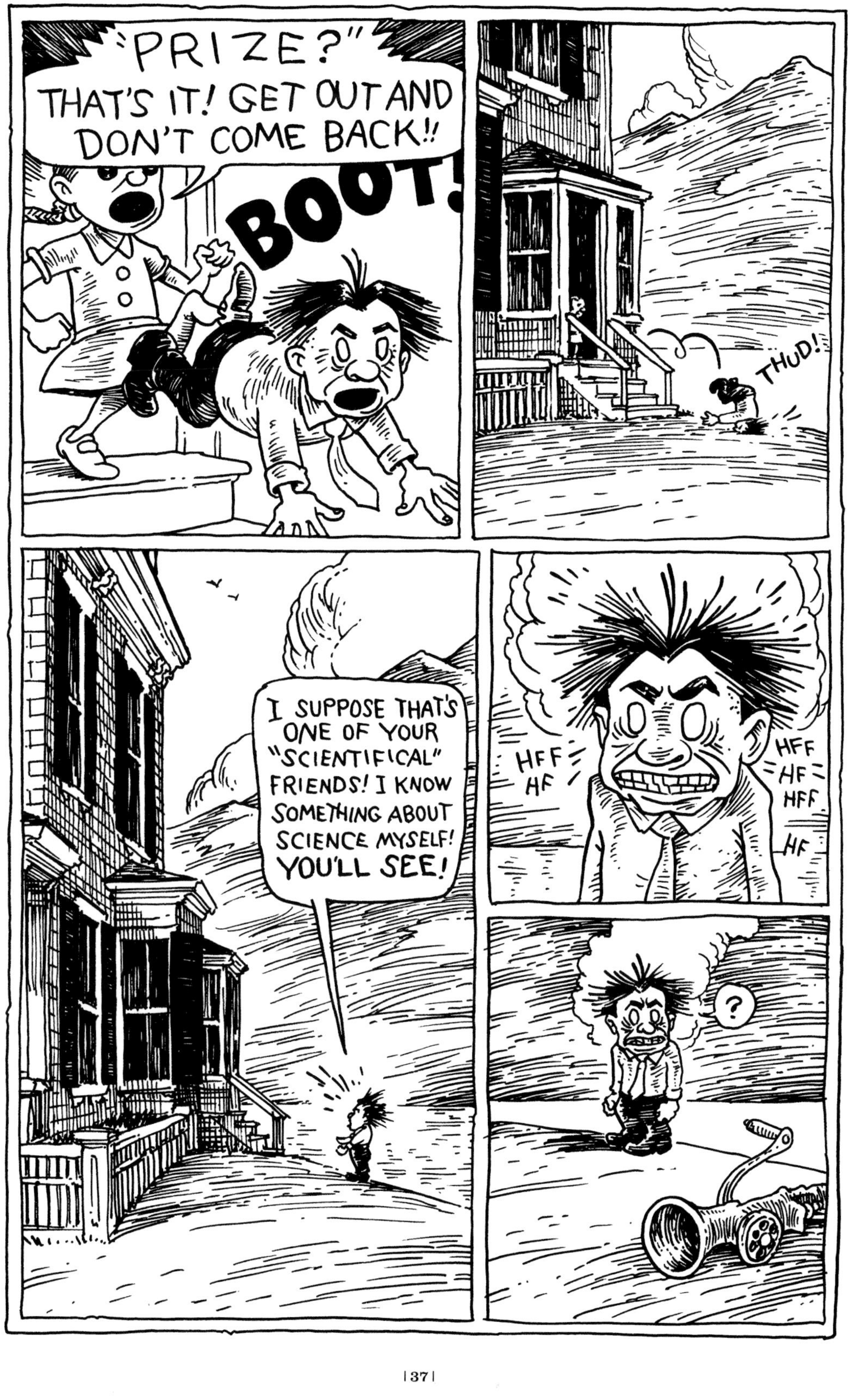
"PRIZE?"
THAT'S IT! GET OUT AND DON'T COME BACK!!
BOOT!
THUD!
I SUPPOSE THAT'S ONE OF YOUR "SCIENTIFICAL" FRIENDS! I KNOW SOMETHING ABOUT SCIENCE MYSELF! YOU'LL SEE!
HFF HF
HFF HF HFF
HF
?

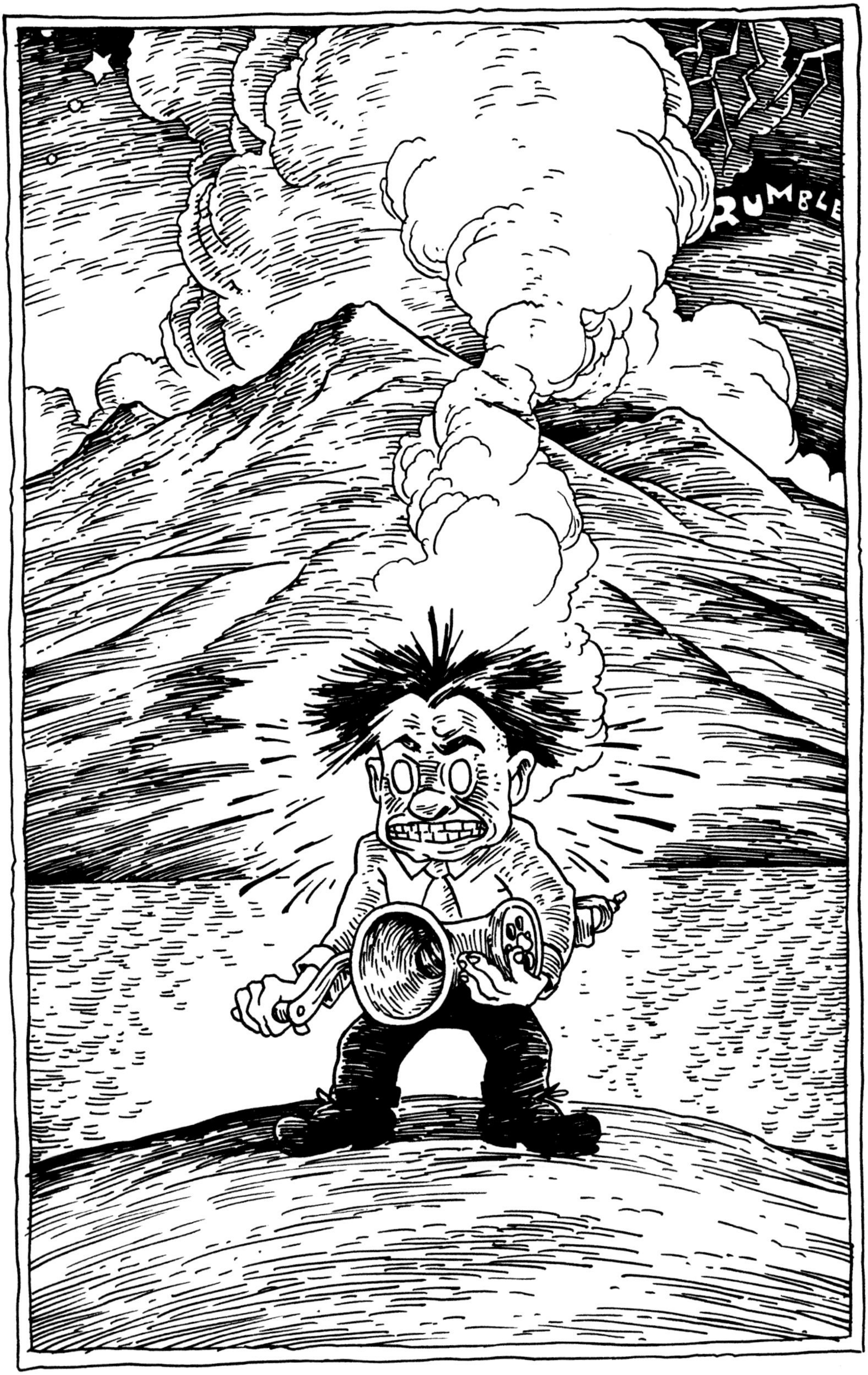
RUMBLE

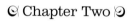 Chapter Two

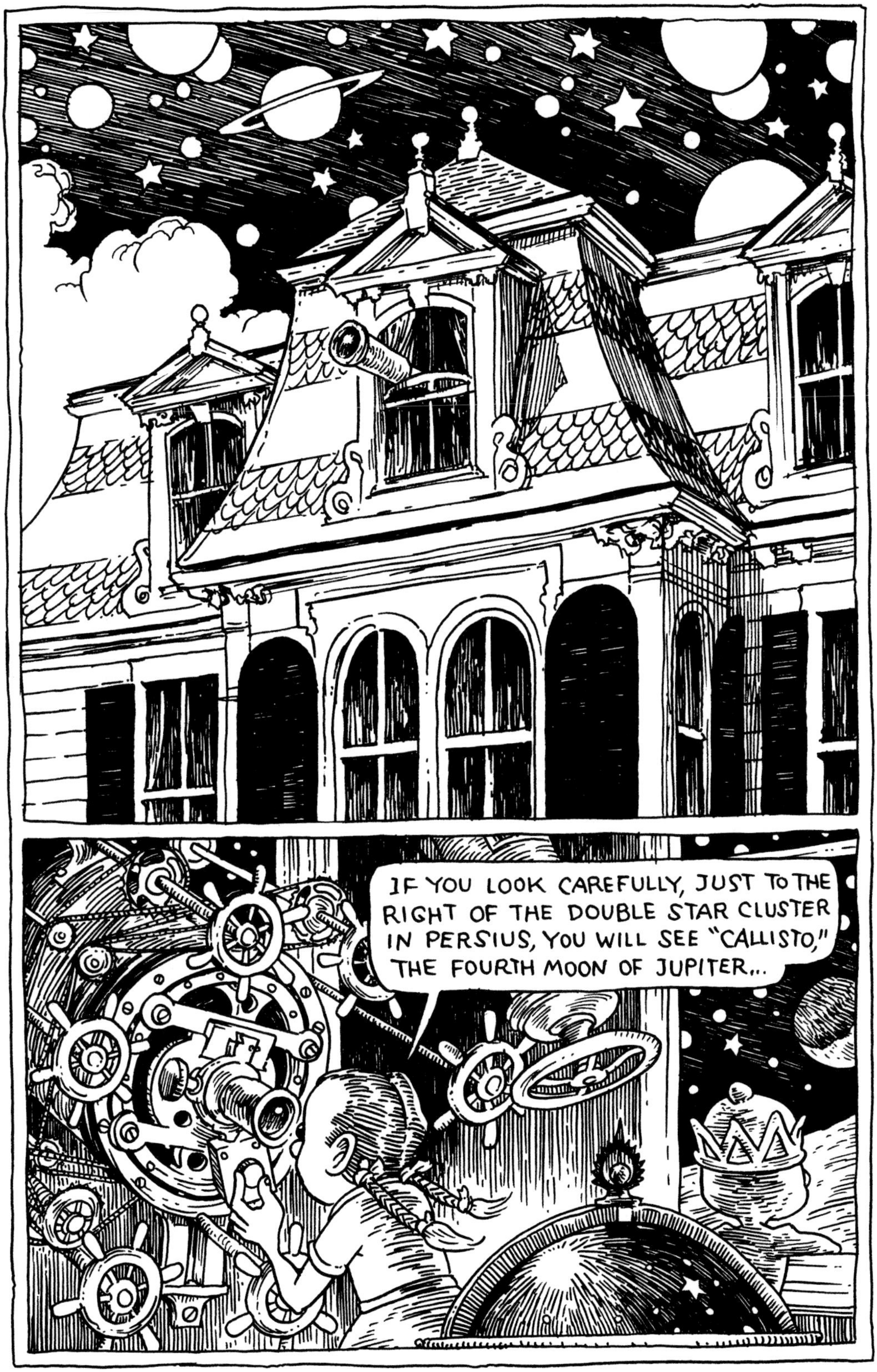
IF YOU LOOK CAREFULLY, JUST TO THE RIGHT OF THE DOUBLE STAR CLUSTER IN PERSIUS, YOU WILL SEE "CALLISTO," THE FOURTH MOON OF JUPITER...

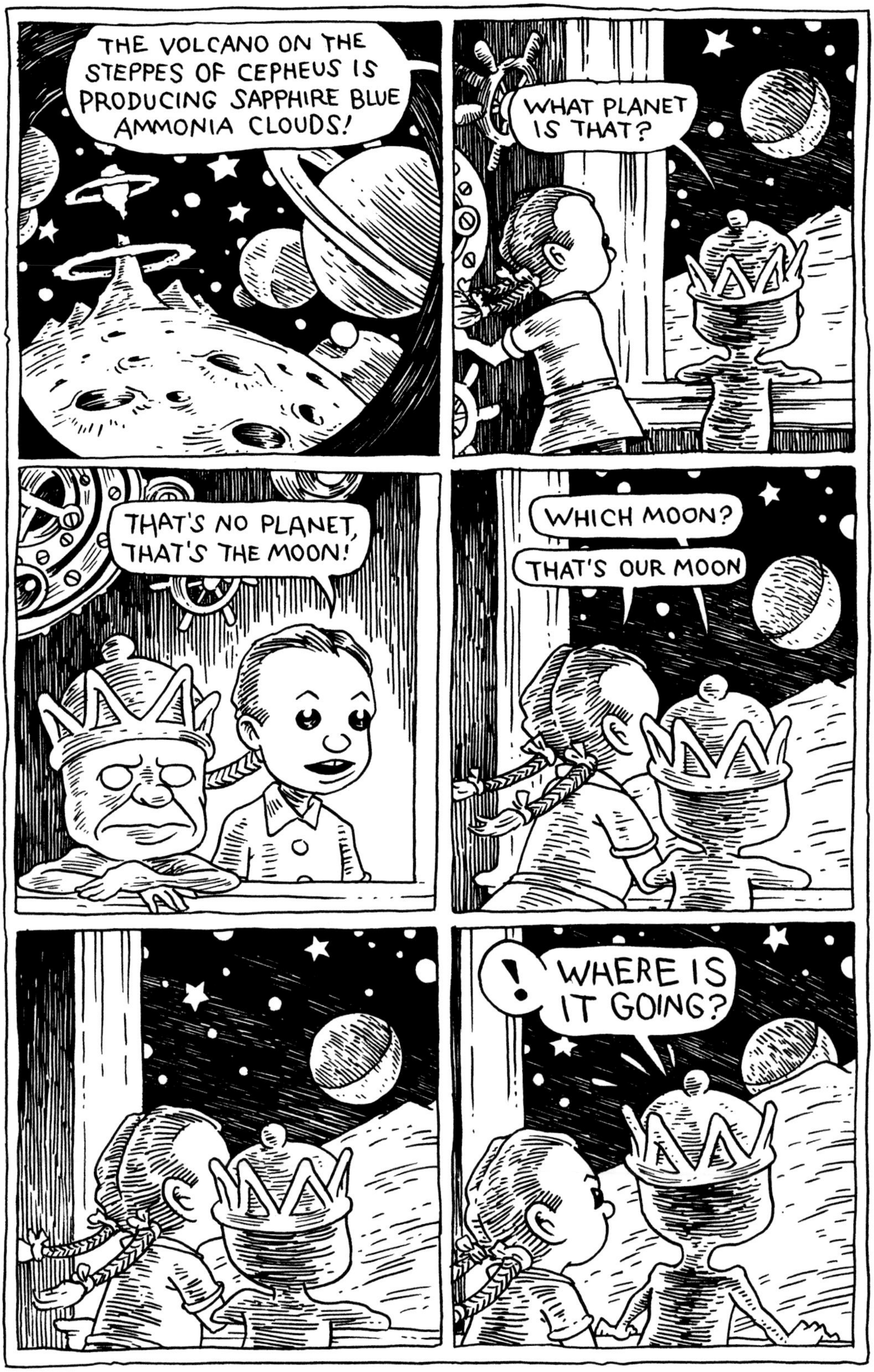
THE VOLCANO ON THE STEPPES OF CEPHEUS IS PRODUCING SAPPHIRE BLUE AMMONIA CLOUDS!
WHAT PLANET IS THAT?
THAT'S NO PLANET, THAT'S THE MOON!
WHICH MOON?
THAT'S OUR MOON
!
WHERE IS IT GOING?

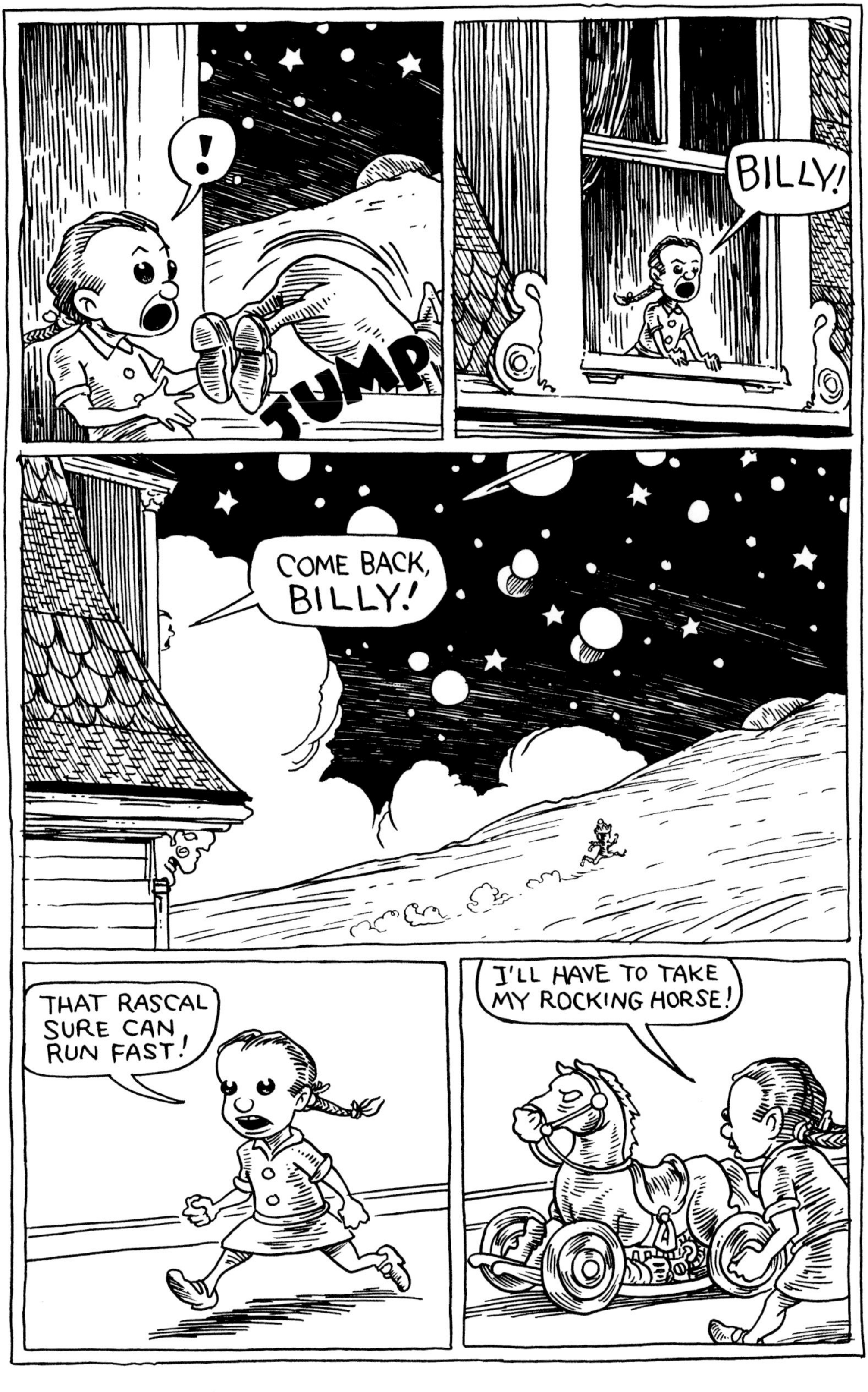
!
JUMP
BILLY!
COME BACK, BILLY!
THAT RASCAL SURE CAN RUN FAST!
I'LL HAVE TO TAKE MY ROCKING HORSE!

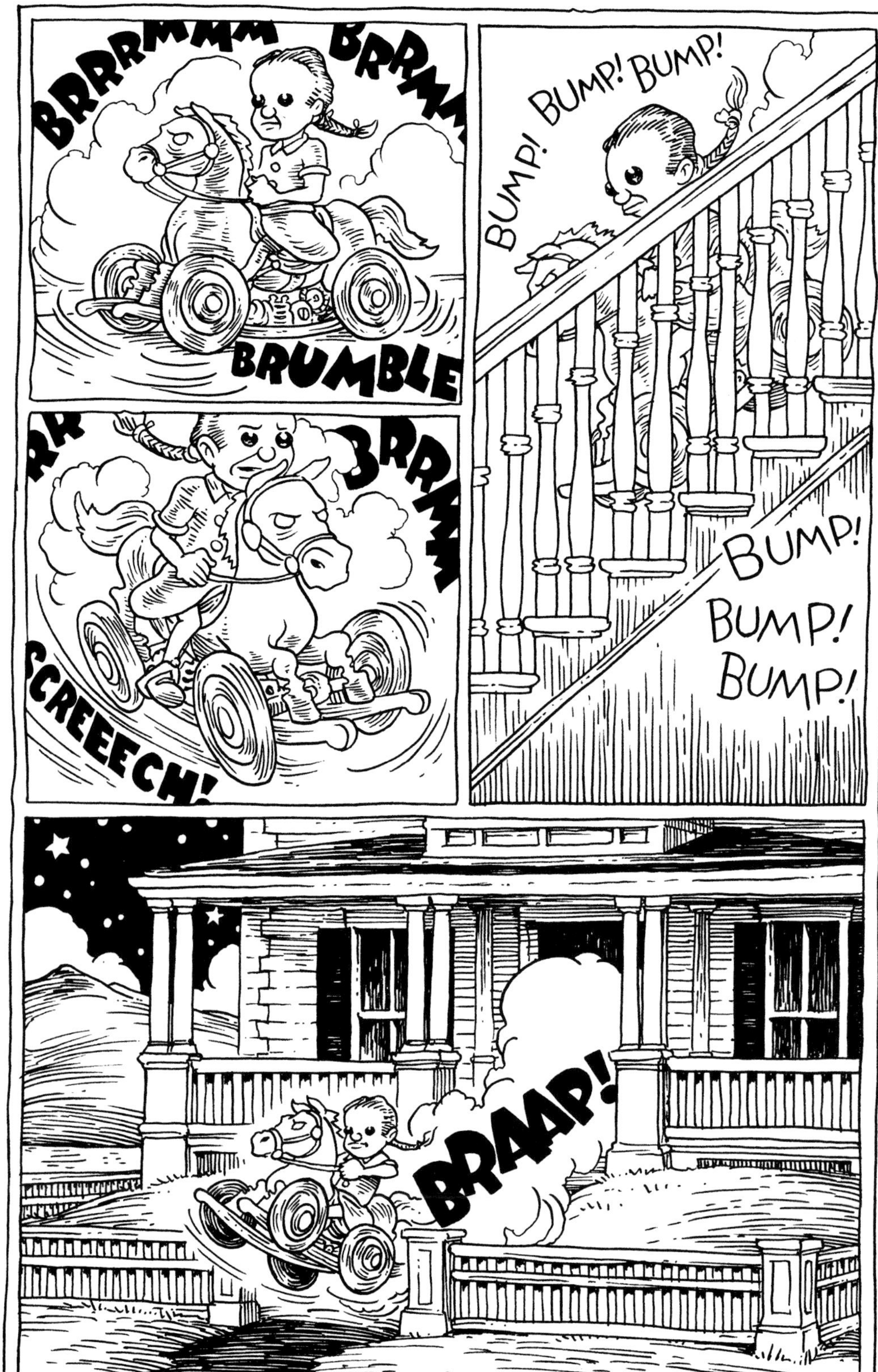
BRRRMMM
BRRMM
BRUMBLE
BUMP! BUMP! BUMP!
RR
BRRMM
SCREEEECH!
BUMP!
BUMP!
BUMP!
BRAAP!

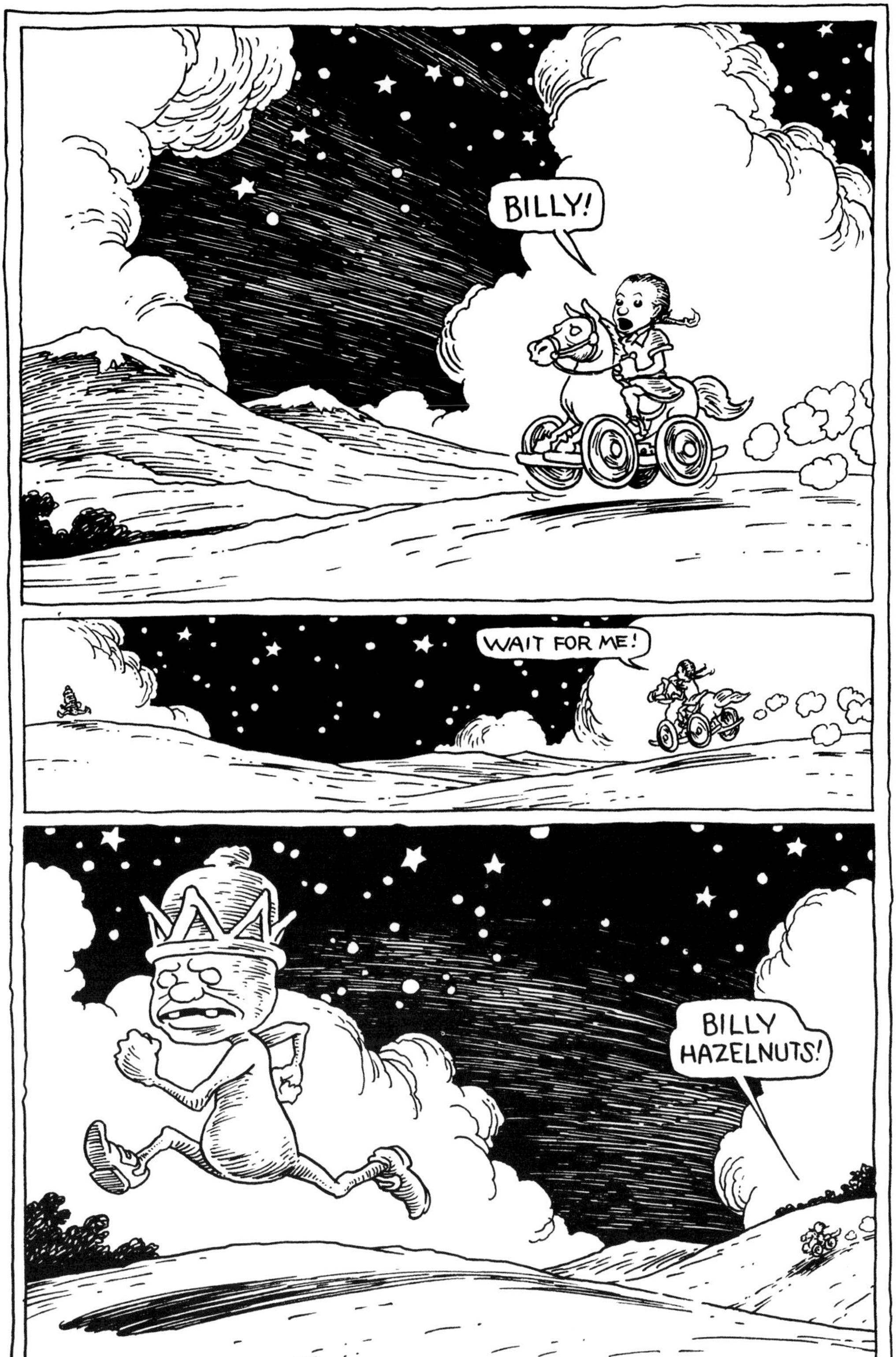
BILLY!
WAIT FOR ME!
BILLY HAZELNUTS!

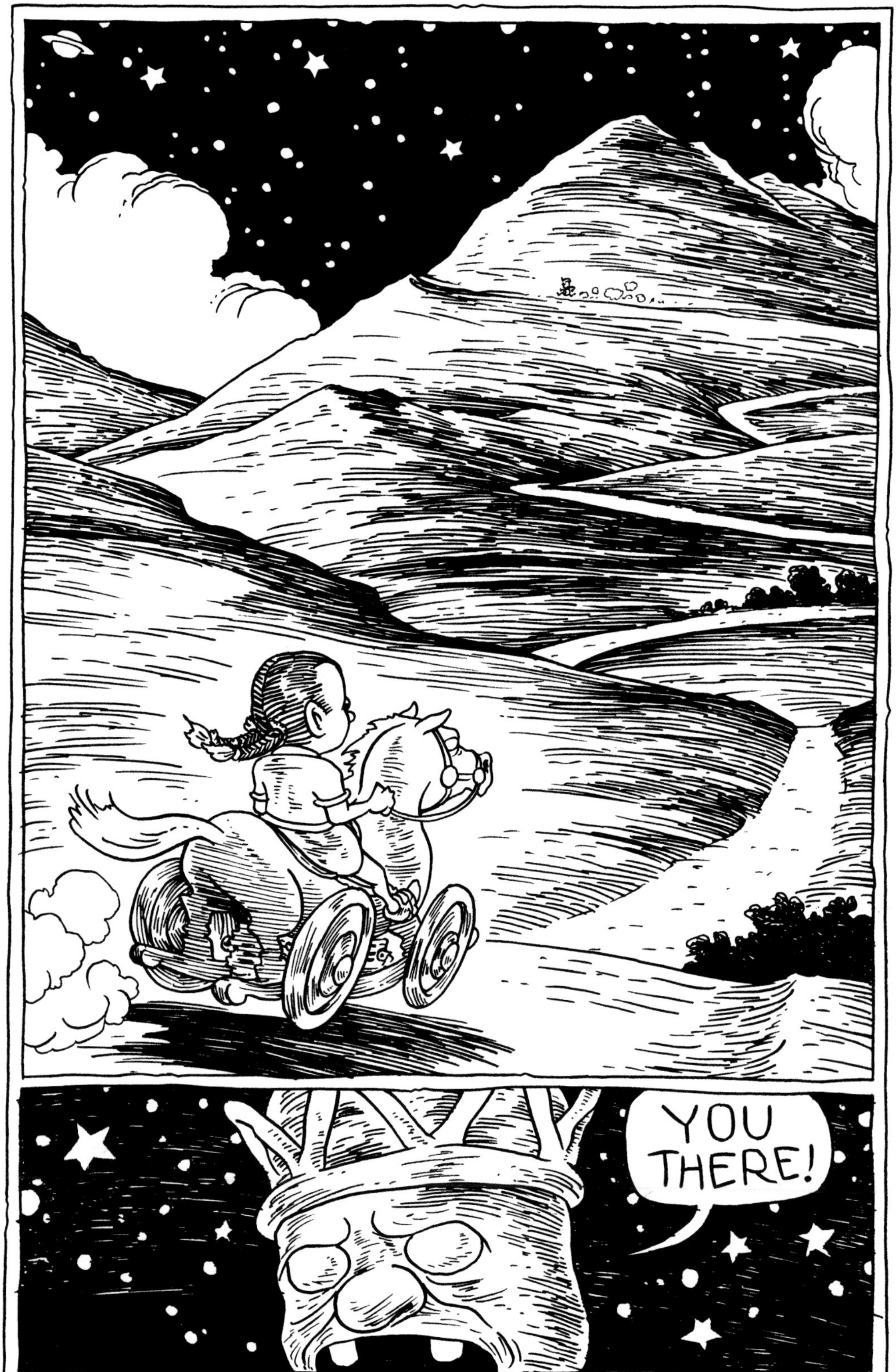
YOU THERE!

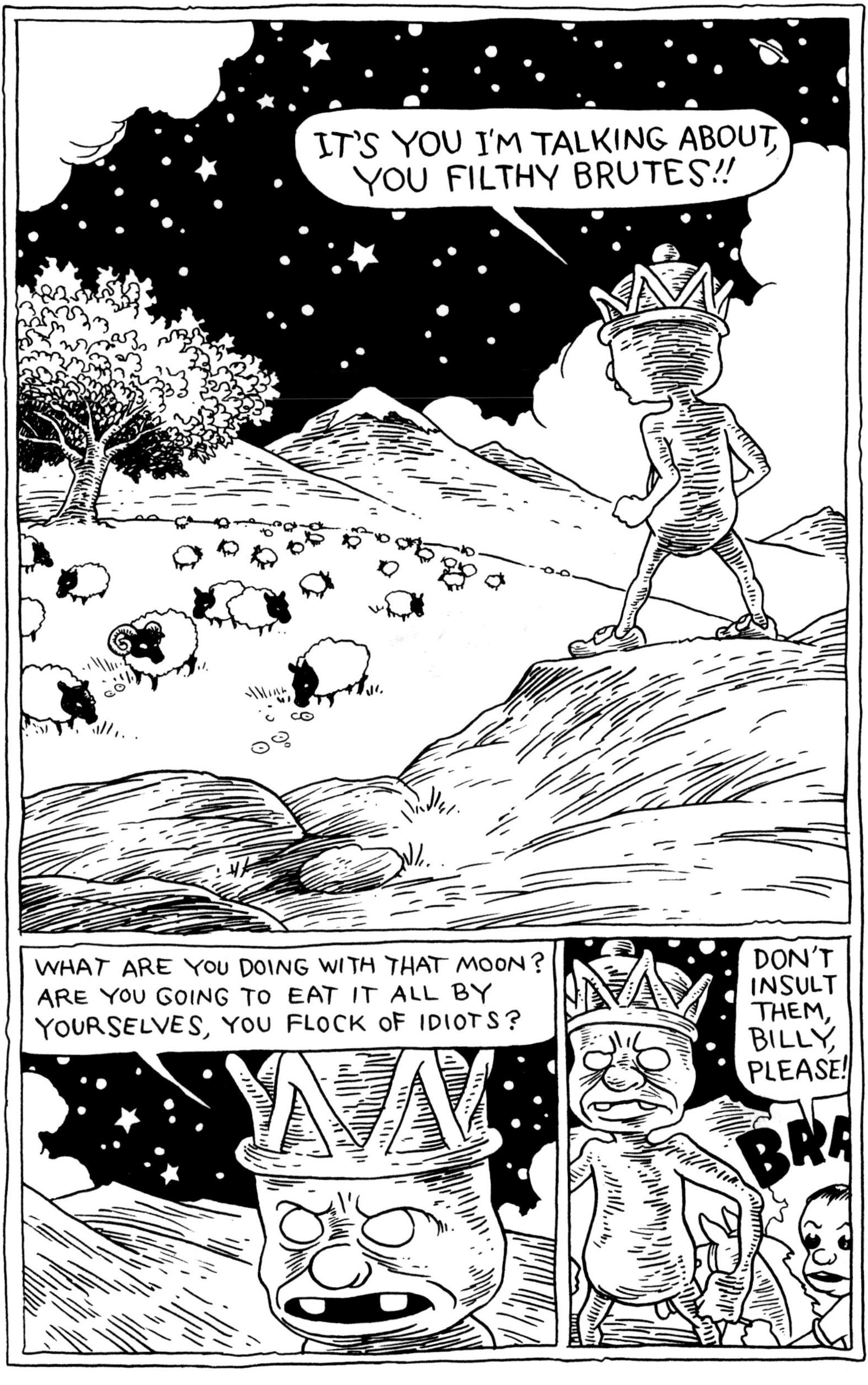
IT'S YOU I'M TALKING ABOUT, YOU FILTHY BRUTES!!
WHAT ARE YOU DOING WITH THAT MOON? ARE YOU GOING TO EAT IT ALL BY YOURSELVES, YOU FLOCK OF IDIOTS?
DON'T INSULT THEM, BILLY, PLEASE!

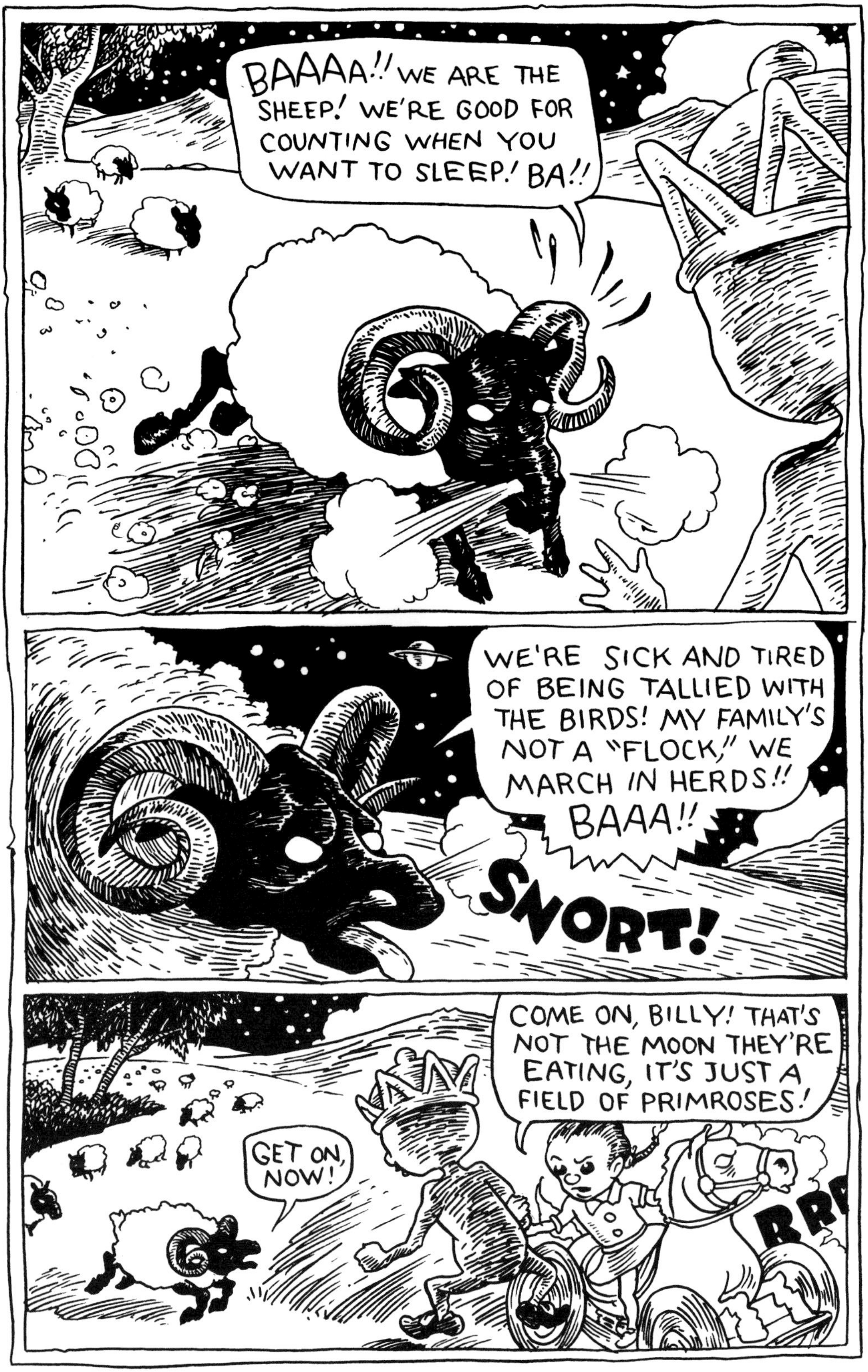
BAAAA!! WE ARE THE SHEEP! WE'RE GOOD FOR COUNTING WHEN YOU WANT TO SLEEP! BA!!
WE'RE SICK AND TIRED OF BEING TALLIED WITH THE BIRDS! MY FAMILY'S NOT A "FLOCK," WE MARCH IN HERDS!! BAAA!!
SNORT!
COME ON, BILLY! THAT'S NOT THE MOON THEY'RE EATING, IT'S JUST A FIELD OF PRIMROSES!
GET ON, NOW!

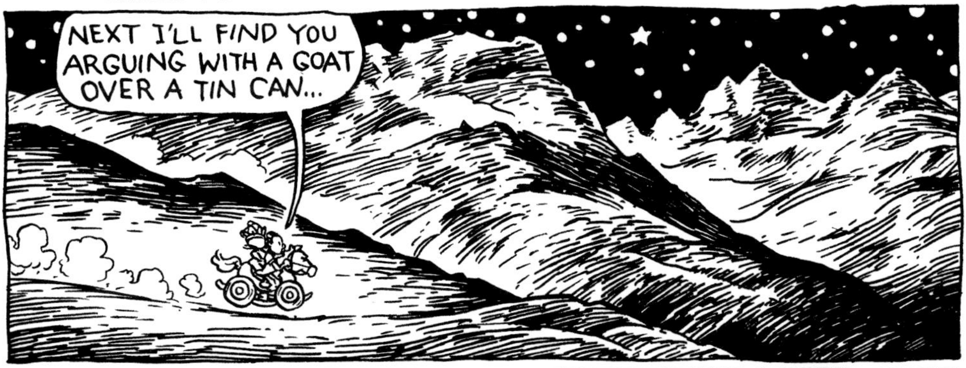
NEXT I'LL FIND YOU ARGUING WITH A GOAT OVER A TIN CAN...

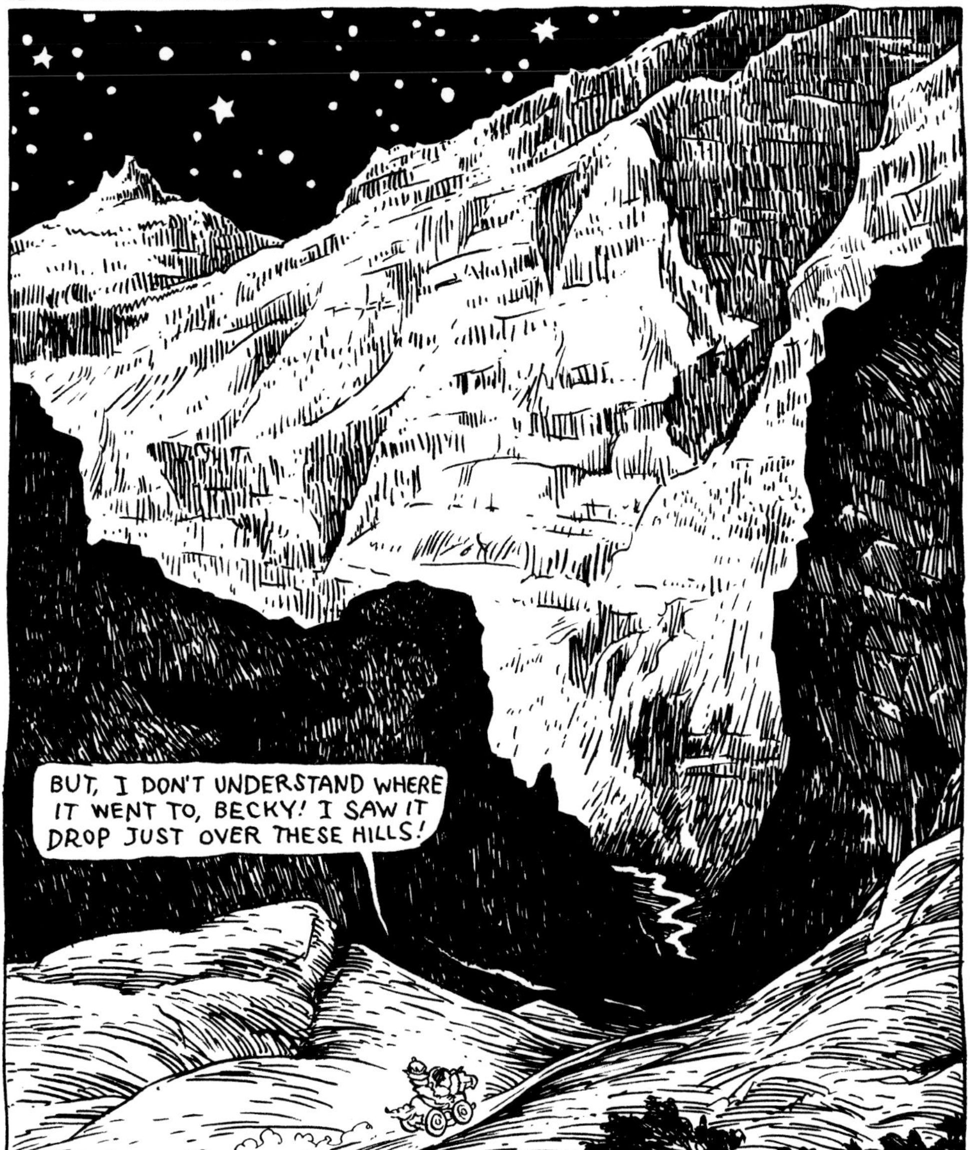
BUT, I DON'T UNDERSTAND WHERE IT WENT TO, BECKY! I SAW IT DROP JUST OVER THESE HILLS!

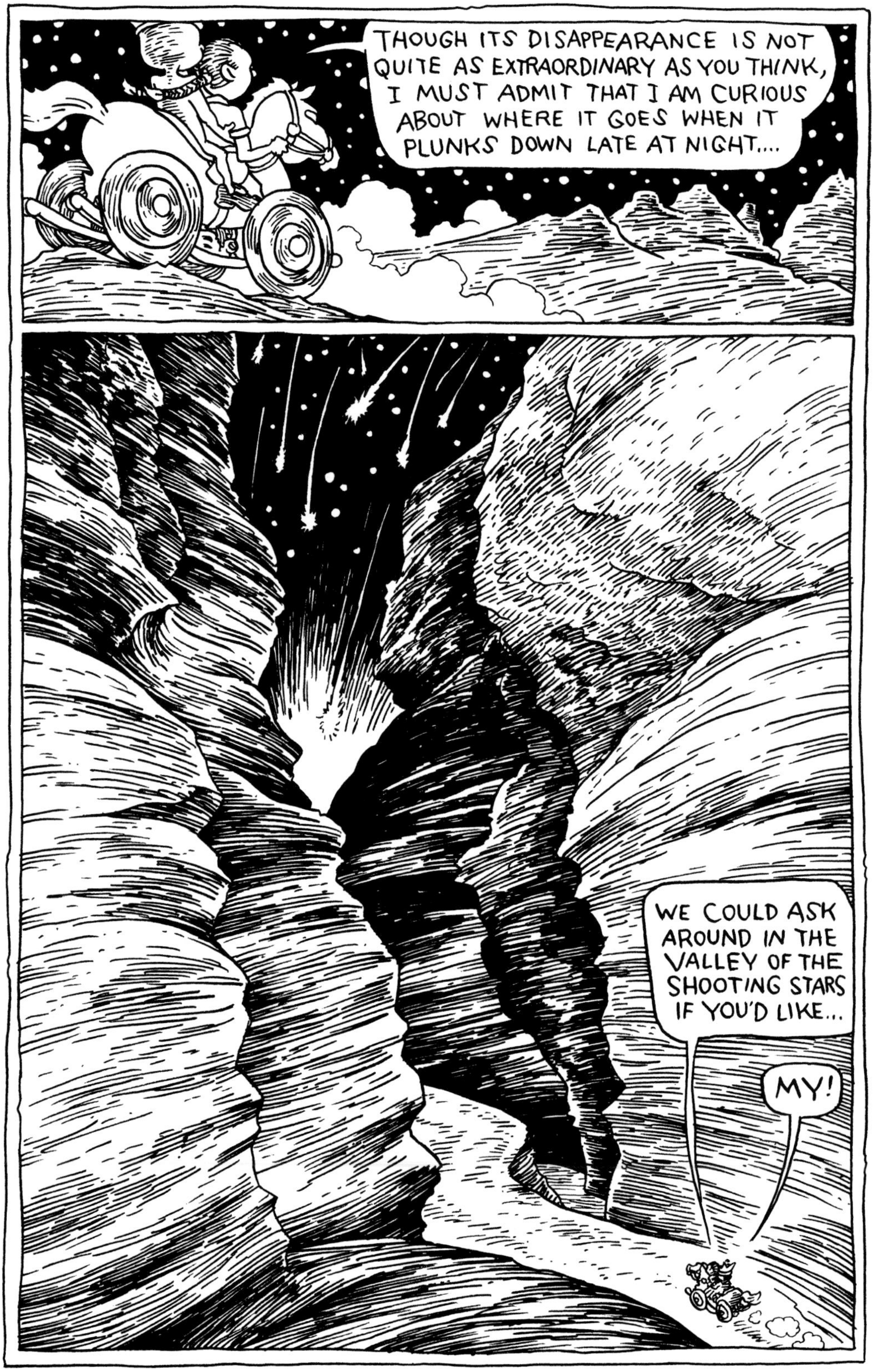
THOUGH ITS DISAPPEARANCE IS NOT QUITE AS EXTRAORDINARY AS YOU THINK, I MUST ADMIT THAT I AM CURIOUS ABOUT WHERE IT GOES WHEN IT PLUNKS DOWN LATE AT NIGHT....
WE COULD ASK AROUND IN THE VALLEY OF THE SHOOTING STARS IF YOU'D LIKE...
MY!

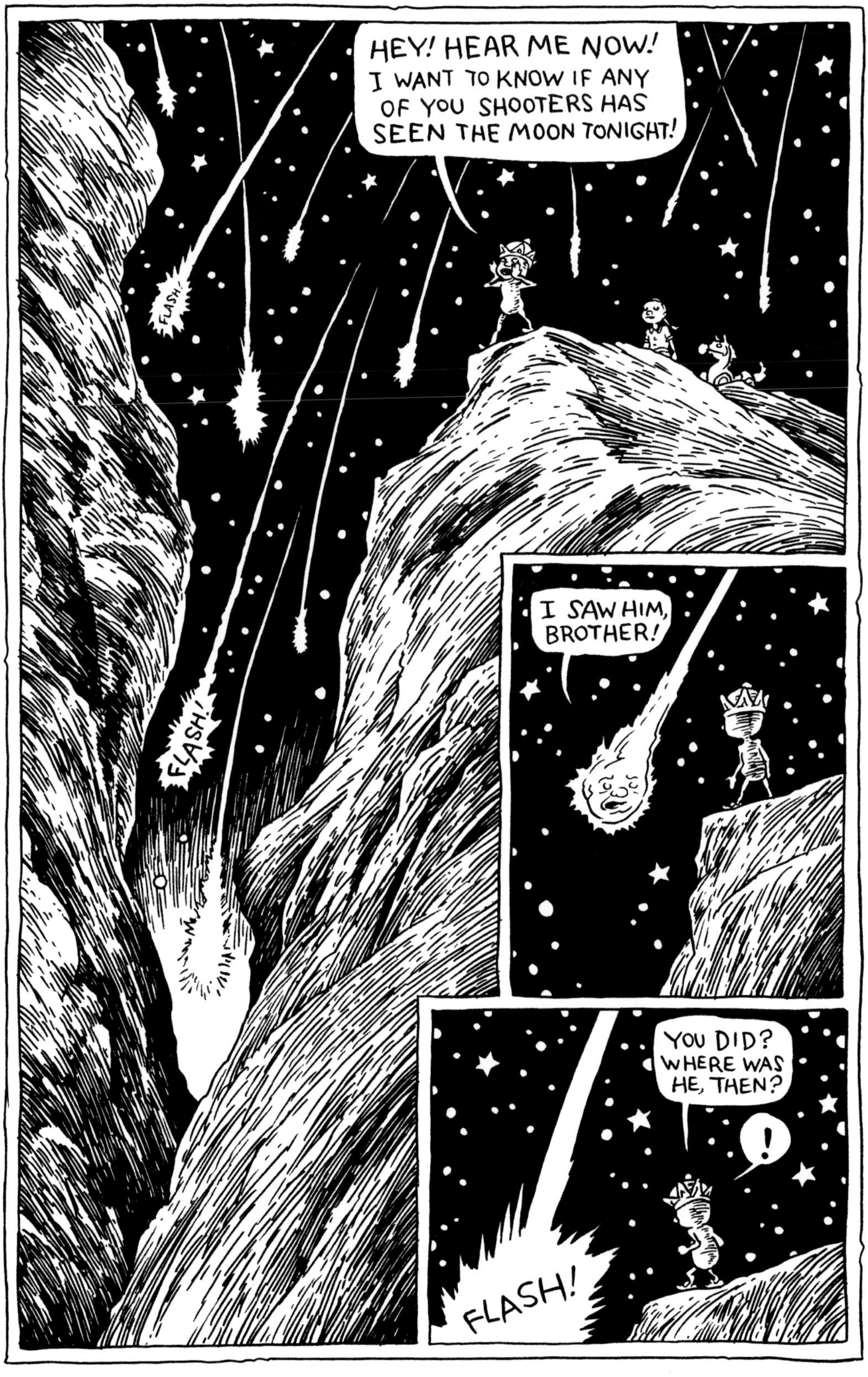
HEY! HEAR ME NOW! I WANT TO KNOW IF ANY OF YOU SHOOTERS HAS SEEN THE MOON TONIGHT!
FLASH!
FLASH!
I SAW HIM, BROTHER!
YOU DID? WHERE WAS HE, THEN?
!
FLASH!

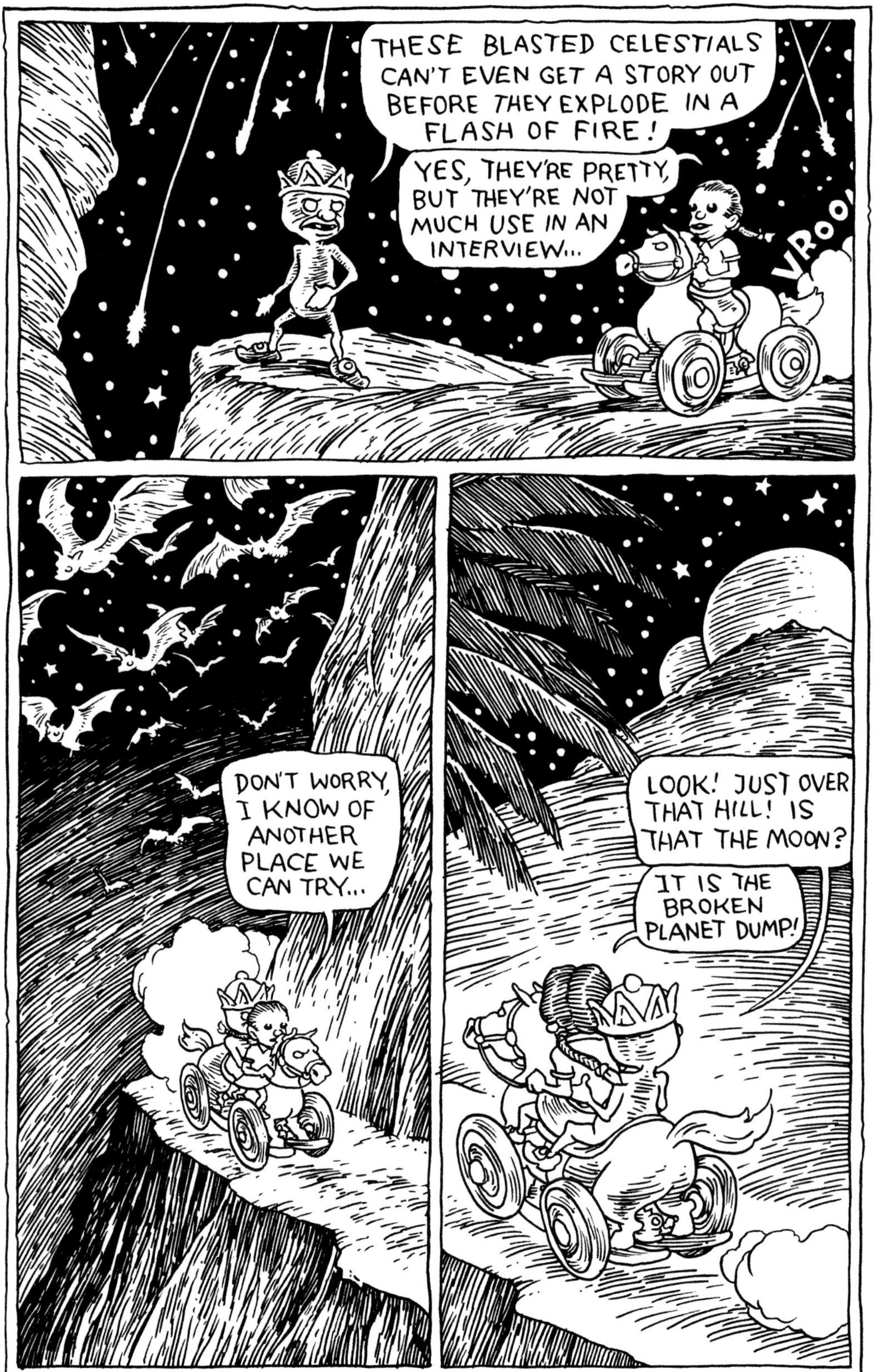
THESE BLASTED CELESTIALS CAN'T EVEN GET A STORY OUT BEFORE *THEY* EXPLODE IN A FLASH OF FIRE!
YES, THEY'RE PRETTY, BUT THEY'RE NOT MUCH USE IN AN INTERVIEW...
VROO
DON'T WORRY, I KNOW OF ANOTHER PLACE WE CAN TRY...
LOOK! JUST OVER THAT HILL! IS THAT THE MOON?
IT IS THE BROKEN PLANET DUMP!

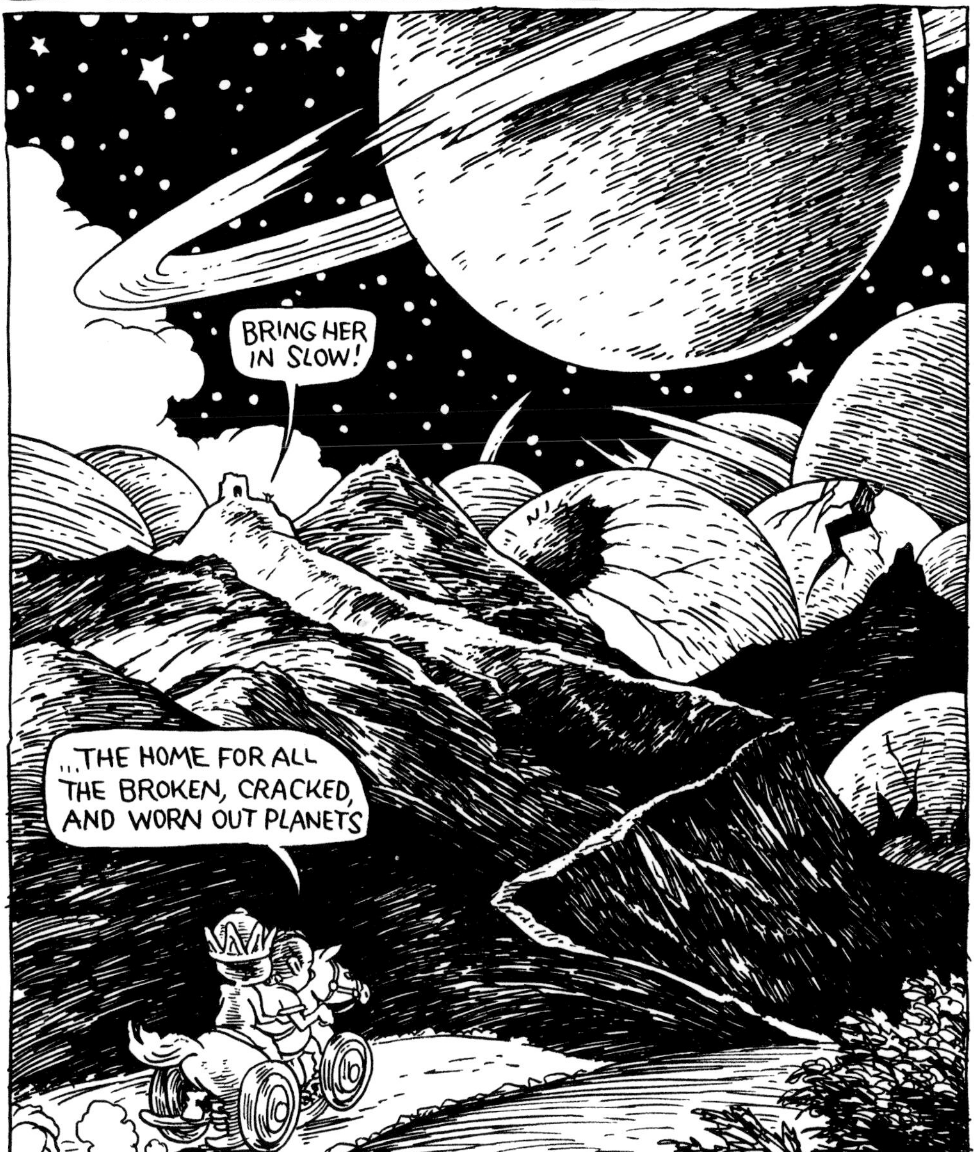
BRING HER IN SLOW!
...THE HOME FOR ALL THE BROKEN, CRACKED, AND WORN OUT PLANETS

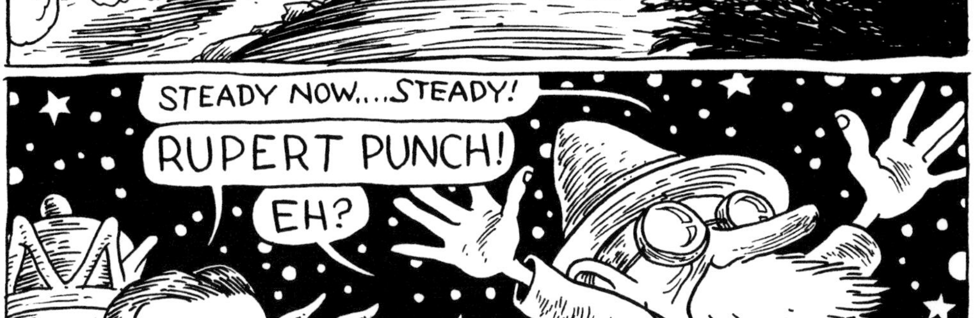
STEADY NOW....STEADY!
RUPERT PUNCH!
EH?

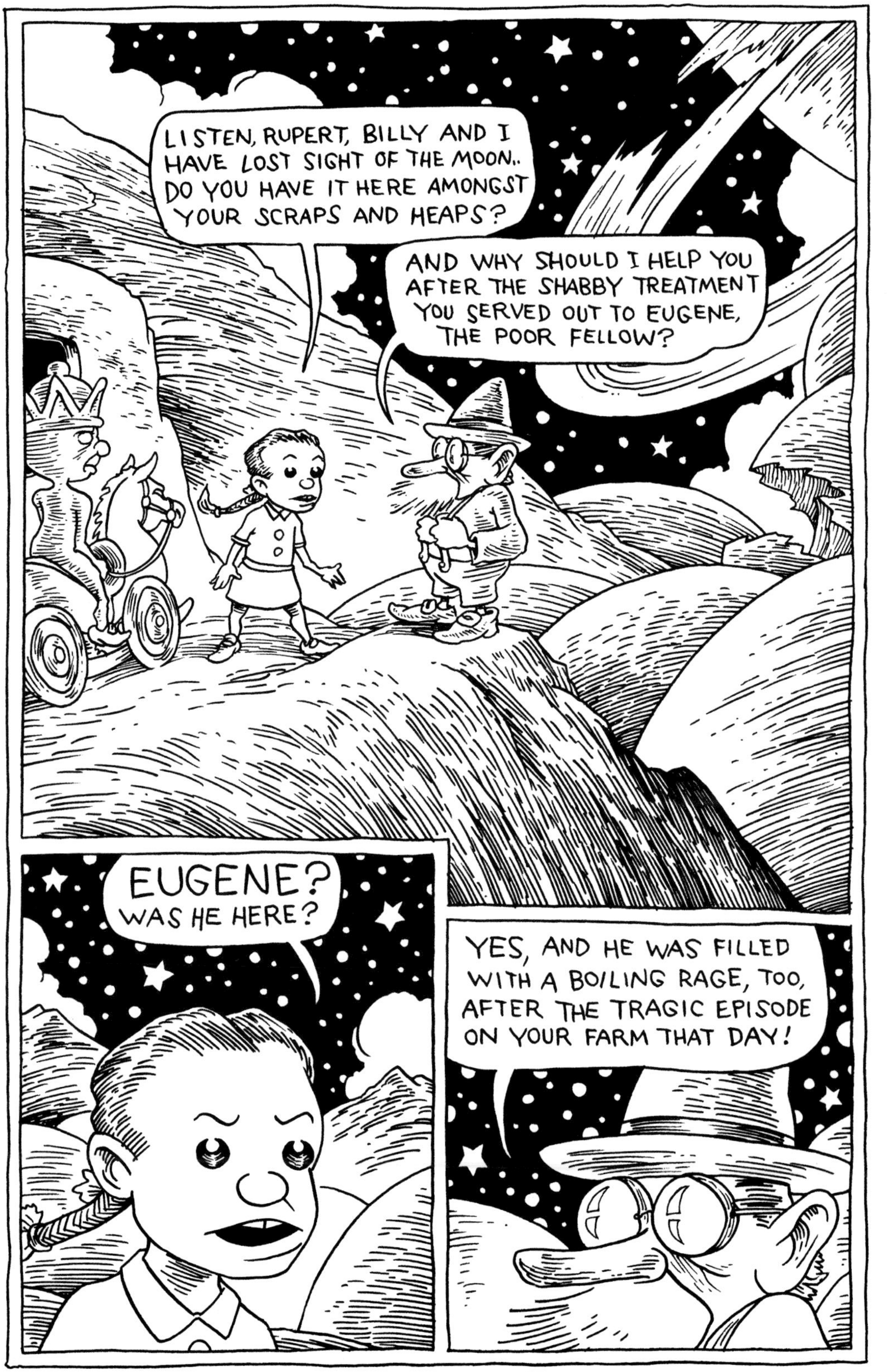
LISTEN, RUPERT, BILLY AND I HAVE LOST SIGHT OF THE MOON.. DO YOU HAVE IT HERE AMONGST YOUR SCRAPS AND HEAPS?
AND WHY SHOULD I HELP YOU AFTER THE SHABBY TREATMENT YOU SERVED OUT TO EUGENE, THE POOR FELLOW?
EUGENE? WAS HE HERE?
YES, AND HE WAS FILLED WITH A BOILING RAGE, TOO, AFTER THE TRAGIC EPISODE ON YOUR FARM THAT DAY!

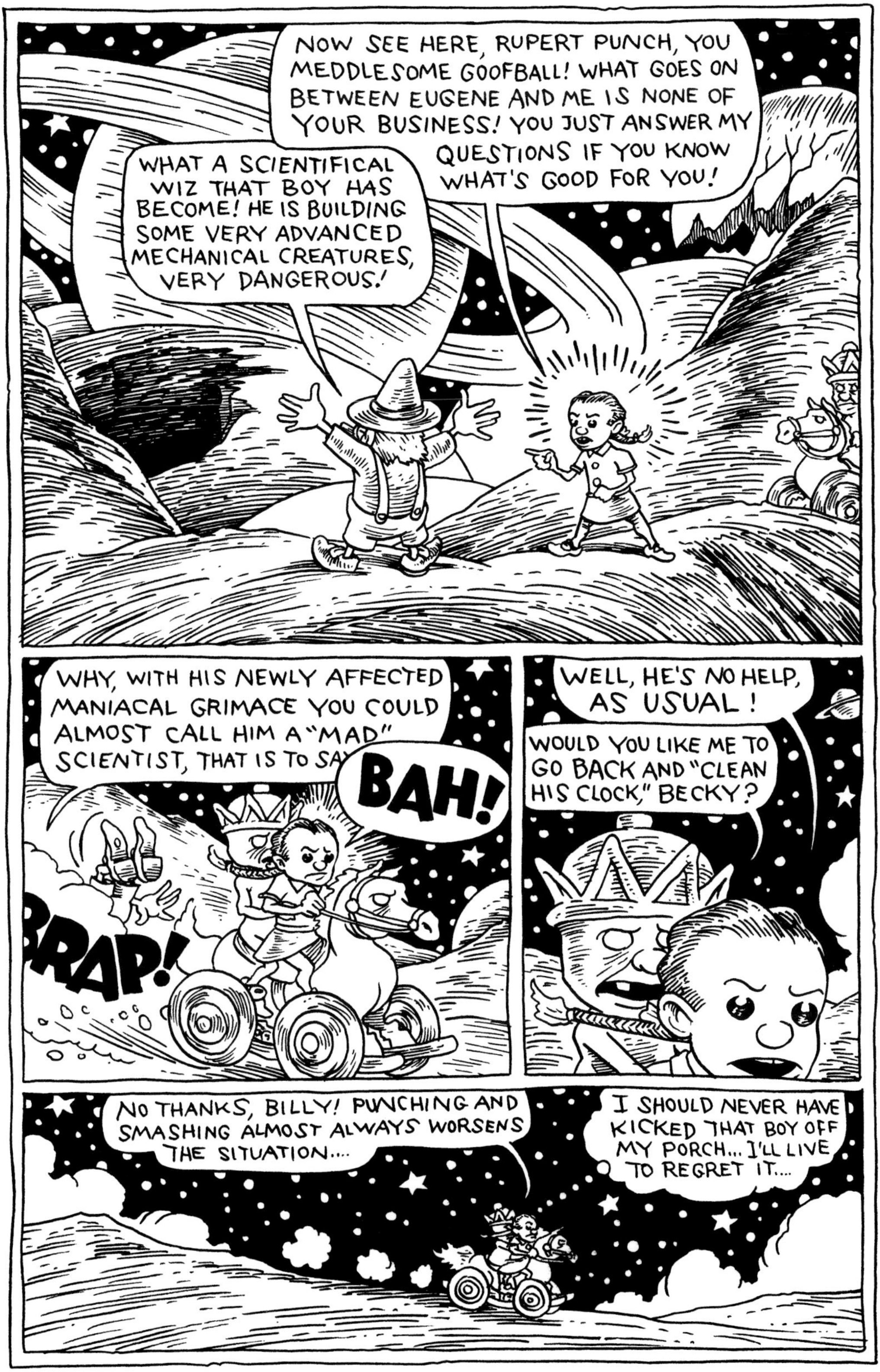
NOW SEE HERE, RUPERT PUNCH, YOU MEDDLESOME GOOFBALL! WHAT GOES ON BETWEEN EUGENE AND ME IS NONE OF YOUR BUSINESS! YOU JUST ANSWER MY QUESTIONS IF YOU KNOW WHAT'S GOOD FOR YOU!
WHAT A SCIENTIFICAL WIZ THAT BOY HAS BECOME! HE IS BUILDING SOME VERY ADVANCED MECHANICAL CREATURES, VERY DANGEROUS!
WHY, WITH HIS NEWLY AFFECTED MANIACAL GRIMACE YOU COULD ALMOST CALL HIM A "MAD" SCIENTIST, THAT IS TO SA
BAH!
BRAP!
WELL, HE'S NO HELP, AS USUAL!
WOULD YOU LIKE ME TO GO BACK AND "CLEAN HIS CLOCK," BECKY?
NO THANKS, BILLY! PUNCHING AND SMASHING ALMOST ALWAYS WORSENS THE SITUATION....
I SHOULD NEVER HAVE KICKED THAT BOY OFF MY PORCH... I'LL LIVE TO REGRET IT....

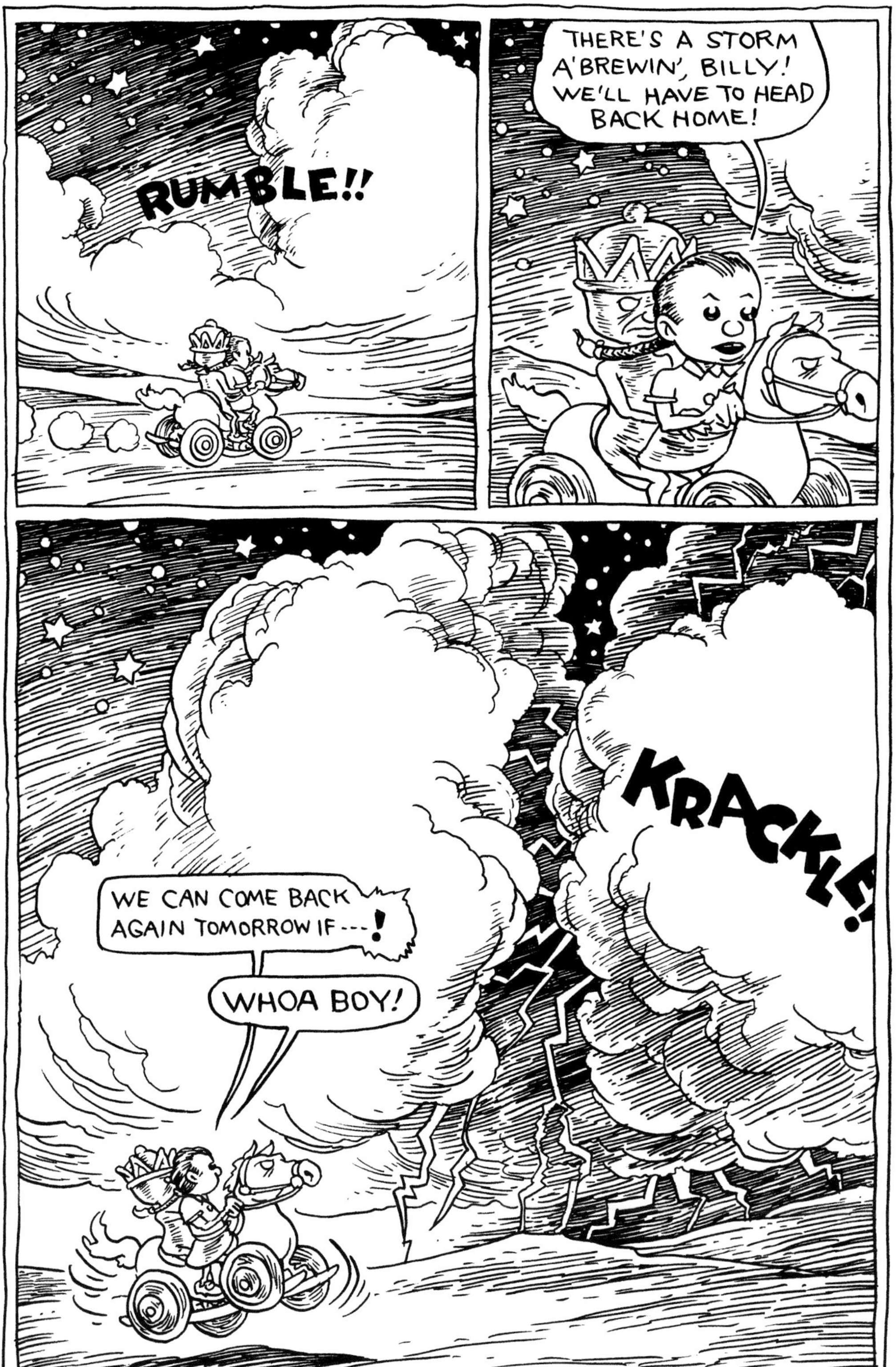
RUMBLE!!
THERE'S A STORM A'BREWIN', BILLY! WE'LL HAVE TO HEAD BACK HOME!
WE CAN COME BACK AGAIN TOMORROW IF---!
WHOA BOY!
KRACKLE!!

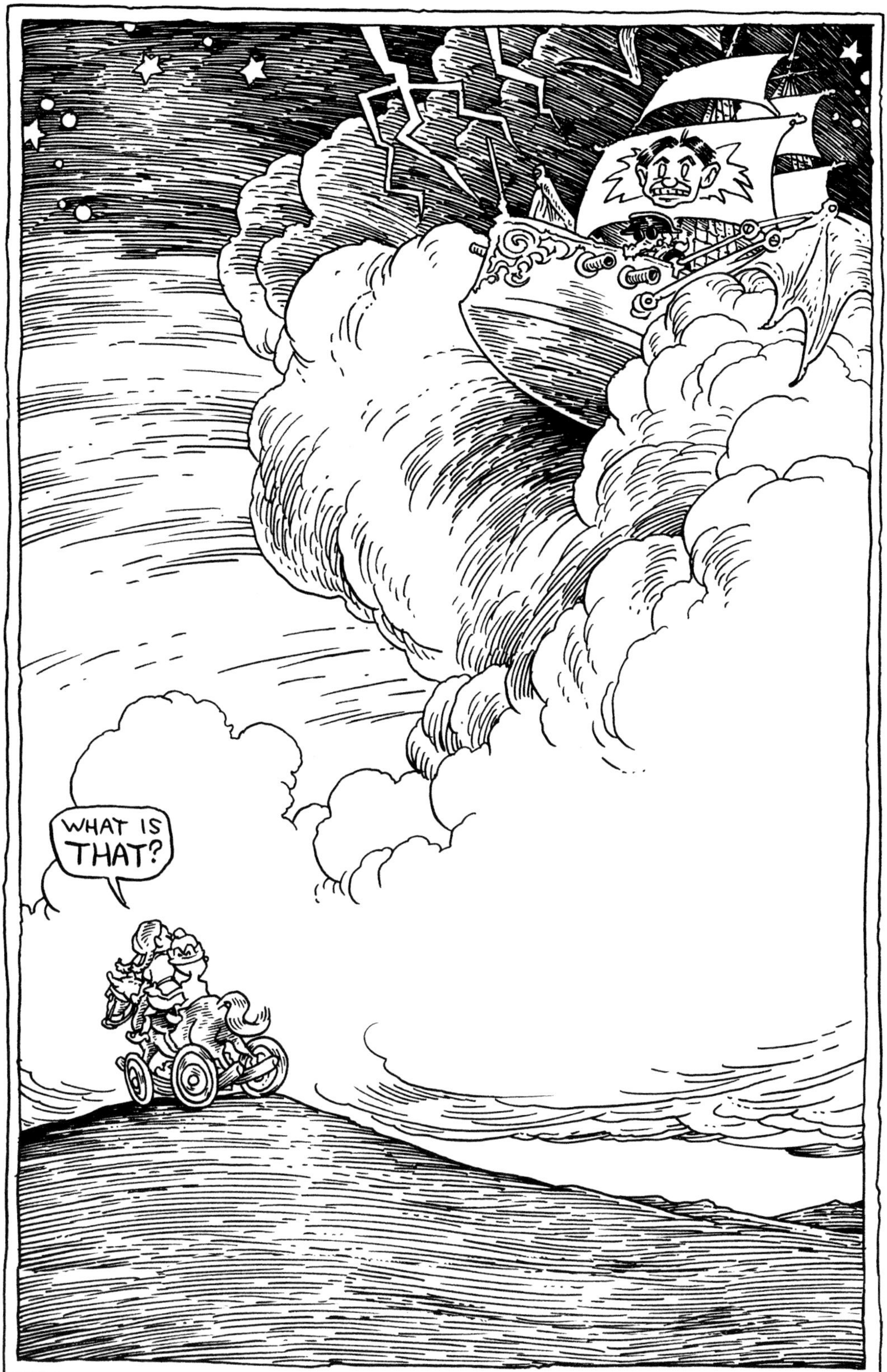
WHAT IS THAT?

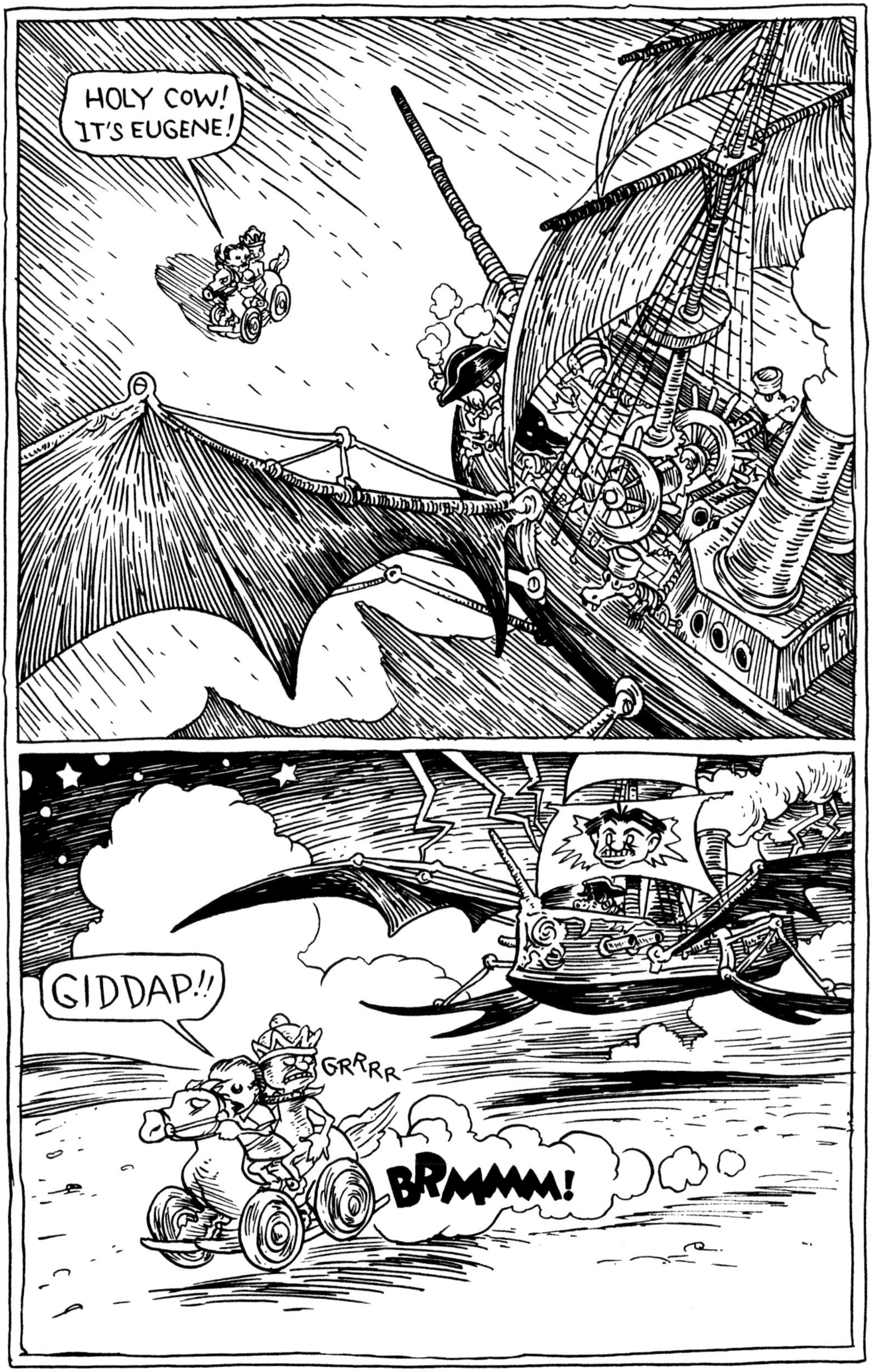
HOLY COW! IT'S EUGENE!
GIDDAP!!
GRRRR
BRMMMM!

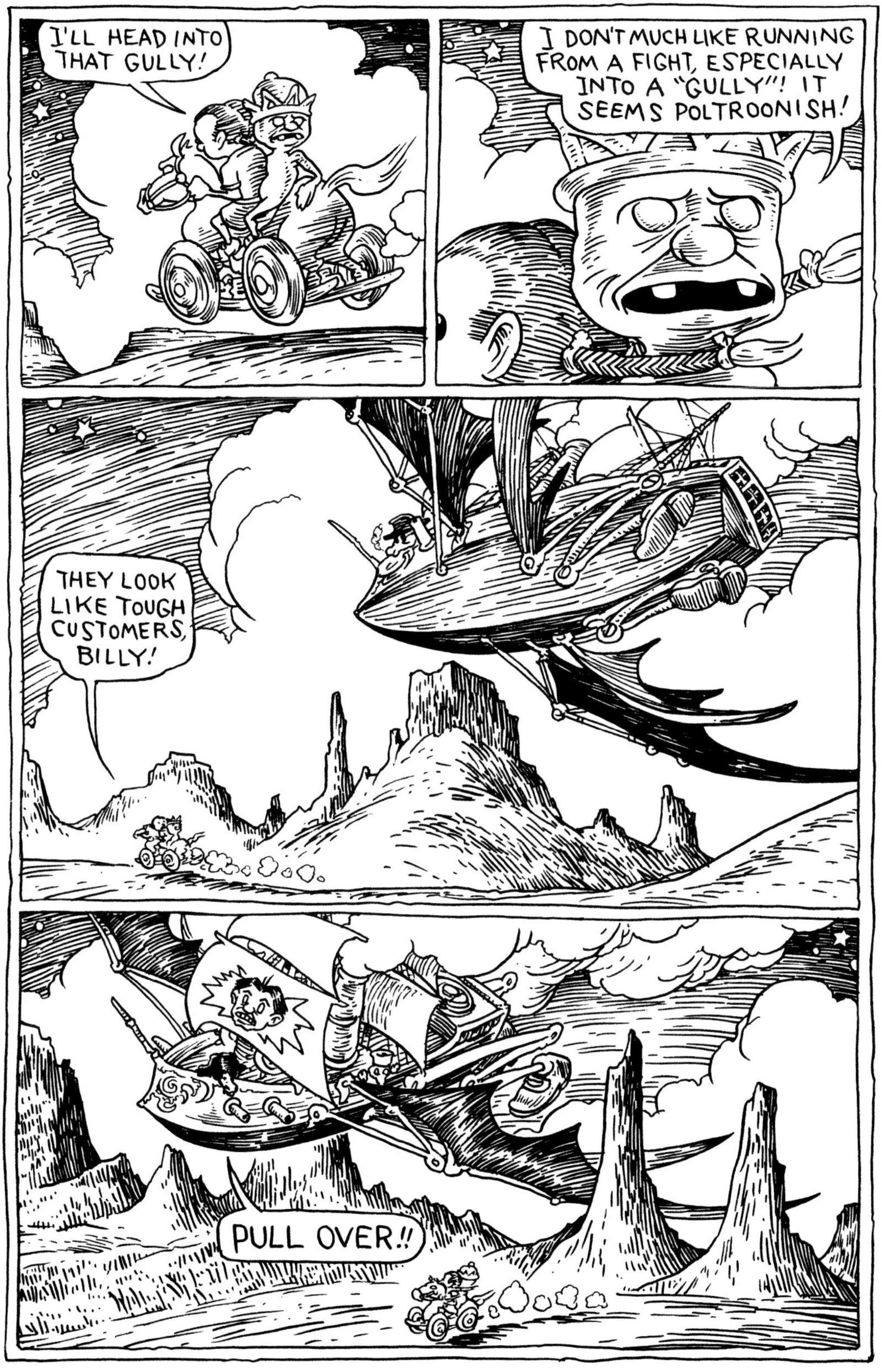
I'LL HEAD INTO THAT GULLY!
I DON'T MUCH LIKE RUNNING FROM A FIGHT, ESPECIALLY INTO A "GULLY"! IT SEEMS POLTROONISH!
THEY LOOK LIKE TOUGH CUSTOMERS, BILLY!
PULL OVER!!

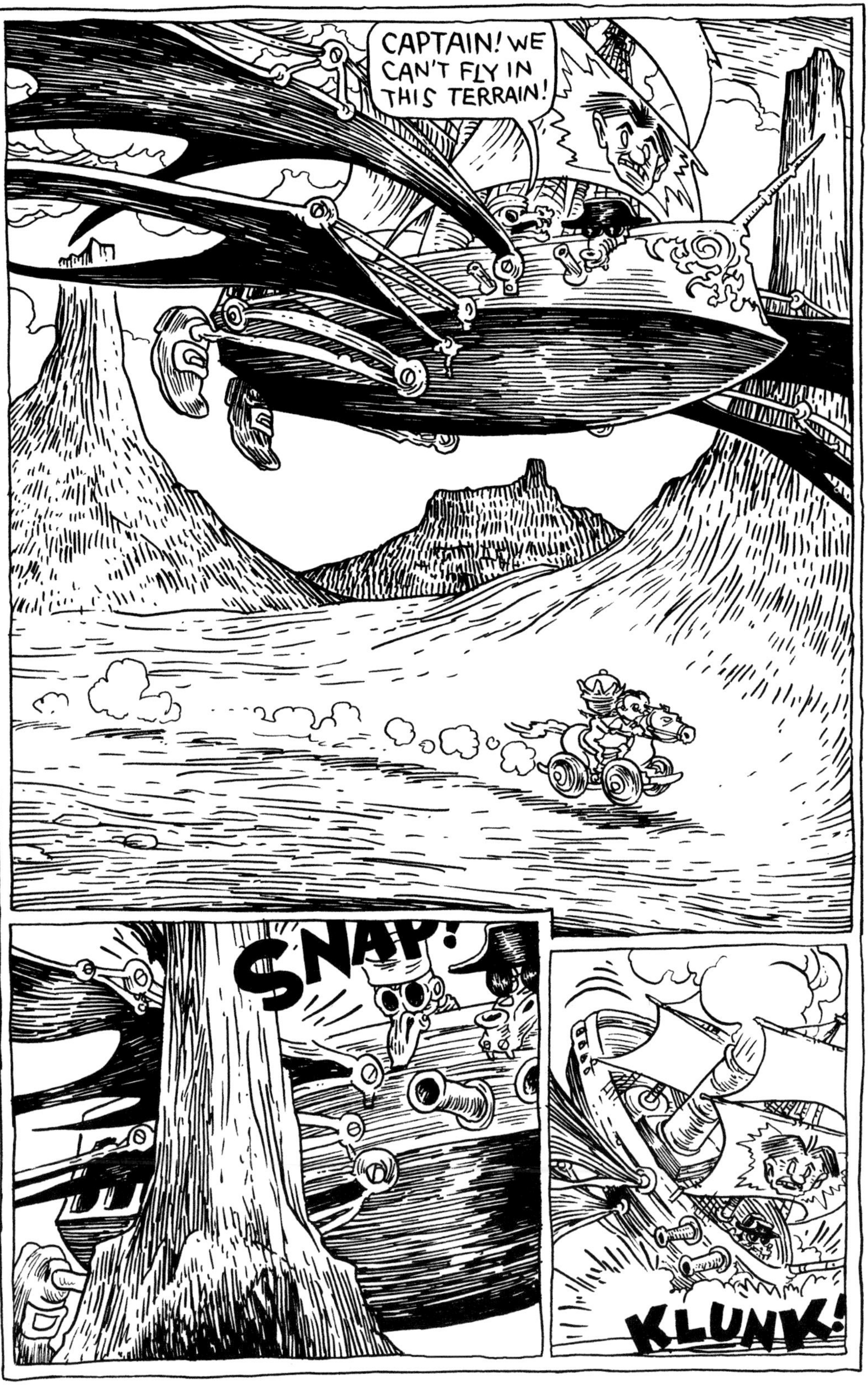
CAPTAIN! WE CAN'T FLY IN THIS TERRAIN!
SNAP!
KLUNK!

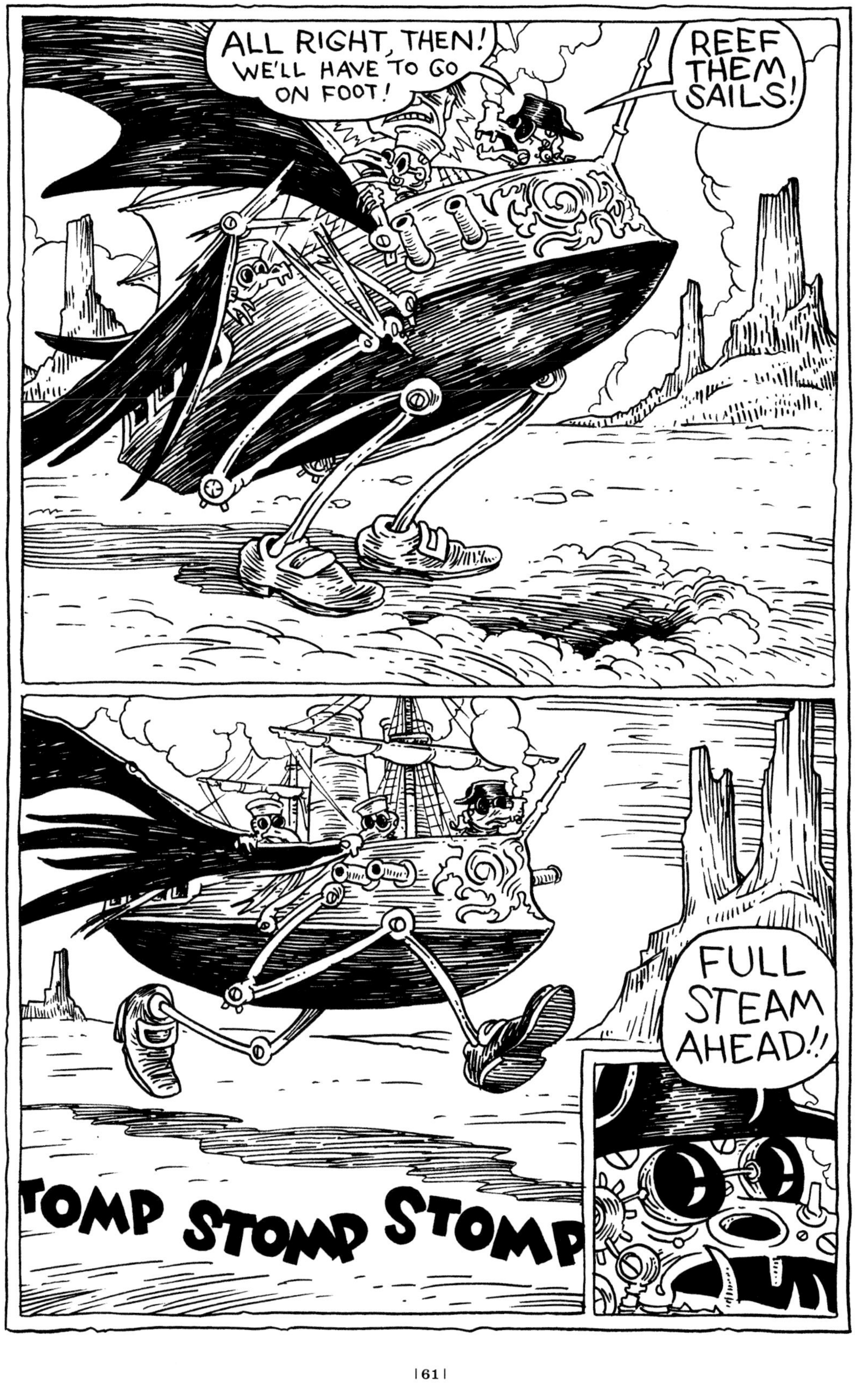
ALL RIGHT, THEN! WE'LL HAVE TO GO ON FOOT!
REEF THEM SAILS!
FULL STEAM AHEAD!!
TOMP STOMP STOMP

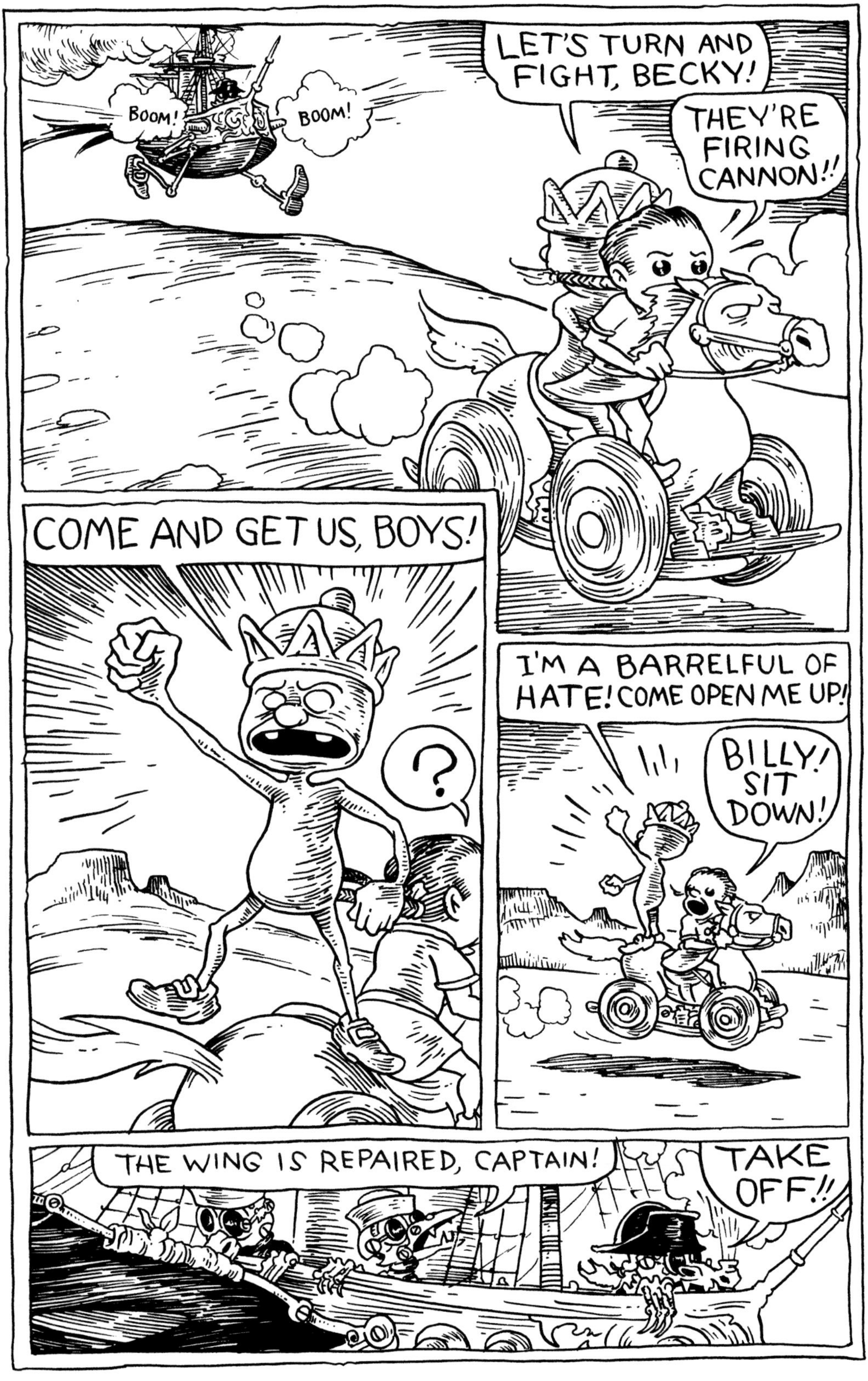
BOOM!
BOOM!
LET'S TURN AND FIGHT, BECKY!
THEY'RE FIRING CANNON!!
COME AND GET US, BOYS!
?
I'M A BARRELFUL OF HATE! COME OPEN ME UP!
BILLY! SIT DOWN!
THE WING IS REPAIRED, CAPTAIN!
TAKE OFF!!

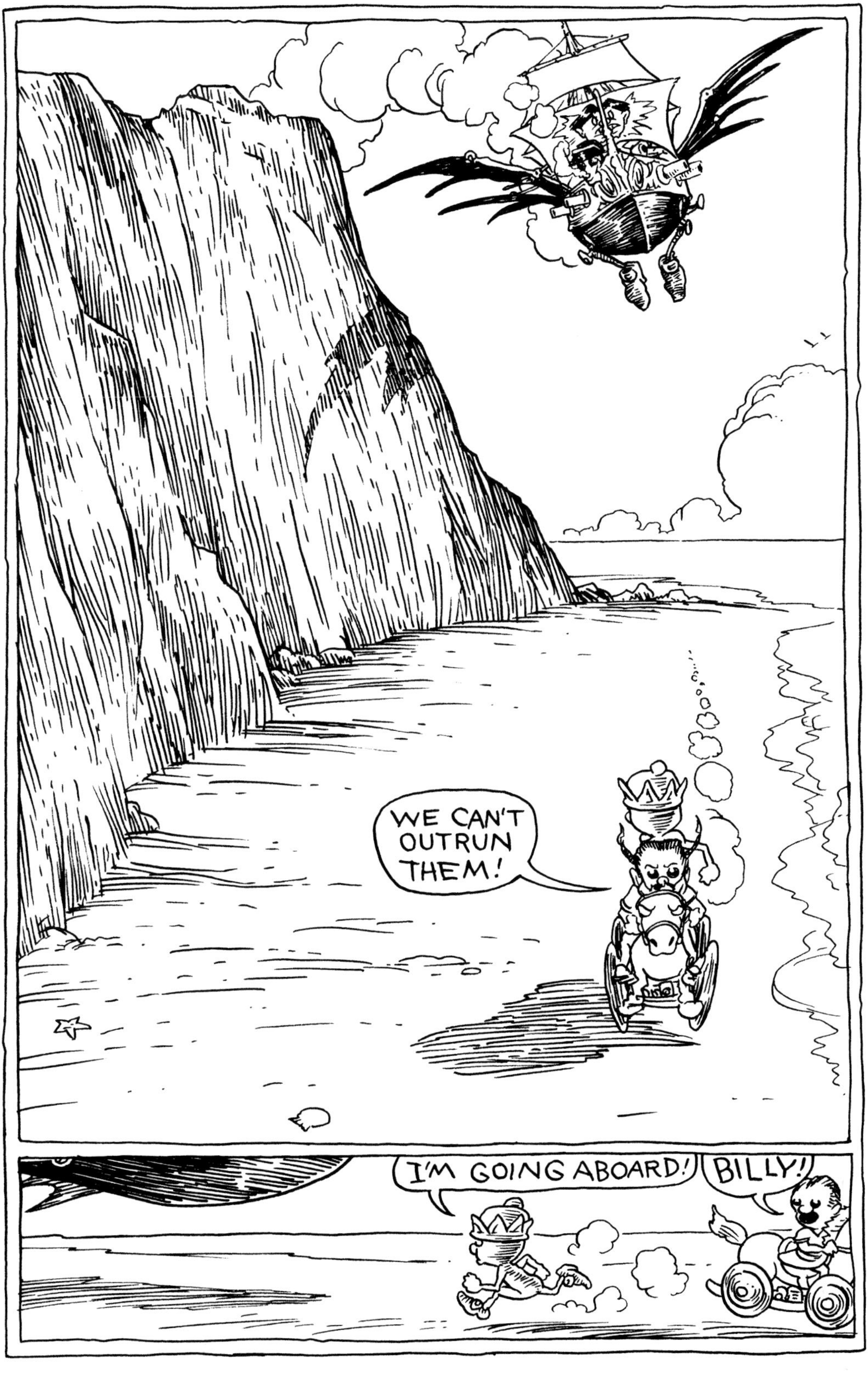
WE CAN'T OUTRUN THEM!
I'M GOING ABOARD!
BILLY!

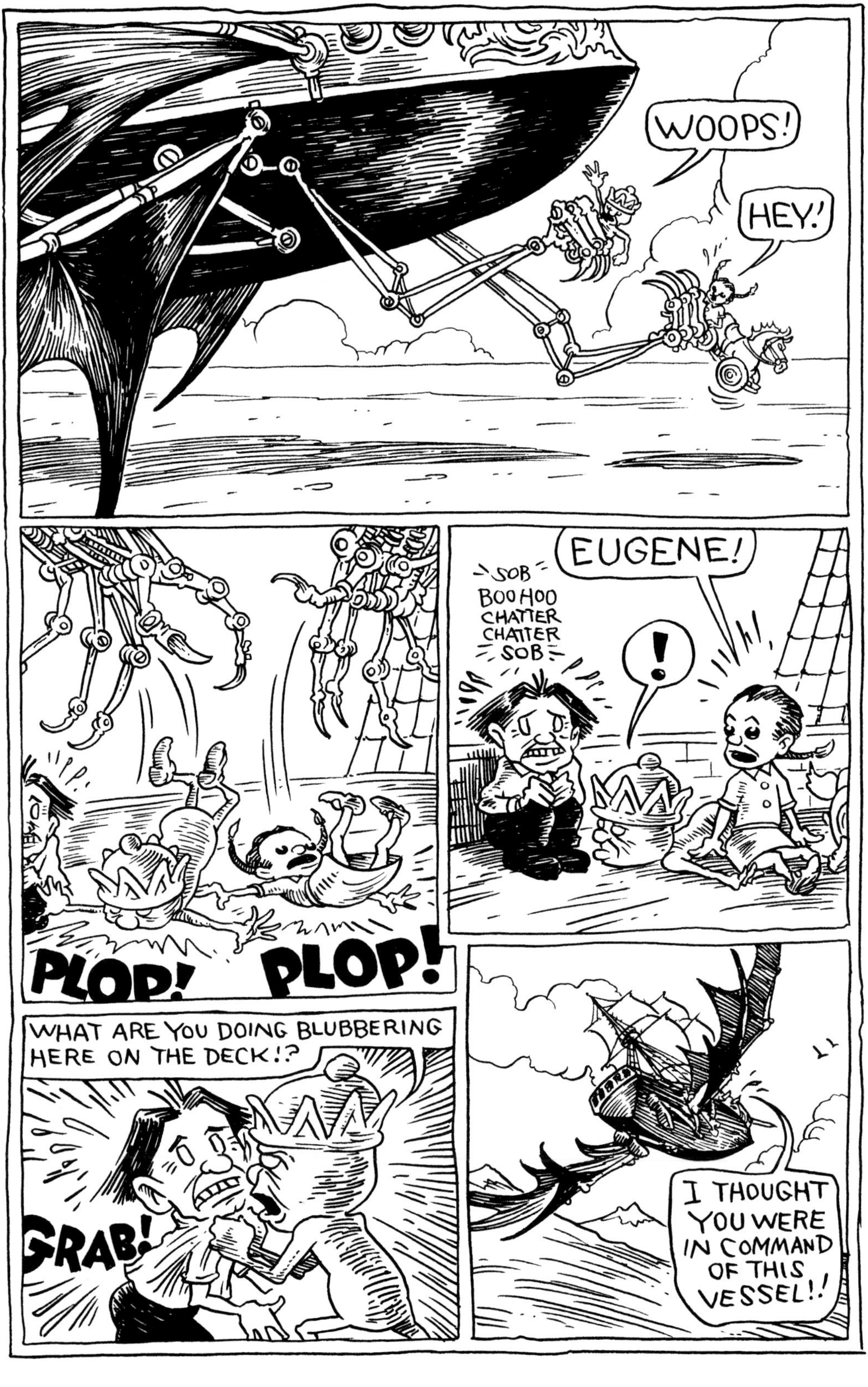
WOOPS!
HEY!
PLOP!
PLOP!
SOB
BOO HOO
CHATTER
CHATTER
SOB
EUGENE!
!
WHAT ARE YOU DOING BLUBBERING HERE ON THE DECK!?
GRAB!
I THOUGHT YOU WERE IN COMMAND OF THIS VESSEL!!

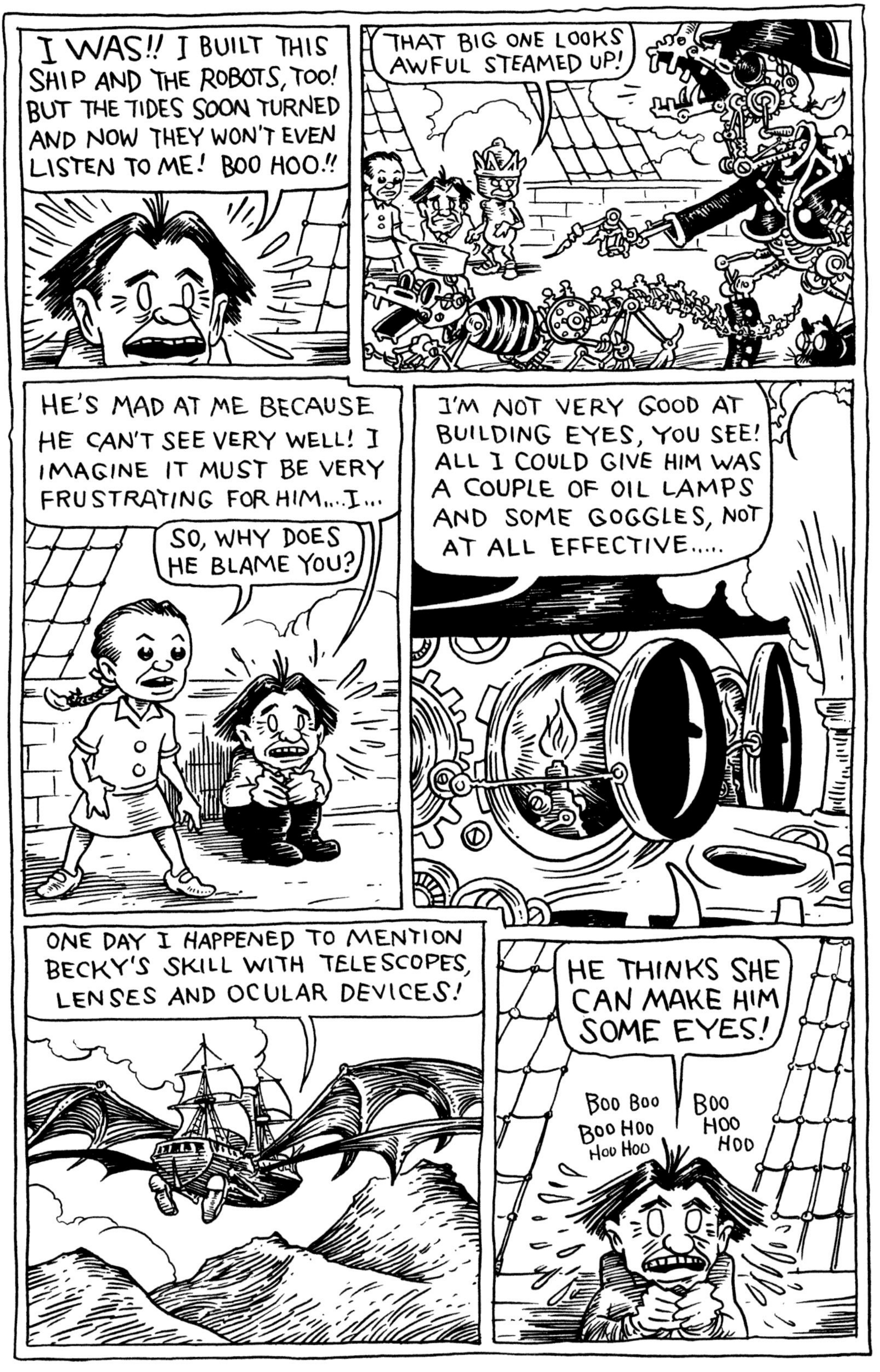

I WAS!! I BUILT THIS SHIP AND THE ROBOTS, TOO! BUT THE TIDES SOON TURNED AND NOW THEY WON'T EVEN LISTEN TO ME! BOO HOO!!
THAT BIG ONE LOOKS AWFUL STEAMED UP!
HE'S MAD AT ME BECAUSE HE CAN'T SEE VERY WELL! I IMAGINE IT MUST BE VERY FRUSTRATING FOR HIM....I...
SO, WHY DOES HE BLAME YOU?
I'M NOT VERY GOOD AT BUILDING EYES, YOU SEE! ALL I COULD GIVE HIM WAS A COUPLE OF OIL LAMPS AND SOME GOGGLES, NOT AT ALL EFFECTIVE.....
ONE DAY I HAPPENED TO MENTION BECKY'S SKILL WITH TELESCOPES, LENSES AND OCULAR DEVICES!
HE THINKS SHE CAN MAKE HIM SOME EYES!
BOO BOO BOO HOO HOO HOO
BOO HOO HOO

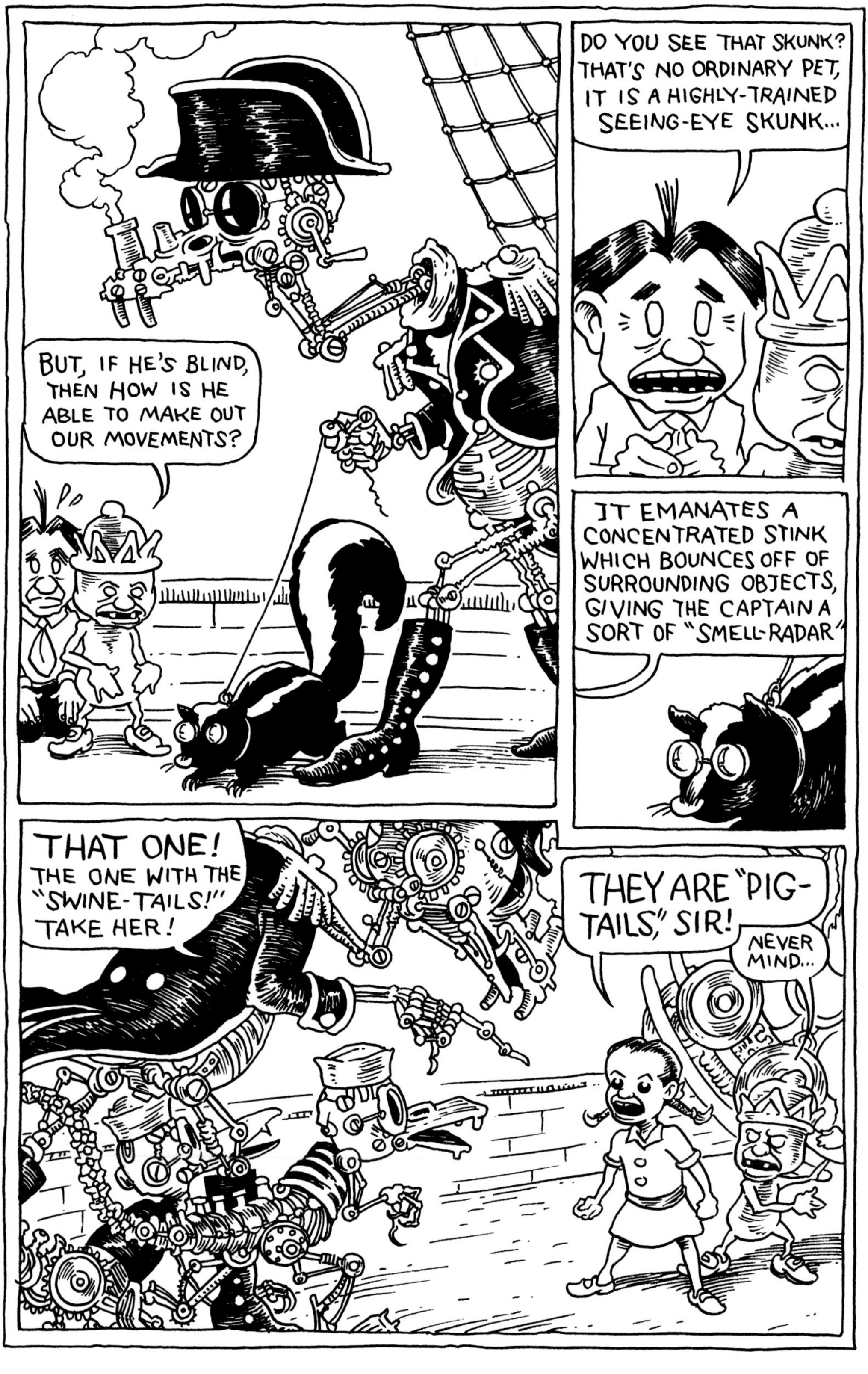
DO YOU SEE THAT SKUNK? THAT'S NO ORDINARY PET, IT IS A HIGHLY-TRAINED SEEING-EYE SKUNK...
BUT, IF HE'S BLIND, THEN HOW IS HE ABLE TO MAKE OUT OUR MOVEMENTS?
IT EMANATES A CONCENTRATED STINK WHICH BOUNCES OFF OF SURROUNDING OBJECTS, GIVING THE CAPTAIN A SORT OF "SMELL-RADAR"
THAT ONE! THE ONE WITH THE "SWINE-TAILS!" TAKE HER!
THEY ARE "PIG-TAILS," SIR!
NEVER MIND...

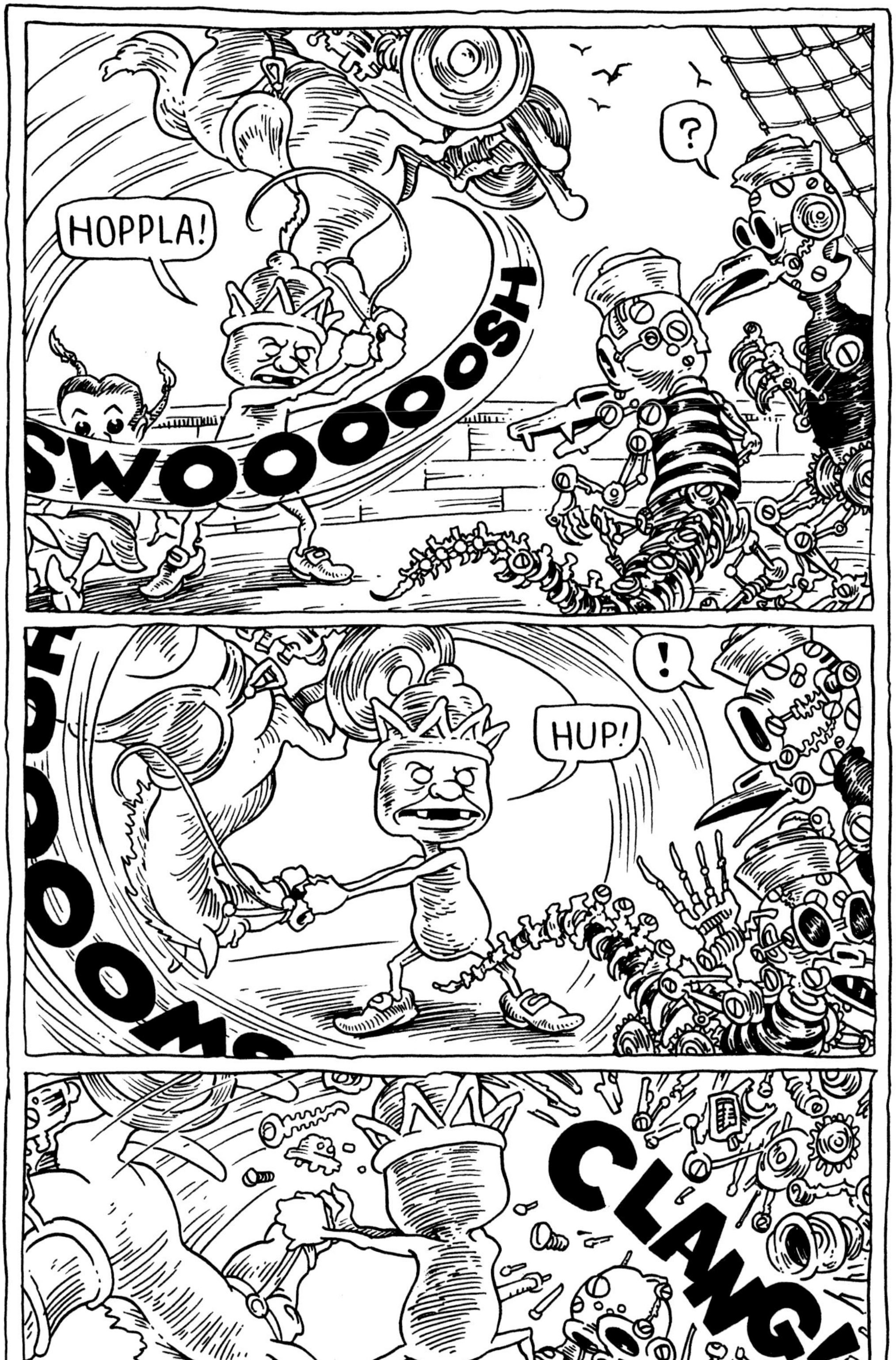
HOPPLA!
?
SWOOOOOOSH
!
HUP!
CLANG!

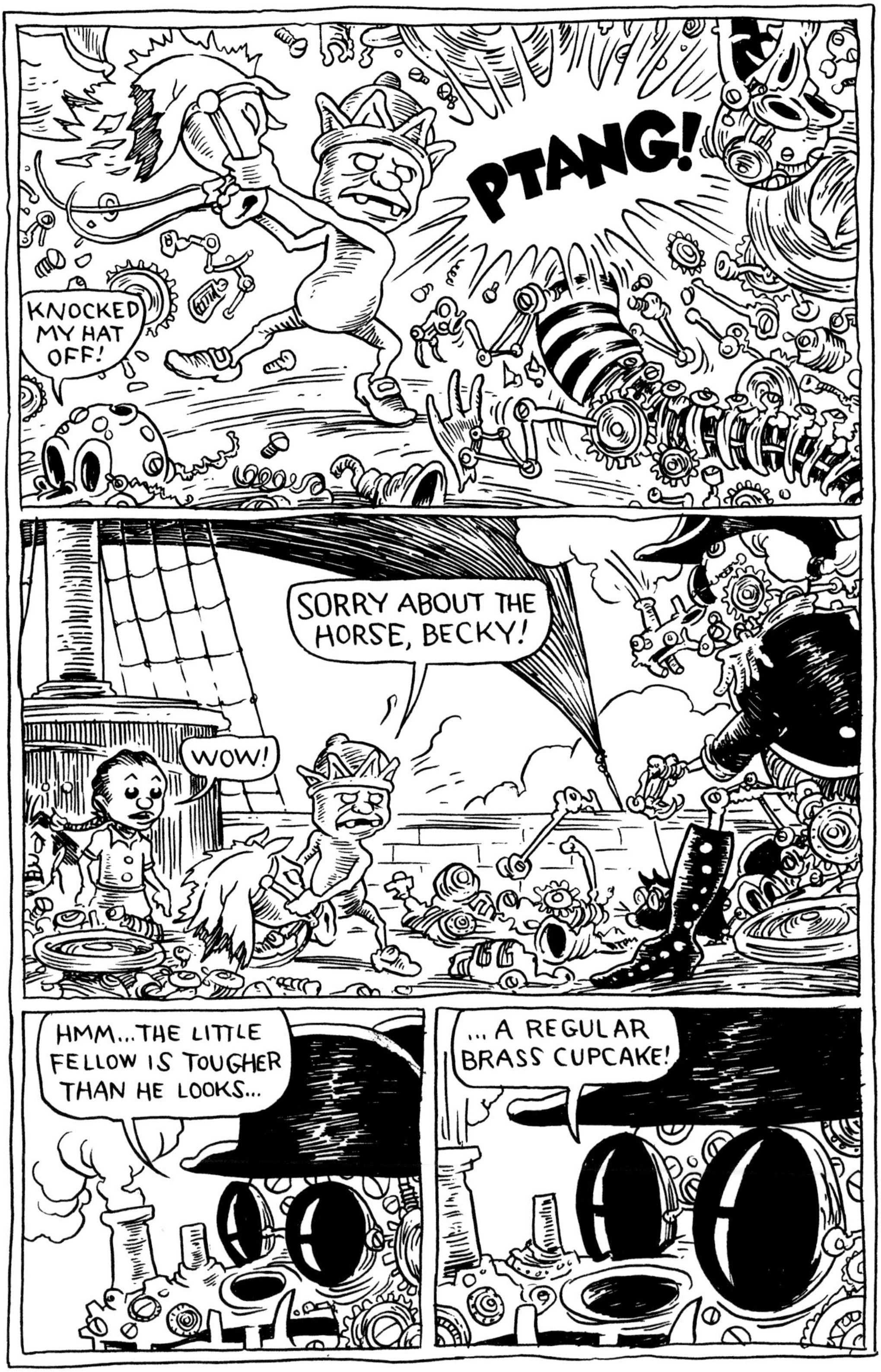
PTANG!
KNOCKED MY HAT OFF!
SORRY ABOUT THE HORSE, BECKY!
WOW!
HMM...THE LITTLE FELLOW IS TOUGHER THAN HE LOOKS...
...A REGULAR BRASS CUPCAKE!

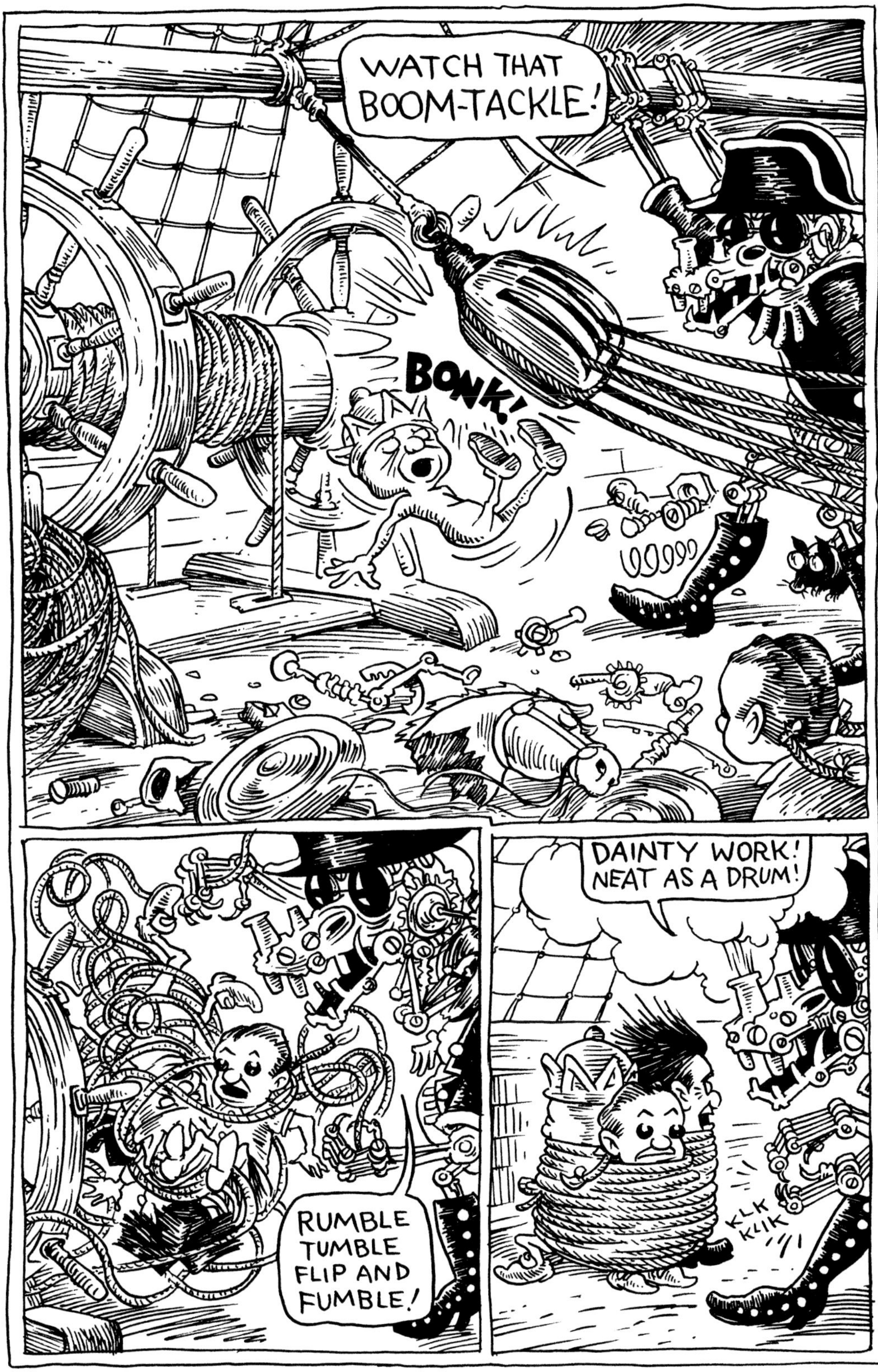
WATCH THAT BOOM-TACKLE!
BONK!
DAINTY WORK! NEAT AS A DRUM!
RUMBLE TUMBLE FLIP AND FUMBLE!
KLK KLIK

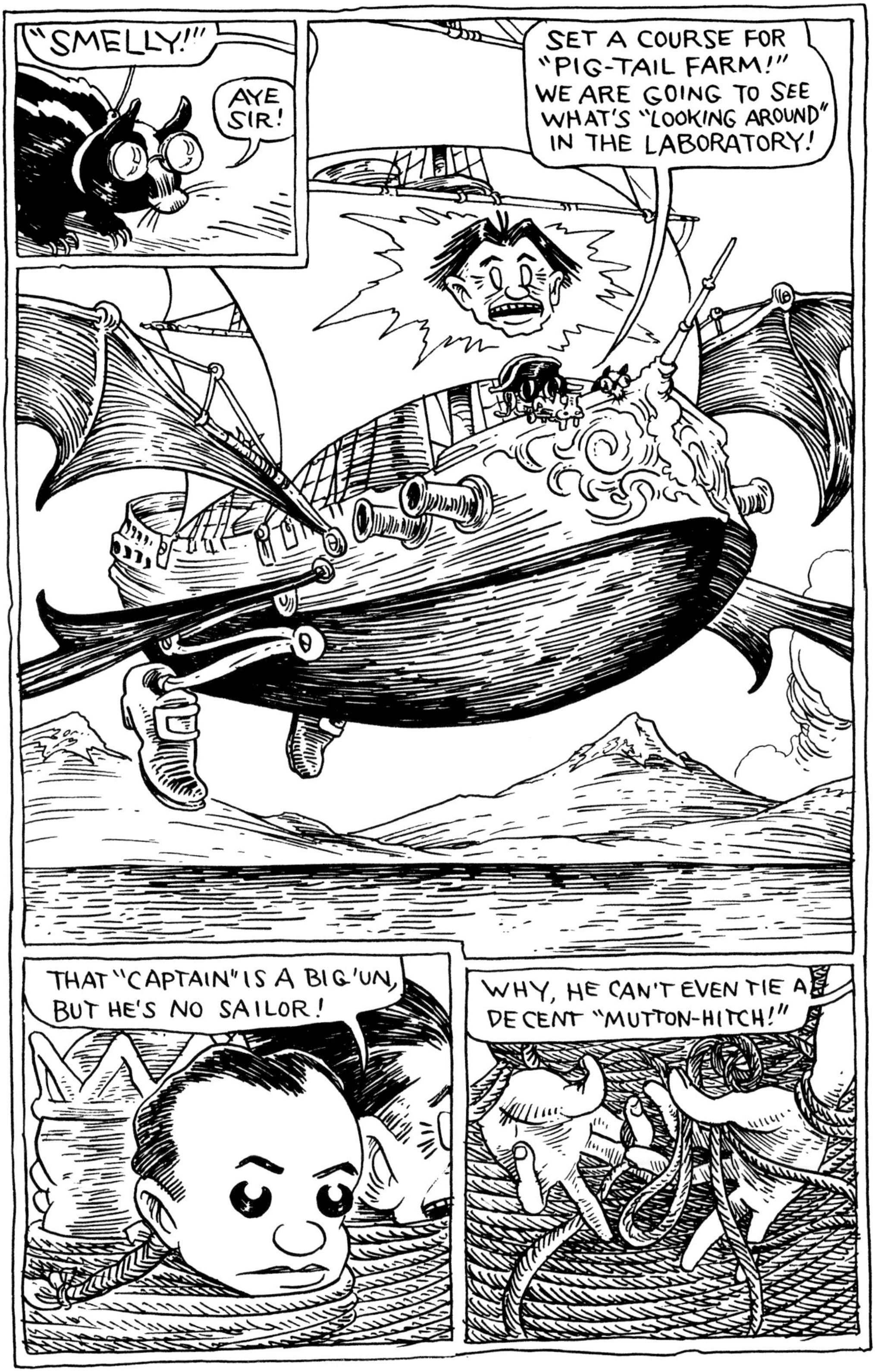
"SMELLY!"
AYE SIR!
SET A COURSE FOR "PIG-TAIL FARM!" WE ARE GOING TO SEE WHAT'S "LOOKING AROUND" IN THE LABORATORY!
THAT "CAPTAIN" IS A BIG'UN, BUT HE'S NO SAILOR!
WHY, HE CAN'T EVEN TIE A DECENT "MUTTON-HITCH!"

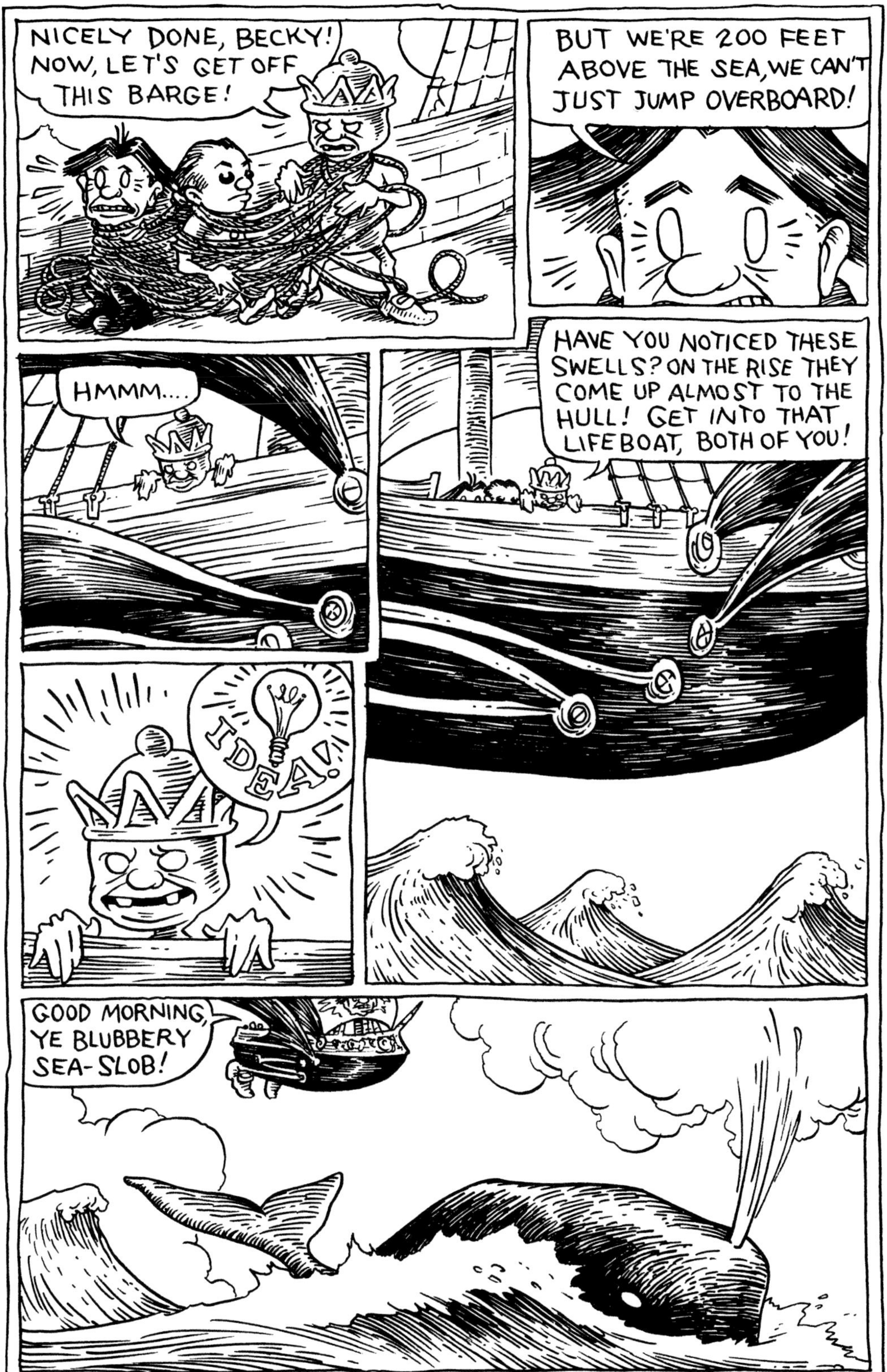
NICELY DONE, BECKY! NOW, LET'S GET OFF THIS BARGE!
BUT WE'RE 200 FEET ABOVE THE SEA, WE CAN'T JUST JUMP OVERBOARD!
HMMM....
HAVE YOU NOTICED THESE SWELLS? ON THE RISE THEY COME UP ALMOST TO THE HULL! GET INTO THAT LIFEBOAT, BOTH OF YOU!
IDEA!
GOOD MORNING, YE BLUBBERY SEA-SLOB!

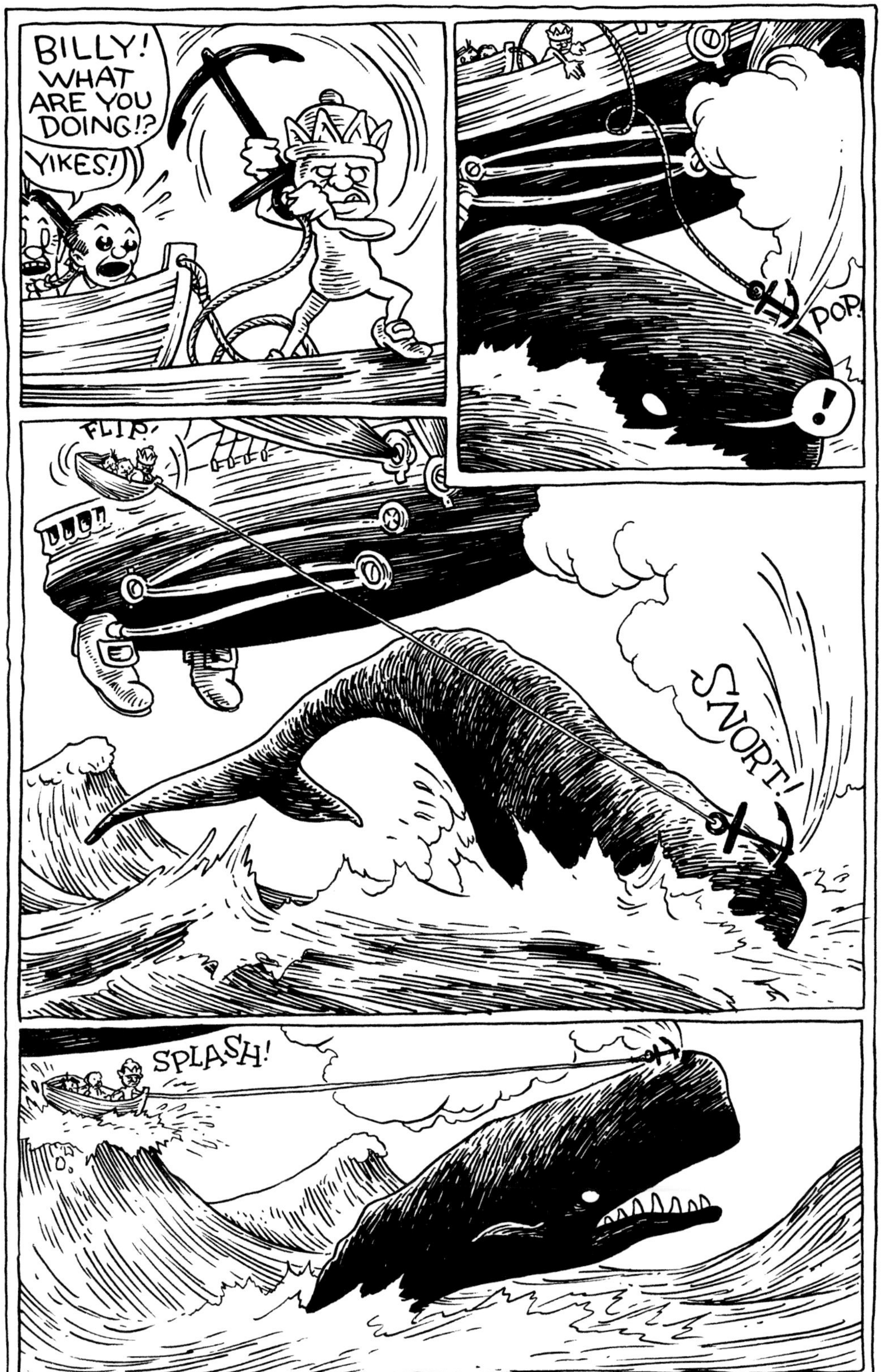
BILLY! WHAT ARE YOU DOING!?
YIKES!
POP!
!
FLIP!
SNORT!
SPLASH!

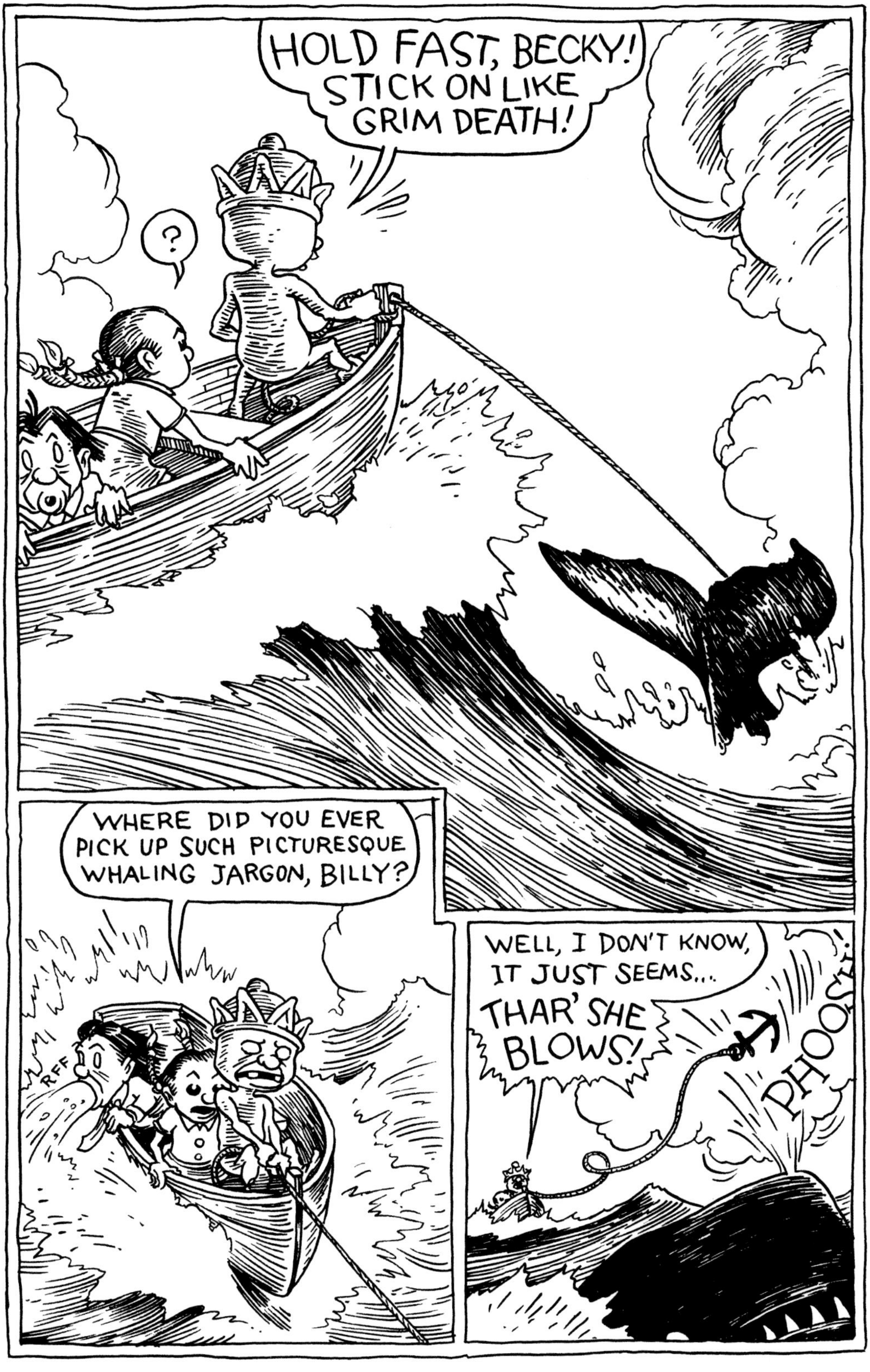
HOLD FAST, BECKY! STICK ON LIKE GRIM DEATH!
?
WHERE DID YOU EVER PICK UP SUCH PICTURESQUE WHALING JARGON, BILLY?
RFF
WELL, I DON'T KNOW, IT JUST SEEMS...
THAR' SHE BLOWS!
PHOOSH!

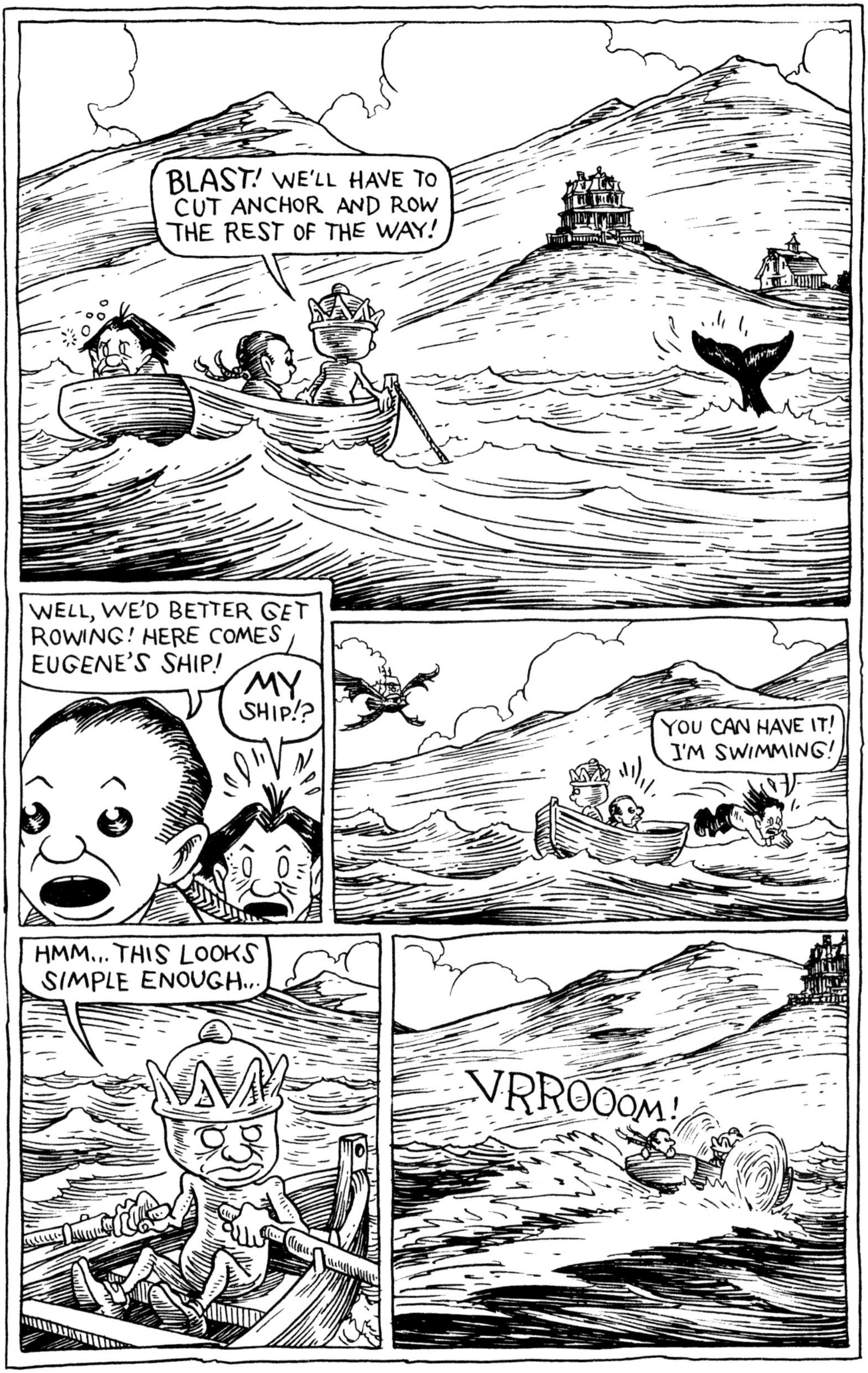
BLAST! WE'LL HAVE TO CUT ANCHOR AND ROW THE REST OF THE WAY!
WELL, WE'D BETTER GET ROWING! HERE COMES EUGENE'S SHIP!
MY SHIP!?
YOU CAN HAVE IT! I'M SWIMMING!
HMM... THIS LOOKS SIMPLE ENOUGH...
VRROOOM!

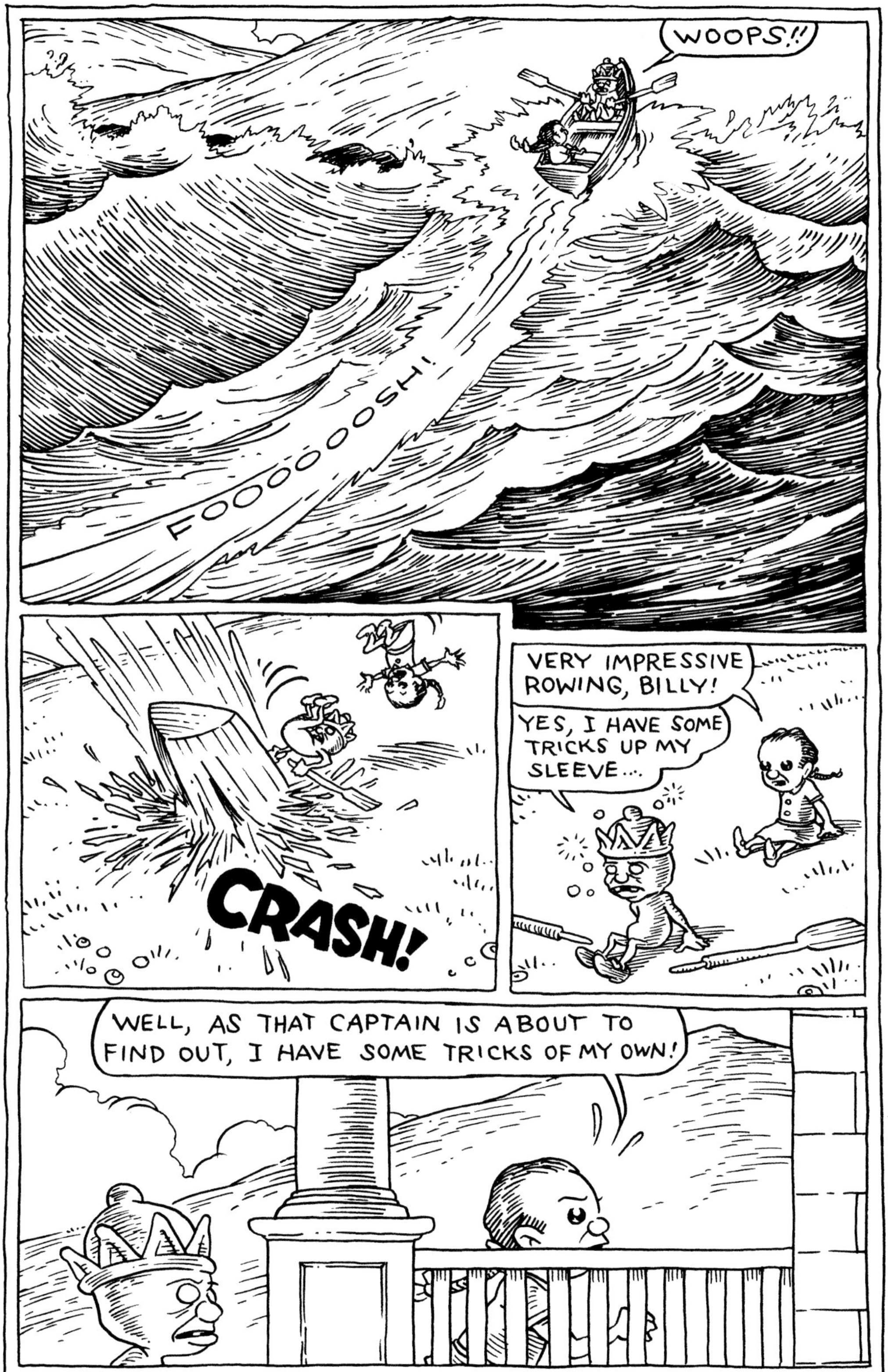

WOOPS!!
FOOOOOOOSH!
CRASH!
VERY IMPRESSIVE ROWING, BILLY!
YES, I HAVE SOME TRICKS UP MY SLEEVE...
WELL, AS THAT CAPTAIN IS ABOUT TO FIND OUT, I HAVE SOME TRICKS OF MY OWN!

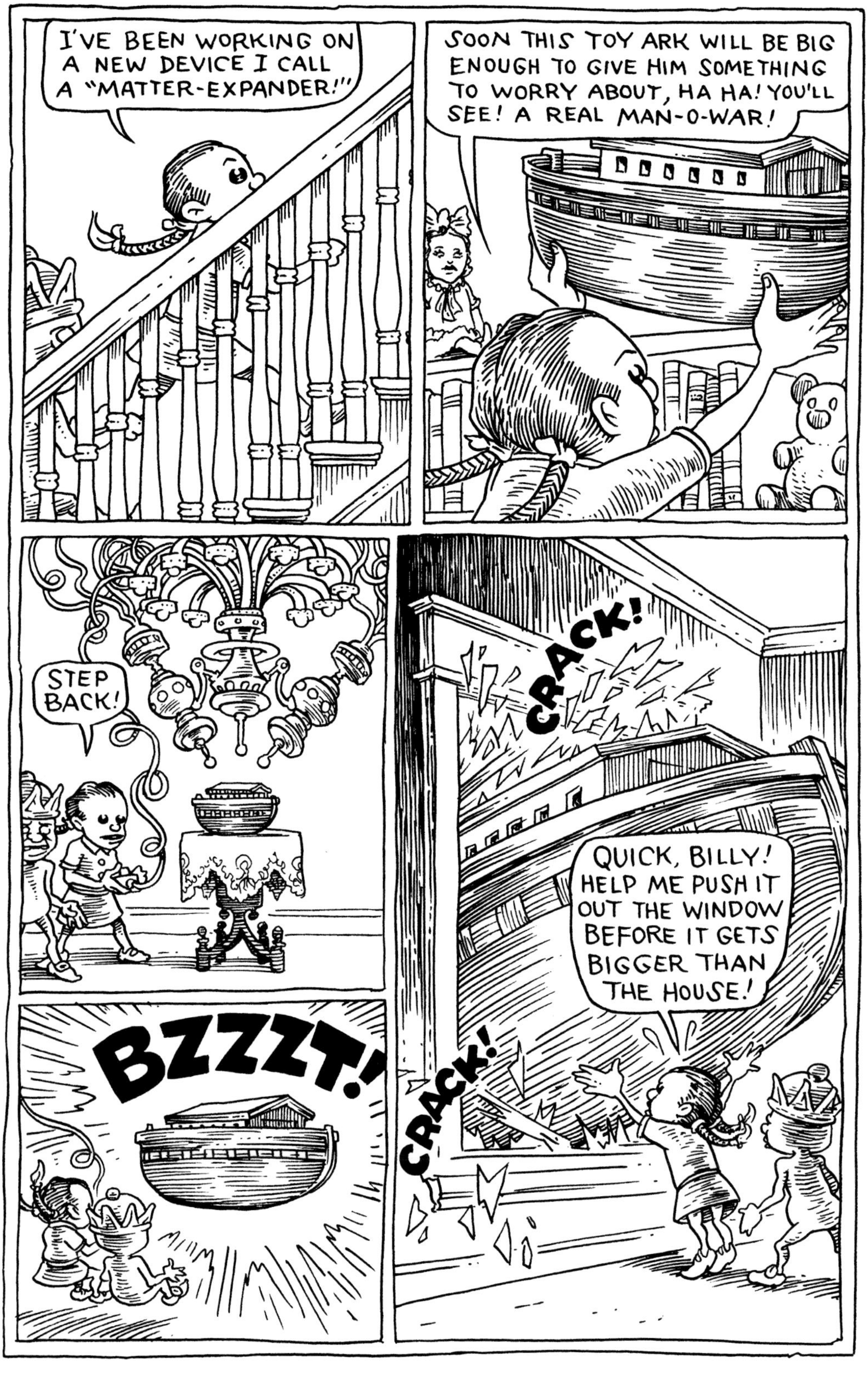
I'VE BEEN WORKING ON A NEW DEVICE I CALL A "MATTER-EXPANDER!"
SOON THIS TOY ARK WILL BE BIG ENOUGH TO GIVE HIM SOMETHING TO WORRY ABOUT, HA HA! YOU'LL SEE! A REAL MAN-O-WAR!
STEP BACK!
BZZZT!
CRACK!
QUICK, BILLY! HELP ME PUSH IT OUT THE WINDOW BEFORE IT GETS BIGGER THAN THE HOUSE!
CRACK!

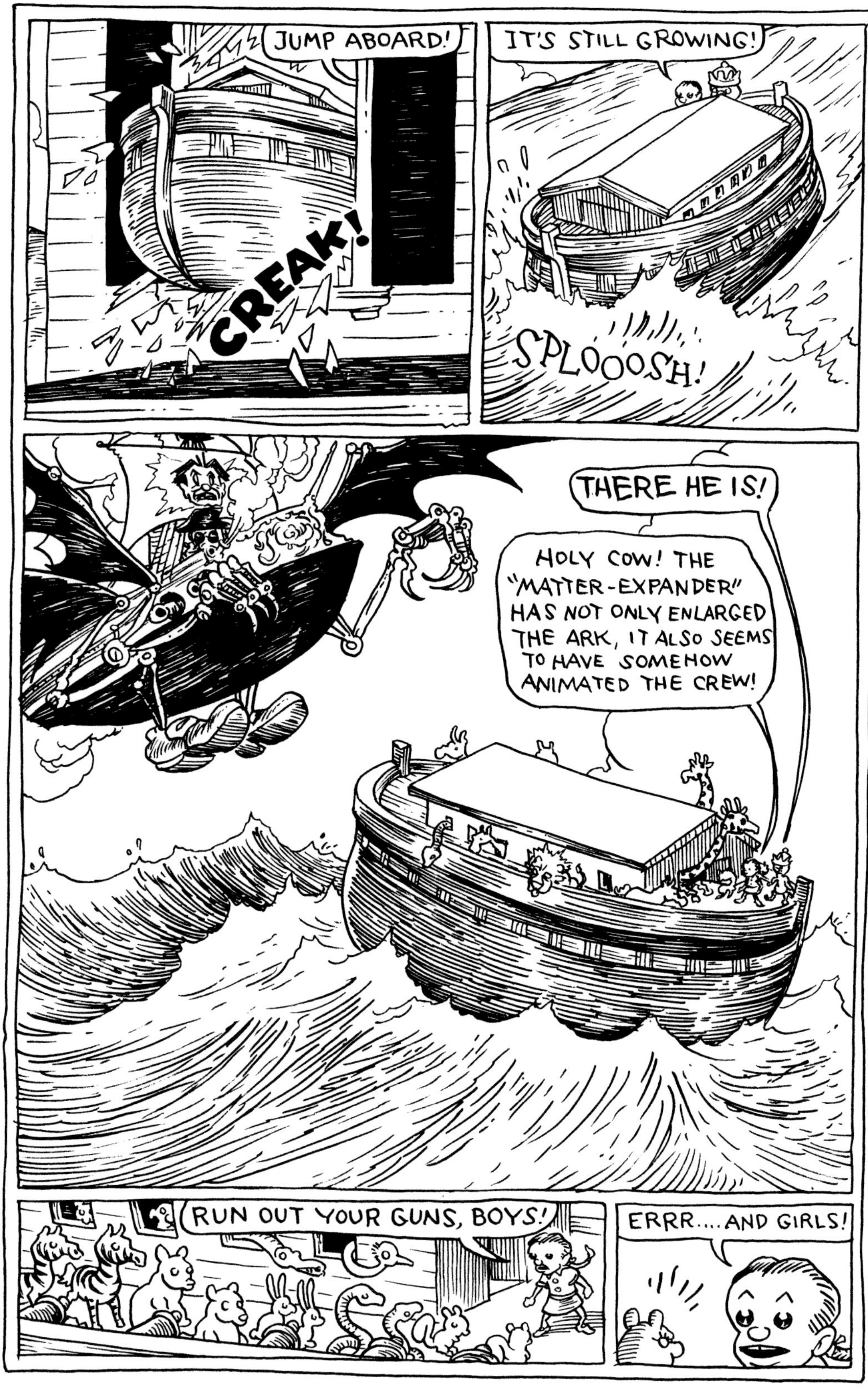
JUMP ABOARD!
CREAK!
IT'S STILL GROWING!
SPLOOOSH!
THERE HE IS!
HOLY COW! THE "MATTER-EXPANDER" HAS NOT ONLY ENLARGED THE ARK, IT ALSO SEEMS TO HAVE SOMEHOW ANIMATED THE CREW!
RUN OUT YOUR GUNS, BOYS!
ERRR.... AND GIRLS!

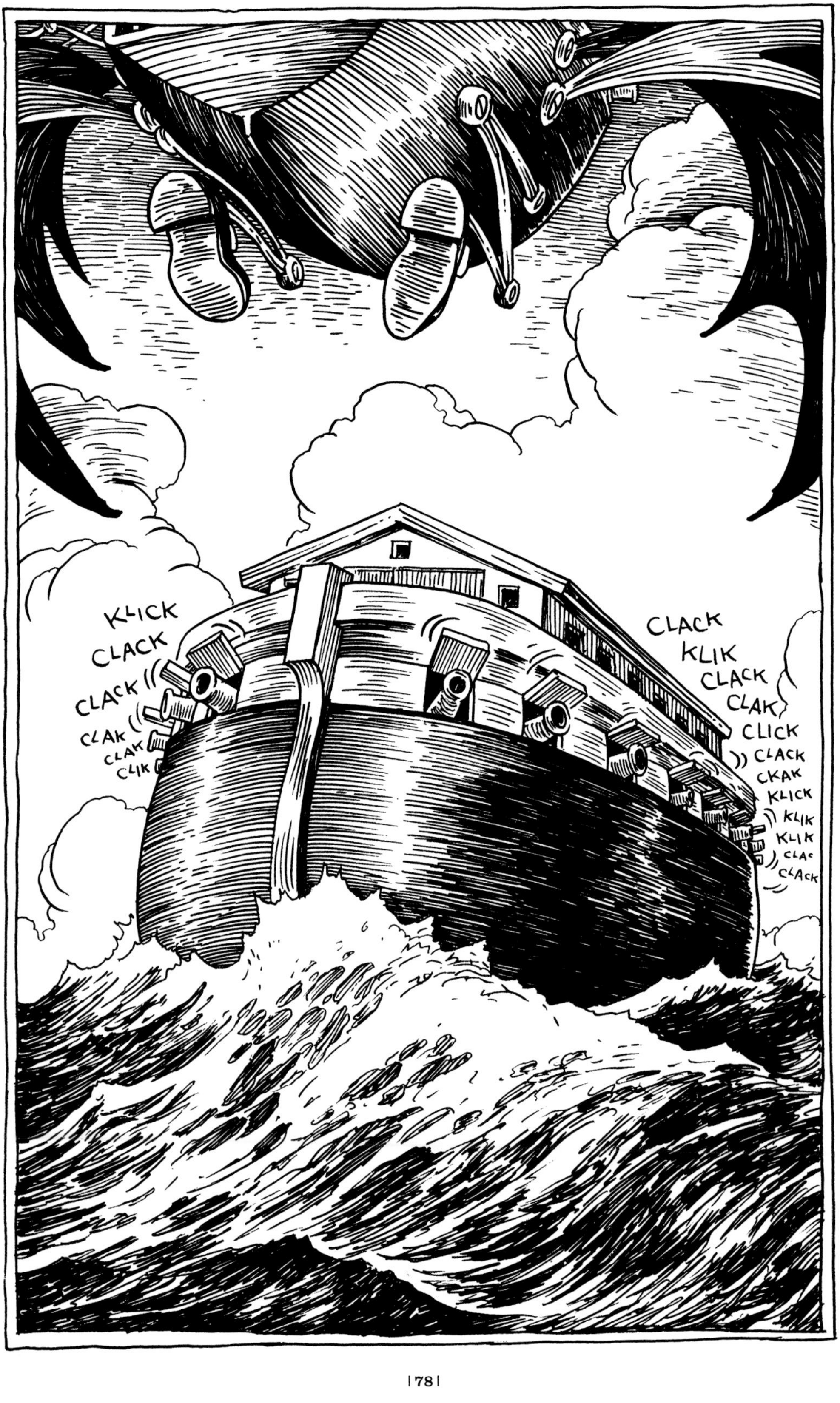
KLICK
CLACK
CLACK
CLAK
CLAK
CLIK
CLACK
KLIK
CLACK
CLAK
CLICK
CLACK
CKAK
KLICK
KLIK
KLIK
CLAC
CLACK

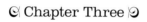Chapter Three

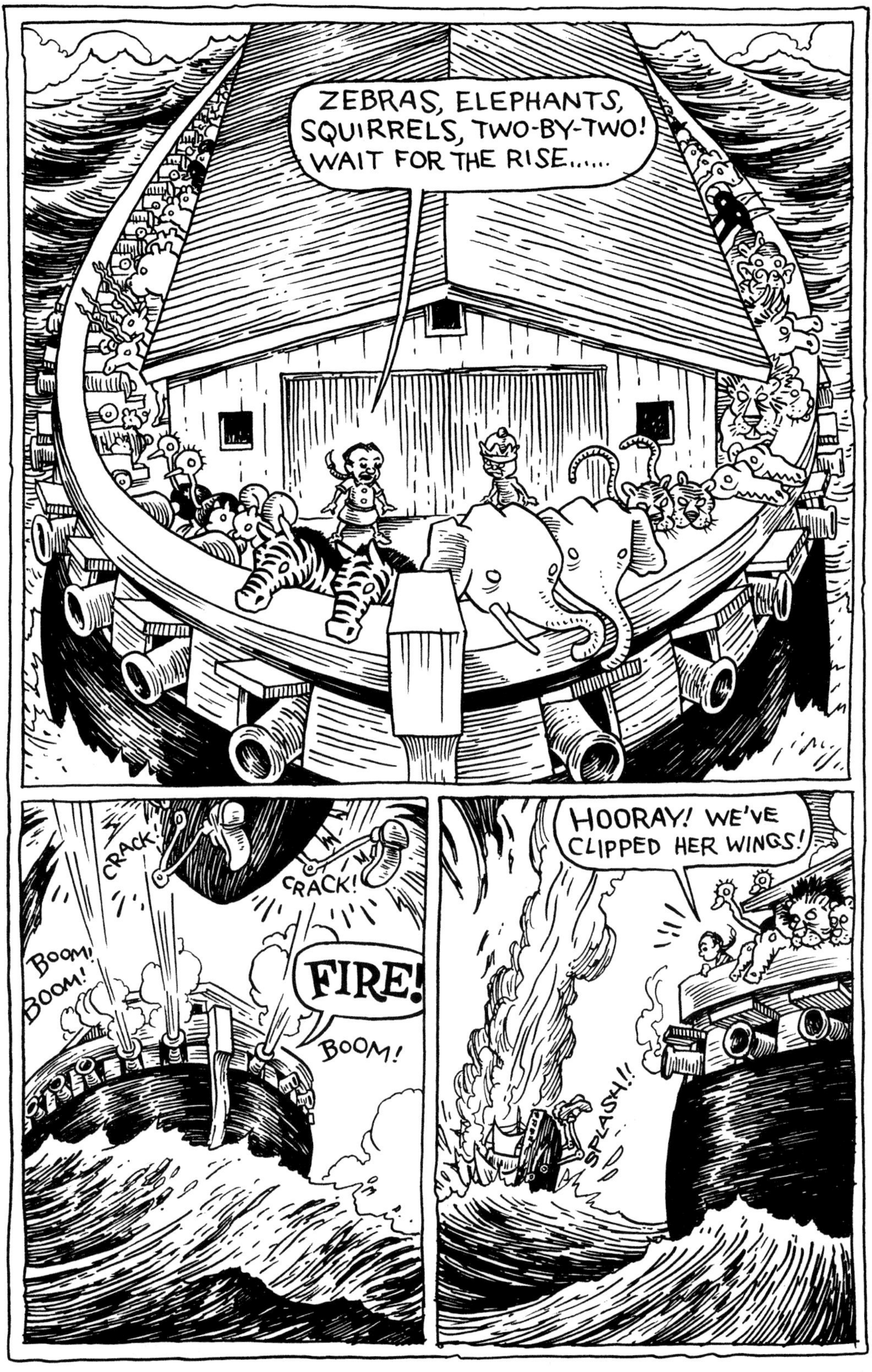

ZEBRAS, ELEPHANTS, SQUIRRELS, TWO-BY-TWO! WAIT FOR THE RISE......
CRACK
CRACK!
BOOM! BOOM!
FIRE!
BOOM!
HOORAY! WE'VE CLIPPED HER WINGS!
SPLASH!!

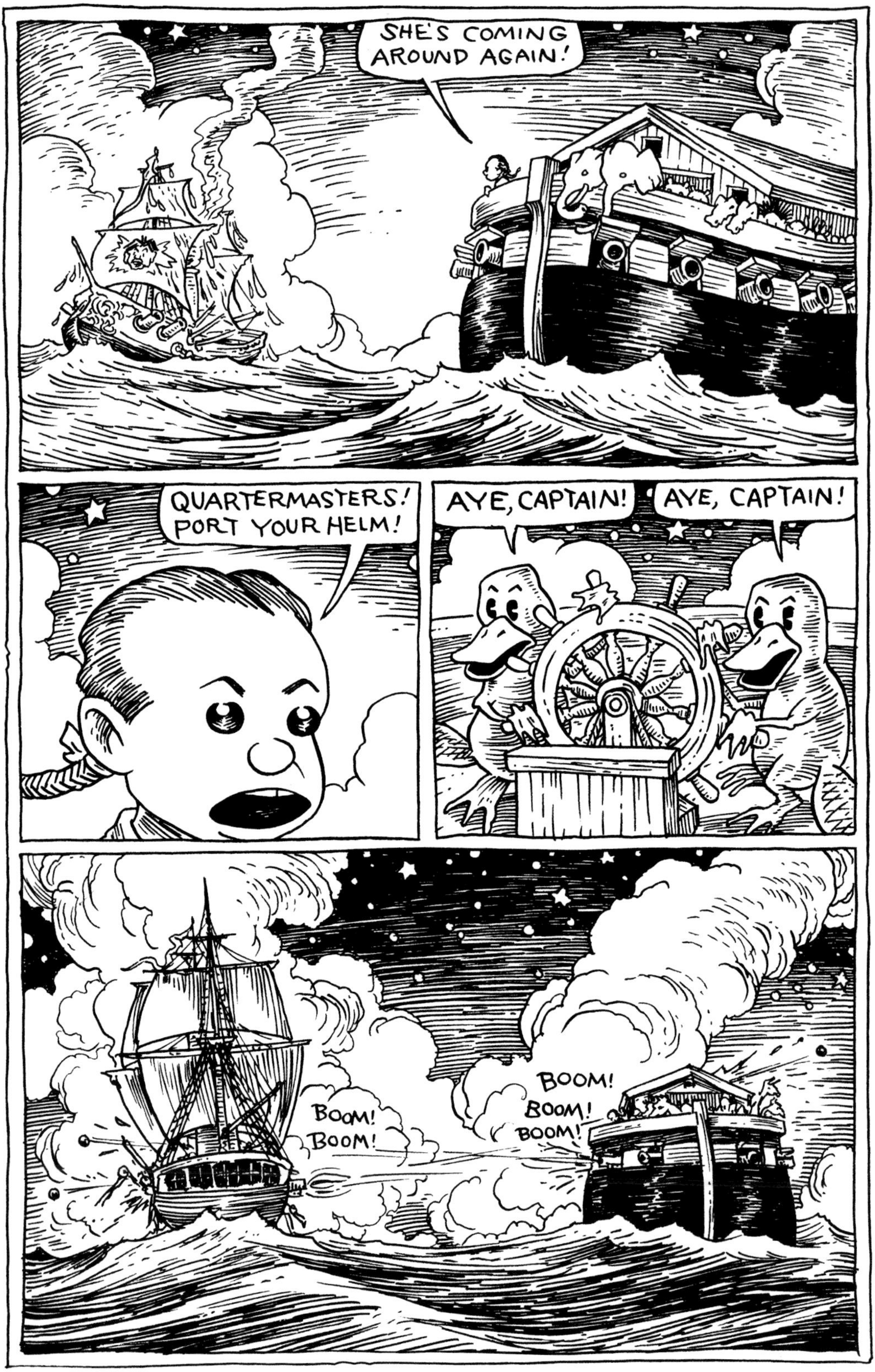
SHE'S COMING AROUND AGAIN!
QUARTERMASTERS! PORT YOUR HELM!
AYE, CAPTAIN!
AYE, CAPTAIN!
BOOM! BOOM!
BOOM! BOOM! BOOM!

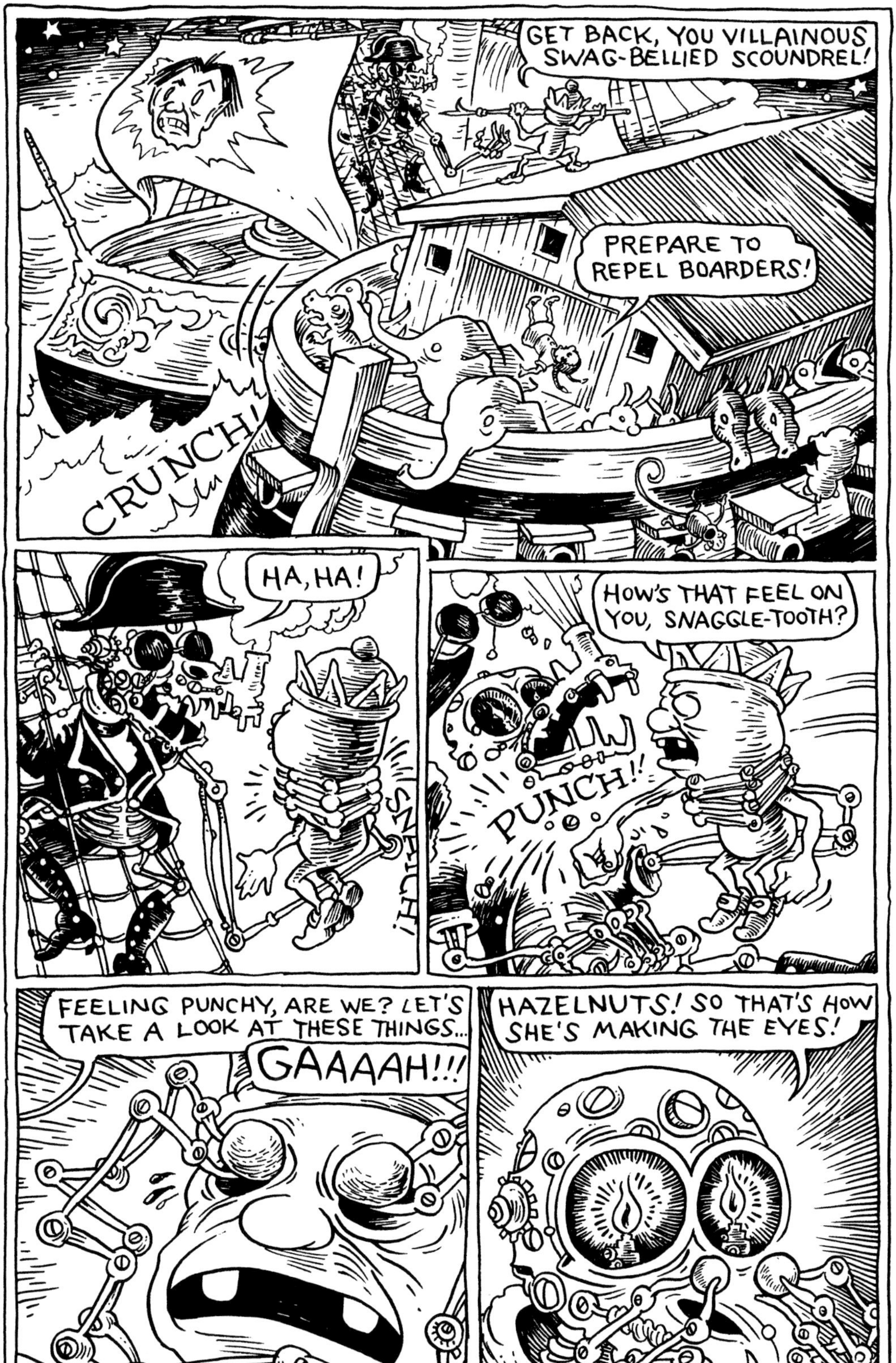
GET BACK, YOU VILLAINOUS SWAG-BELLIED SCOUNDREL!
PREPARE TO REPEL BOARDERS!
CRUNCH!
HA, HA!
SNATCH!
HOW'S THAT FEEL ON YOU, SNAGGLE-TOOTH?
PUNCH!!
FEELING PUNCHY, ARE WE? LET'S TAKE A LOOK AT THESE THINGS...
GAAAAH!!!
HAZELNUTS! SO THAT'S HOW SHE'S MAKING THE EYES!

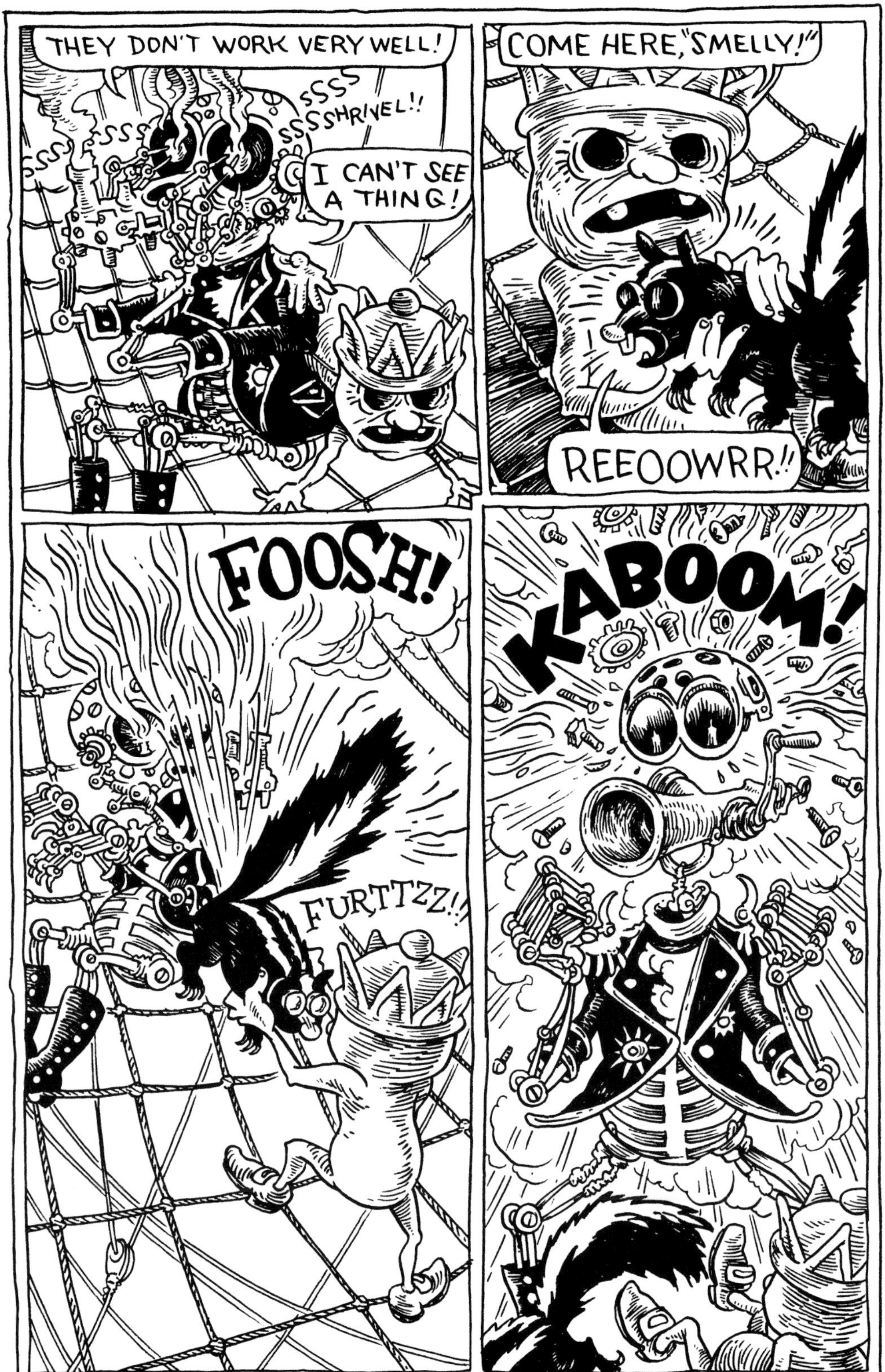
THEY DON'T WORK VERY WELL!
SSSS
SSSSHRIVEL!!
SSS
SSS
SSS
I CAN'T SEE A THING!
COME HERE, "SMELLY!"
REEOOWRR!!
FOOSH!
FURTTZZ!!
KABOOM!!

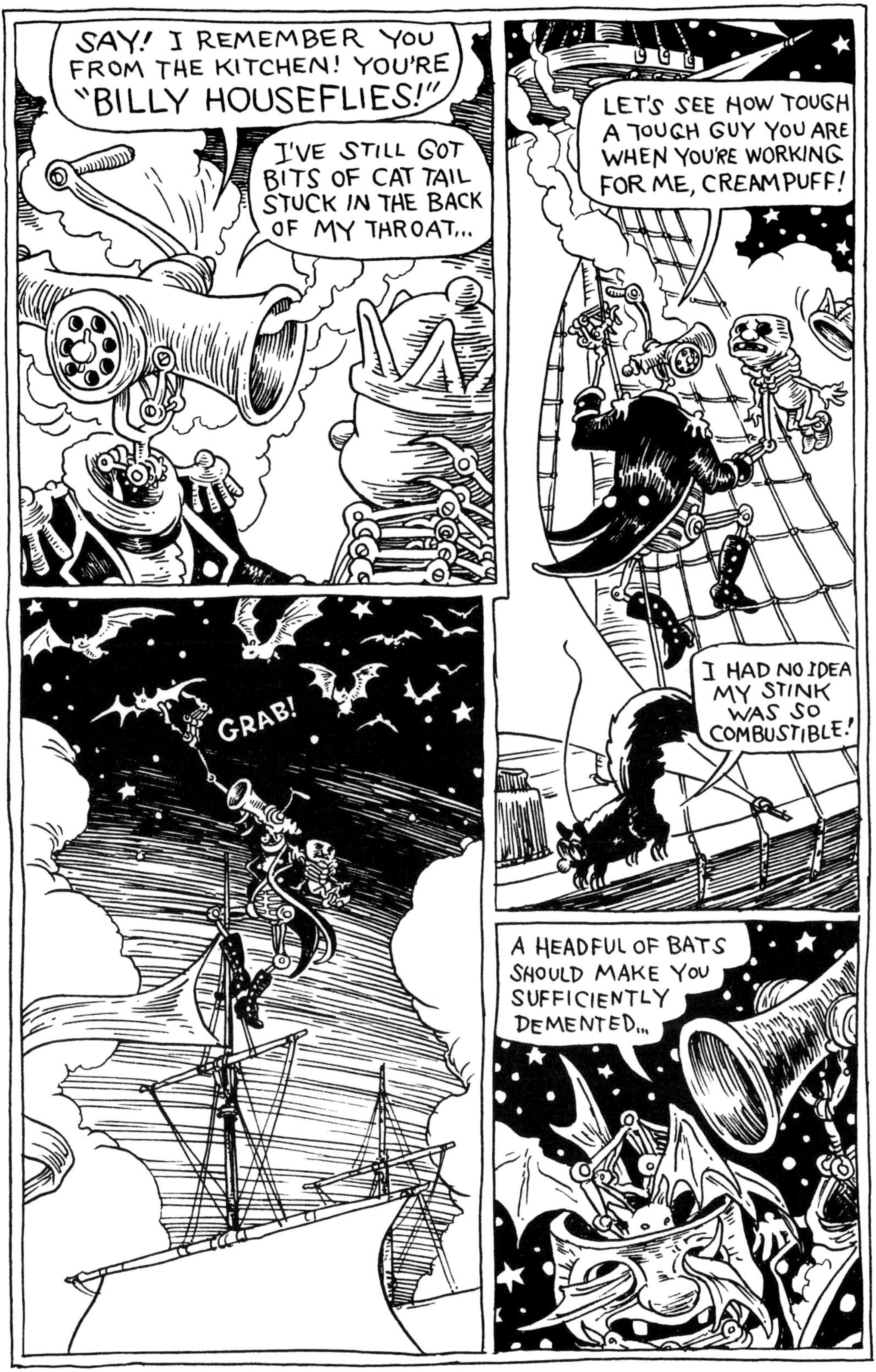
SAY! I REMEMBER YOU FROM THE KITCHEN! YOU'RE "BILLY HOUSEFLIES!"
I'VE STILL GOT BITS OF CAT TAIL STUCK IN THE BACK OF MY THROAT...
LET'S SEE HOW TOUGH A TOUGH GUY YOU ARE WHEN YOU'RE WORKING FOR ME, CREAMPUFF!
I HAD NO IDEA MY STINK WAS SO COMBUSTIBLE!
GRAB!
A HEADFUL OF BATS SHOULD MAKE YOU SUFFICIENTLY DEMENTED...

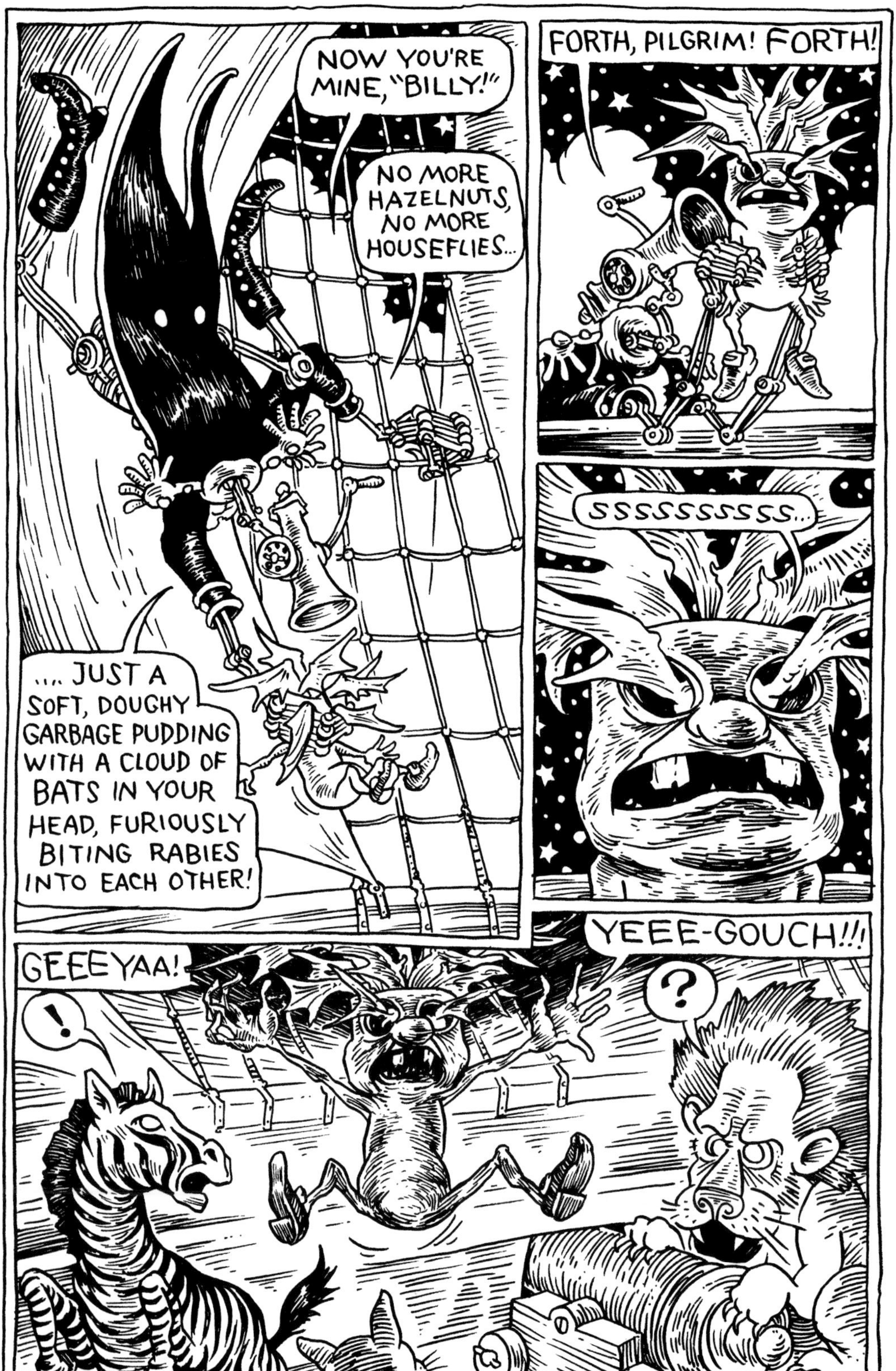
NOW YOU'RE MINE, "BILLY!"
NO MORE HAZELNUTS, NO MORE HOUSEFLIES...
.... JUST A SOFT, DOUGHY GARBAGE PUDDING WITH A CLOUD OF BATS IN YOUR HEAD, FURIOUSLY BITING RABIES INTO EACH OTHER!
FORTH, PILGRIM! FORTH!
SSSSSSSSSS...
YEEE-GOUCH!!!
GEEEYAA!
!
?

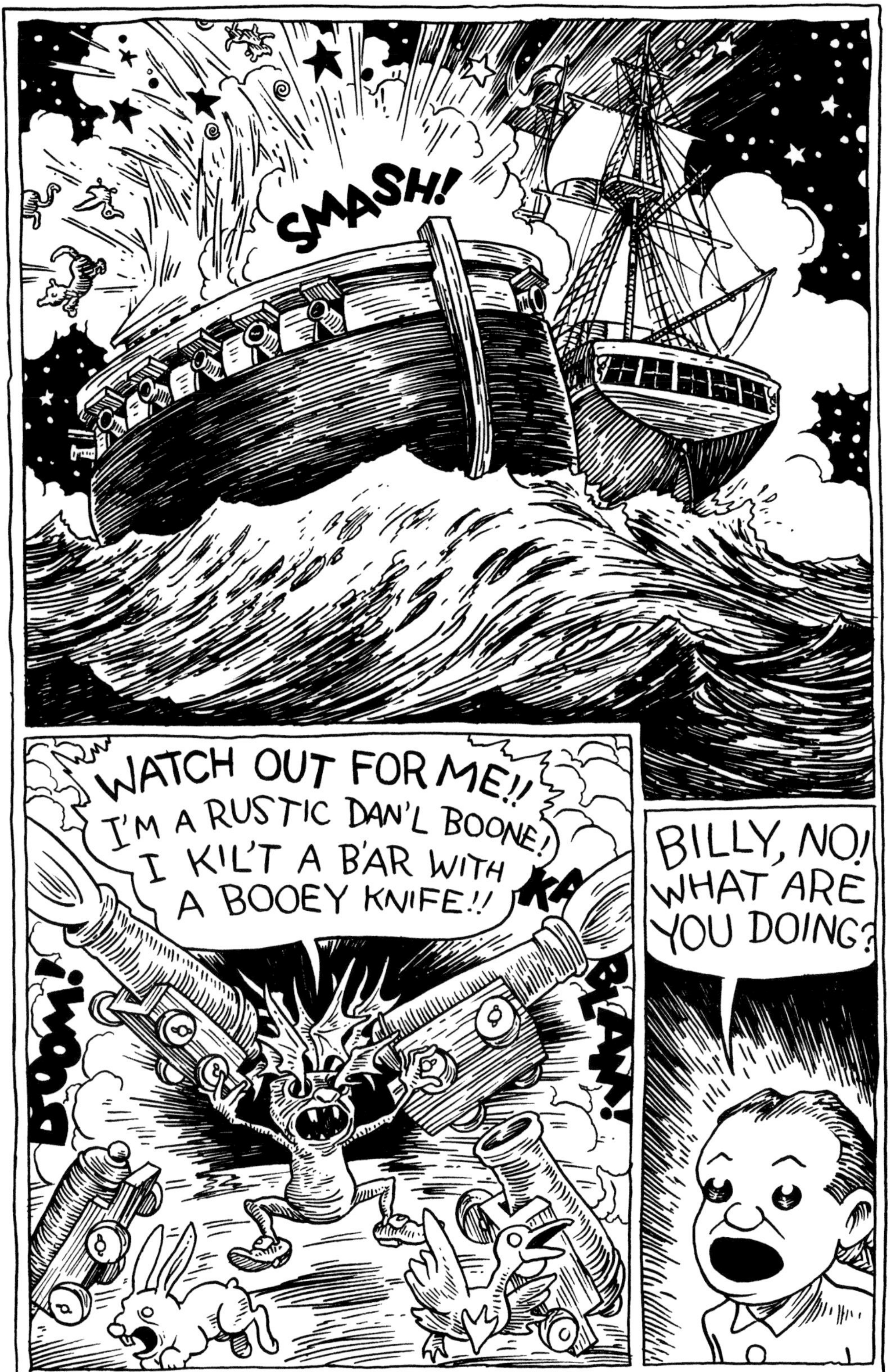
SMASH!
WATCH OUT FOR ME!! I'M A RUSTIC DAN'L BOONE! I KIL'T A B'AR WITH A BOOEY KNIFE!!
KA
BLAM!
BOOM!
BILLY, NO! WHAT ARE YOU DOING?

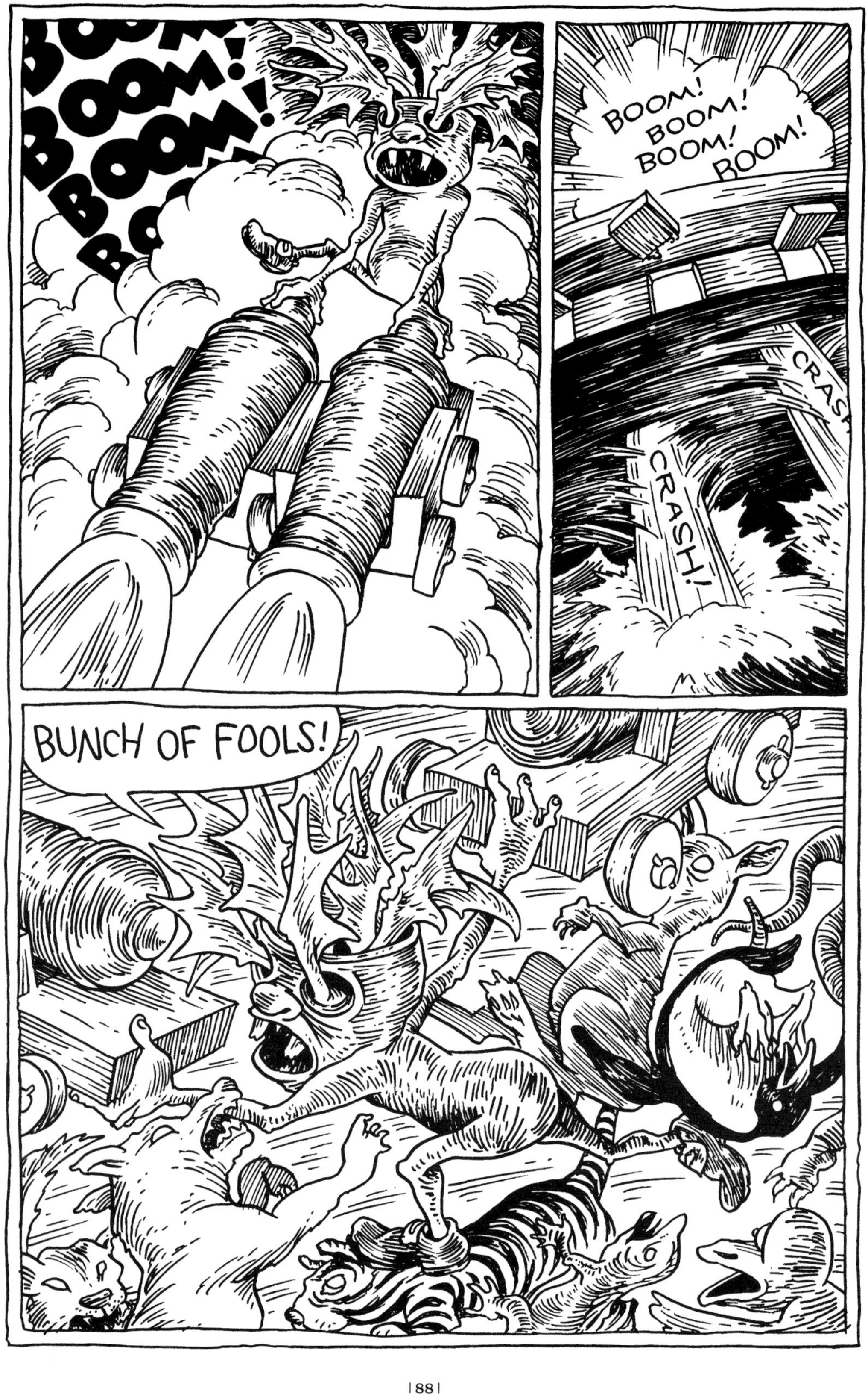
BOOM!
BOOM!
BOOM!
BOOM!
BOOM!
BOOM!
CRASH!
BUNCH OF FOOLS!

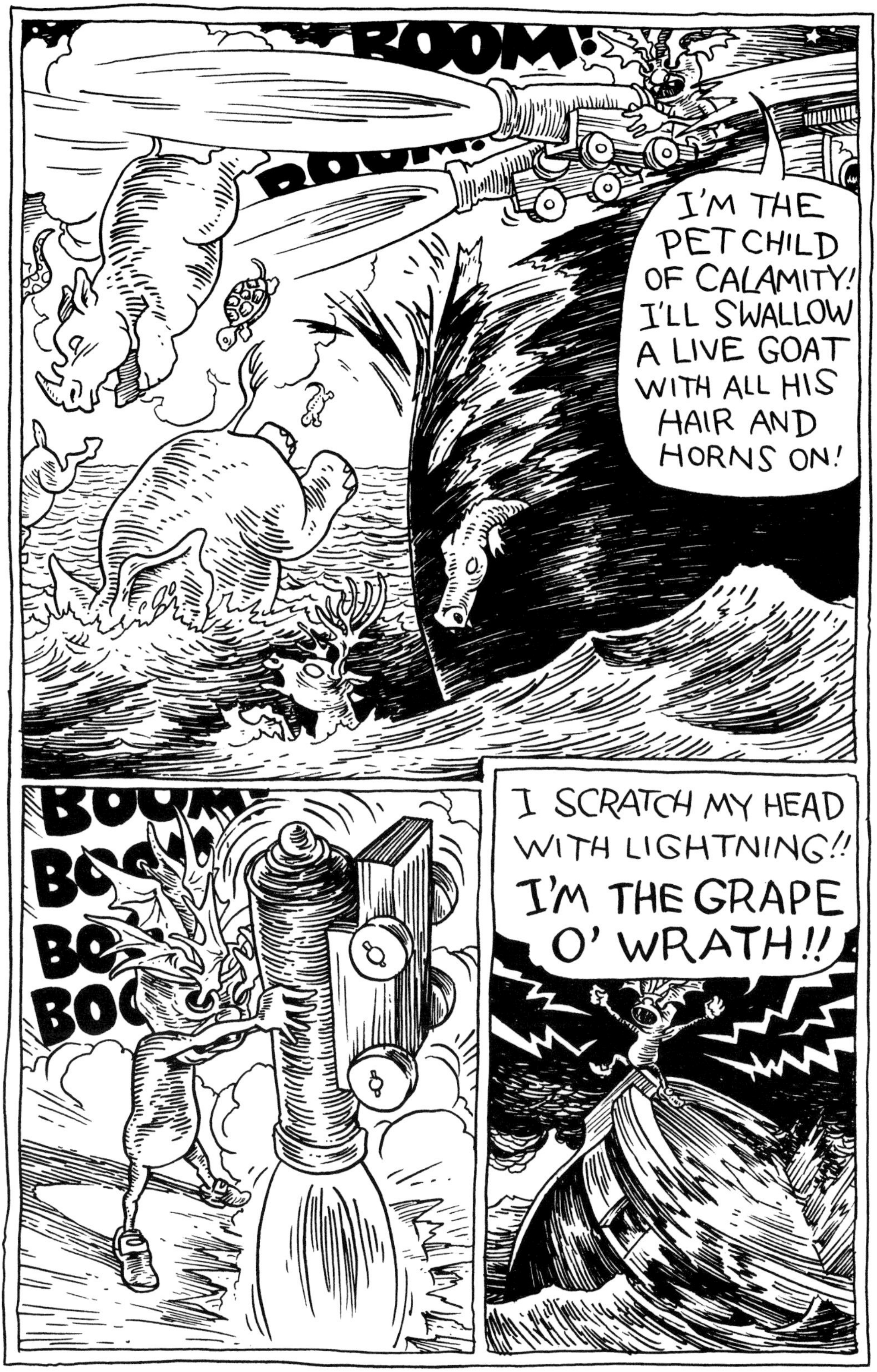
BOOM!
I'M THE PETCHILD OF CALAMITY! I'LL SWALLOW A LIVE GOAT WITH ALL HIS HAIR AND HORNS ON!
I SCRATCH MY HEAD WITH LIGHTNING!! I'M THE GRAPE O' WRATH!!

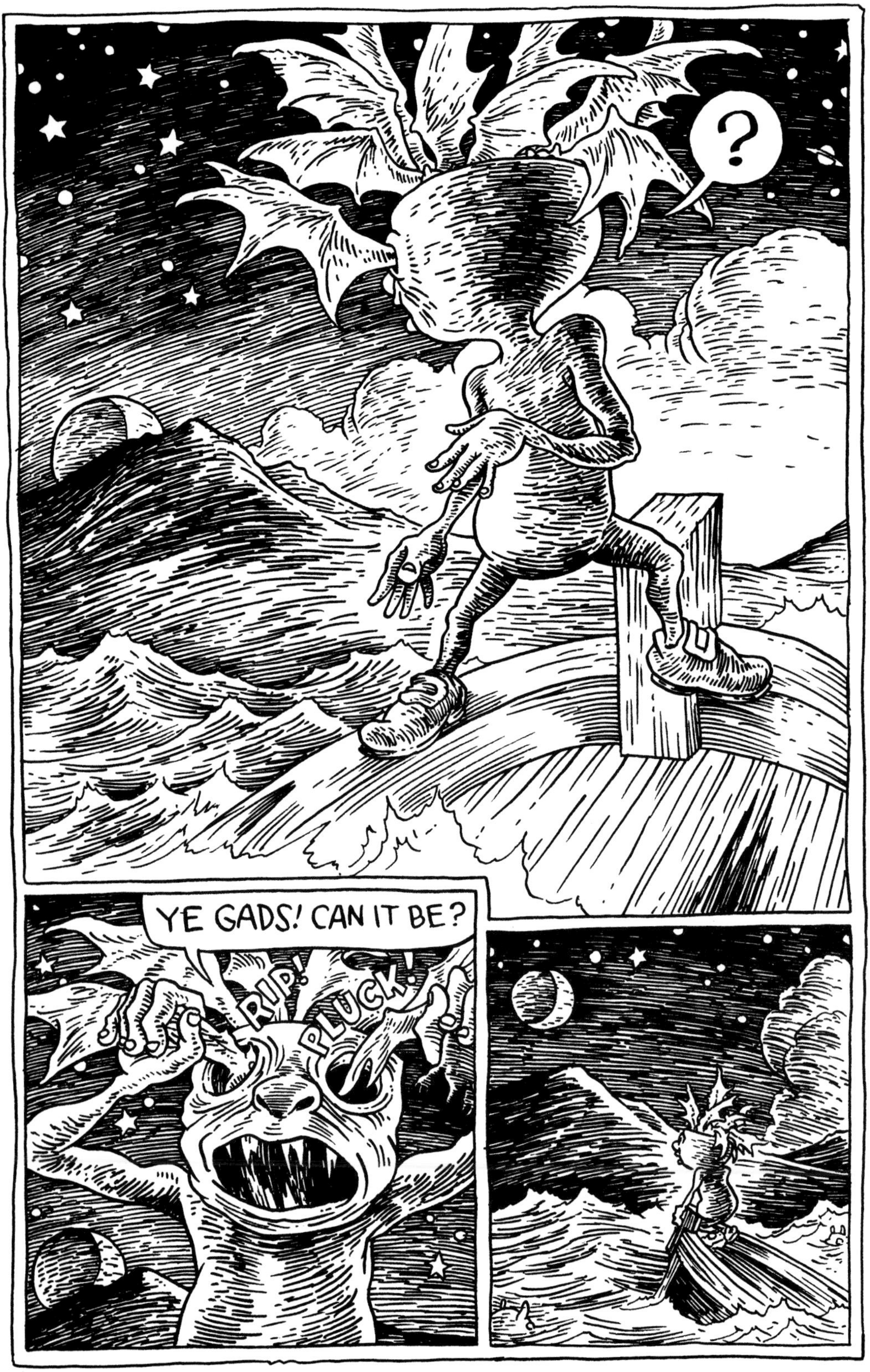
?
YE GADS! CAN IT BE?
RIP!
PLUCK!

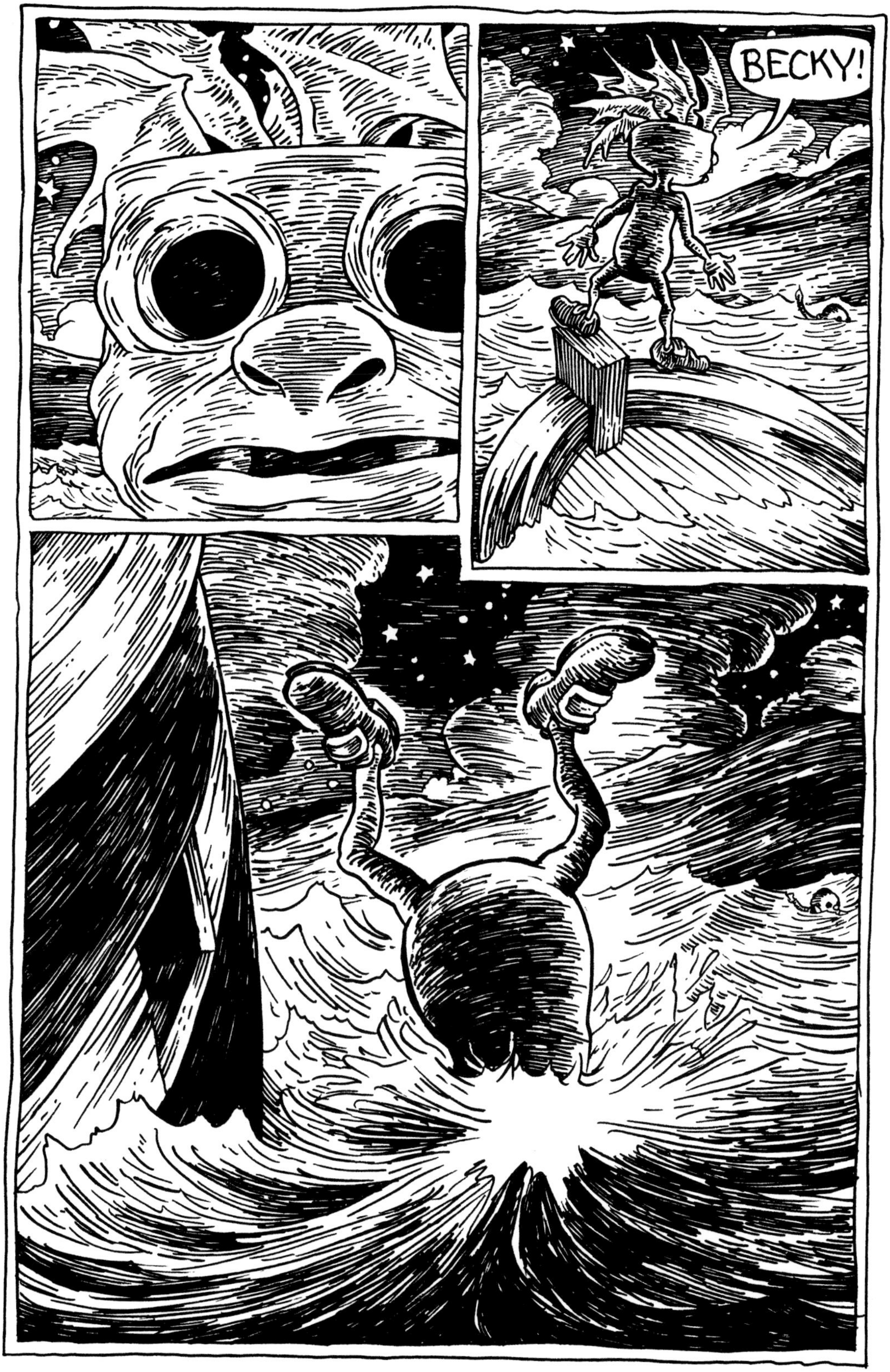
BECKY!

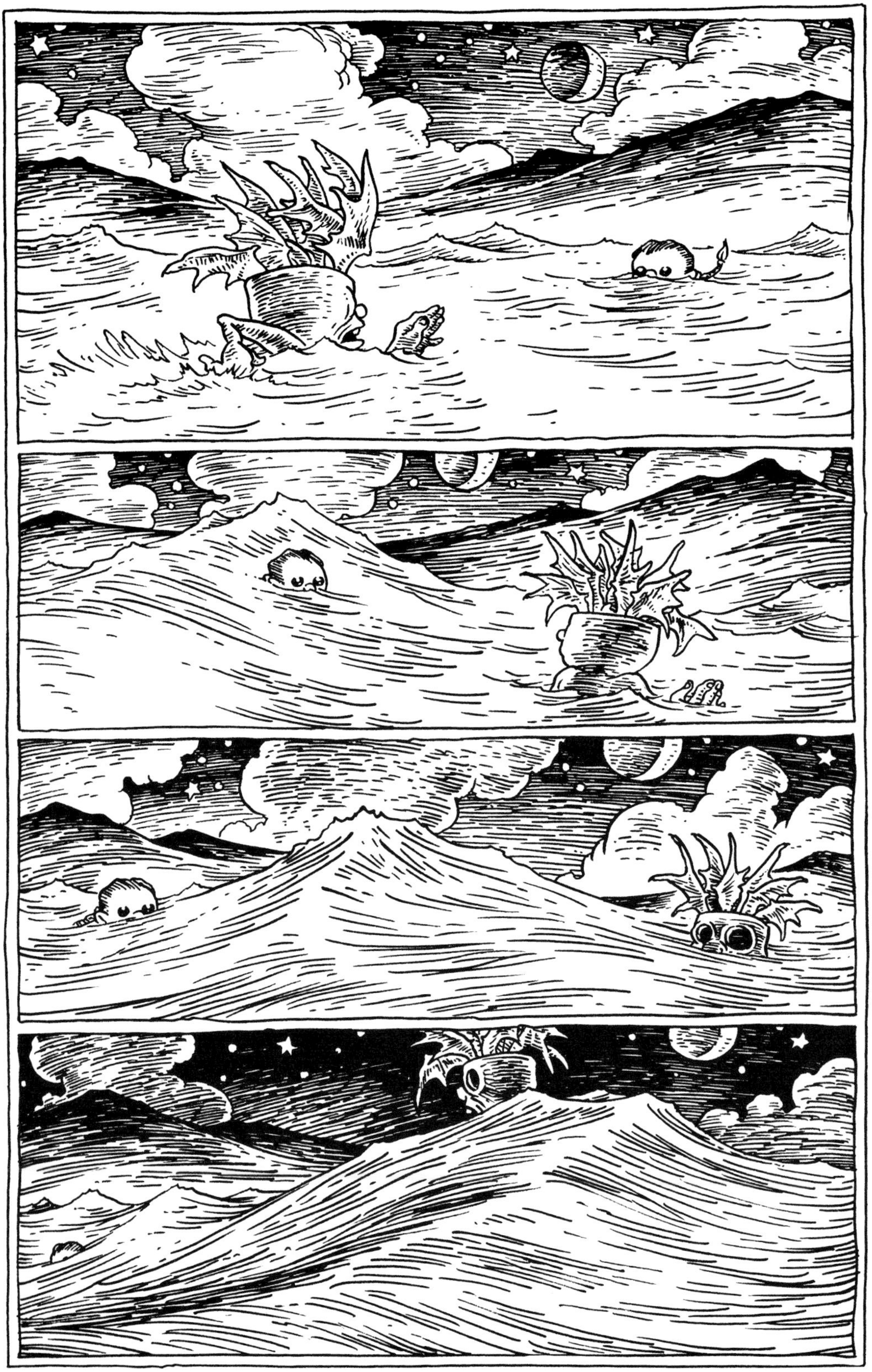

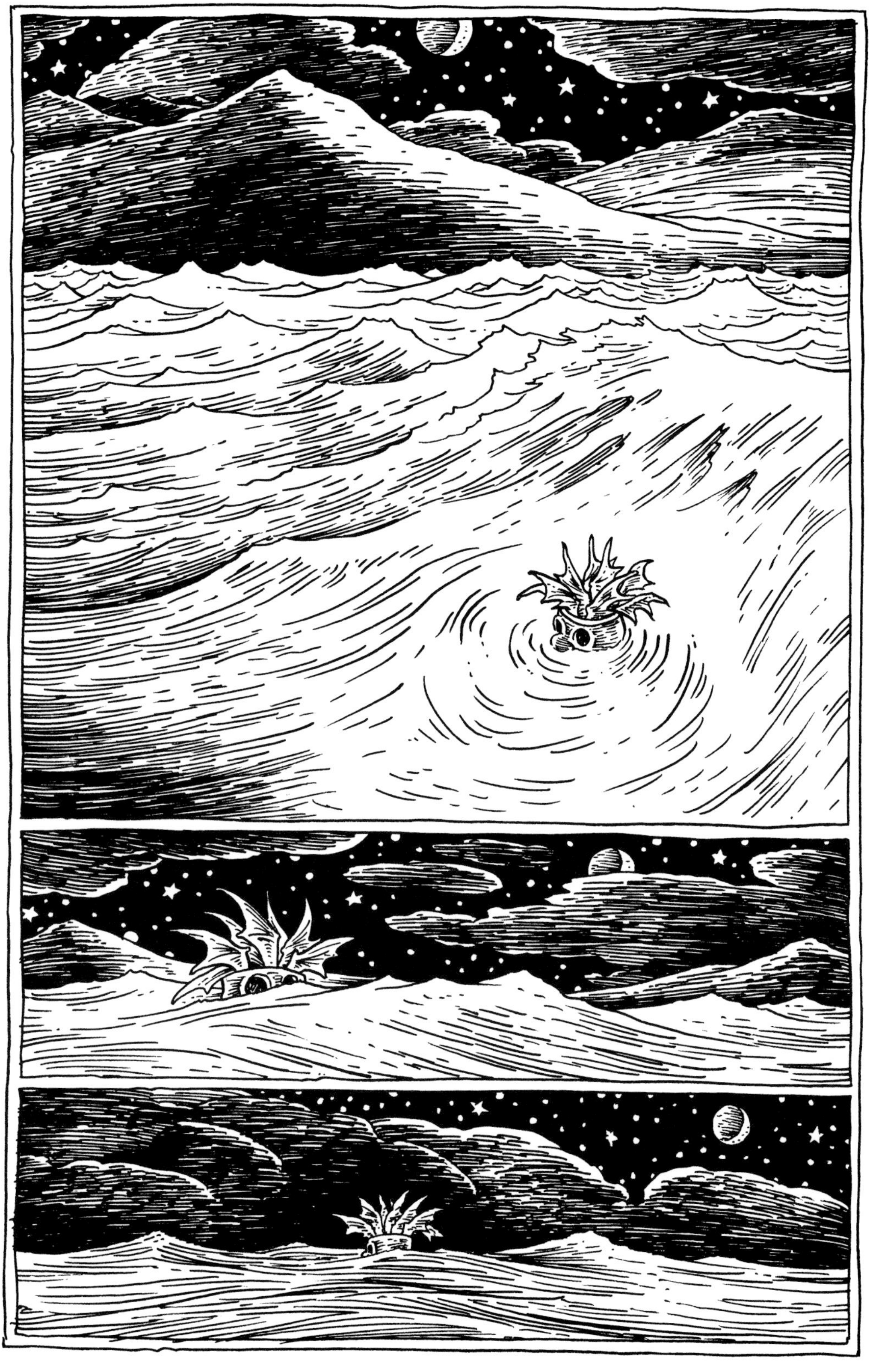

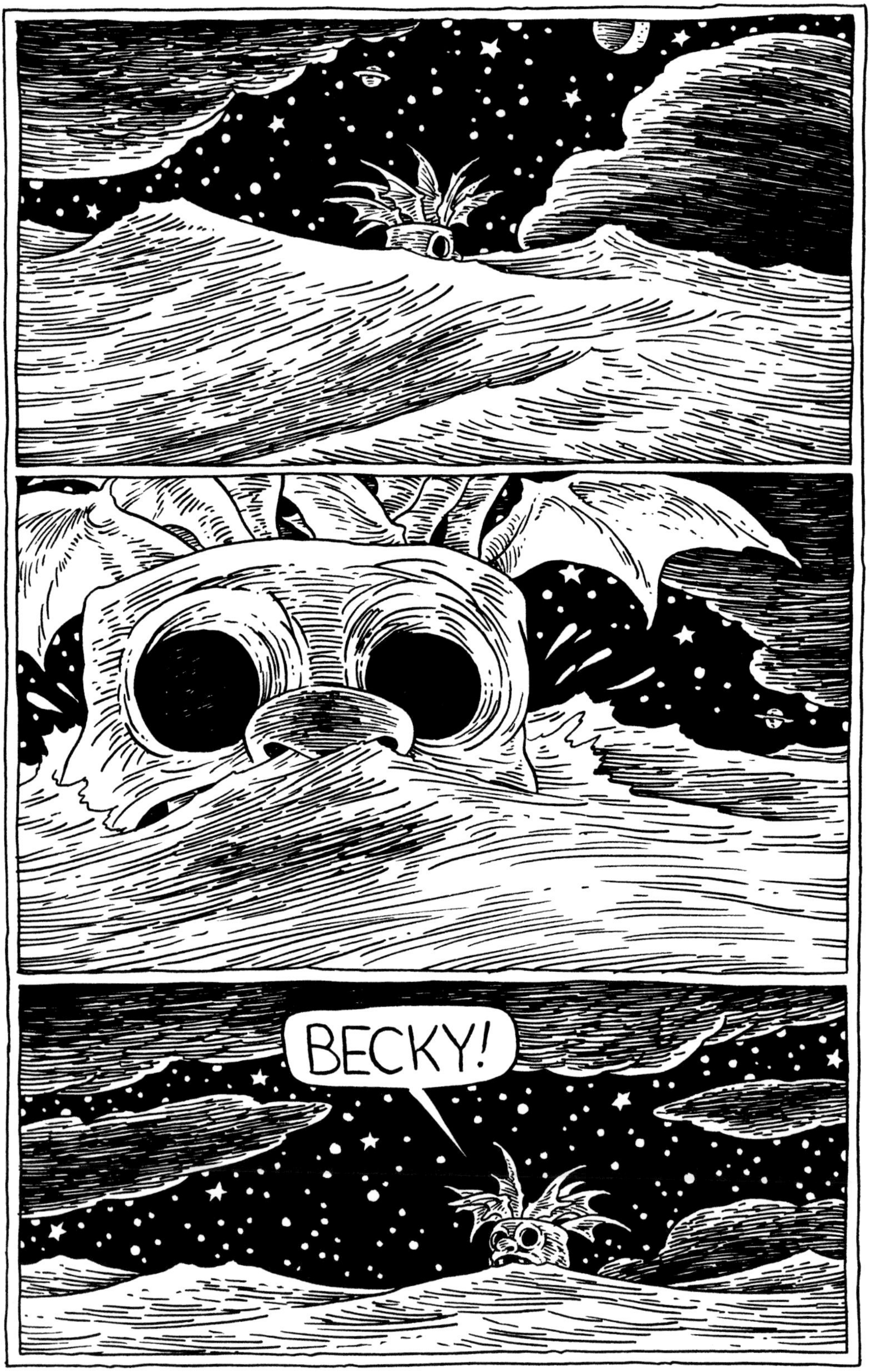
BECKY!

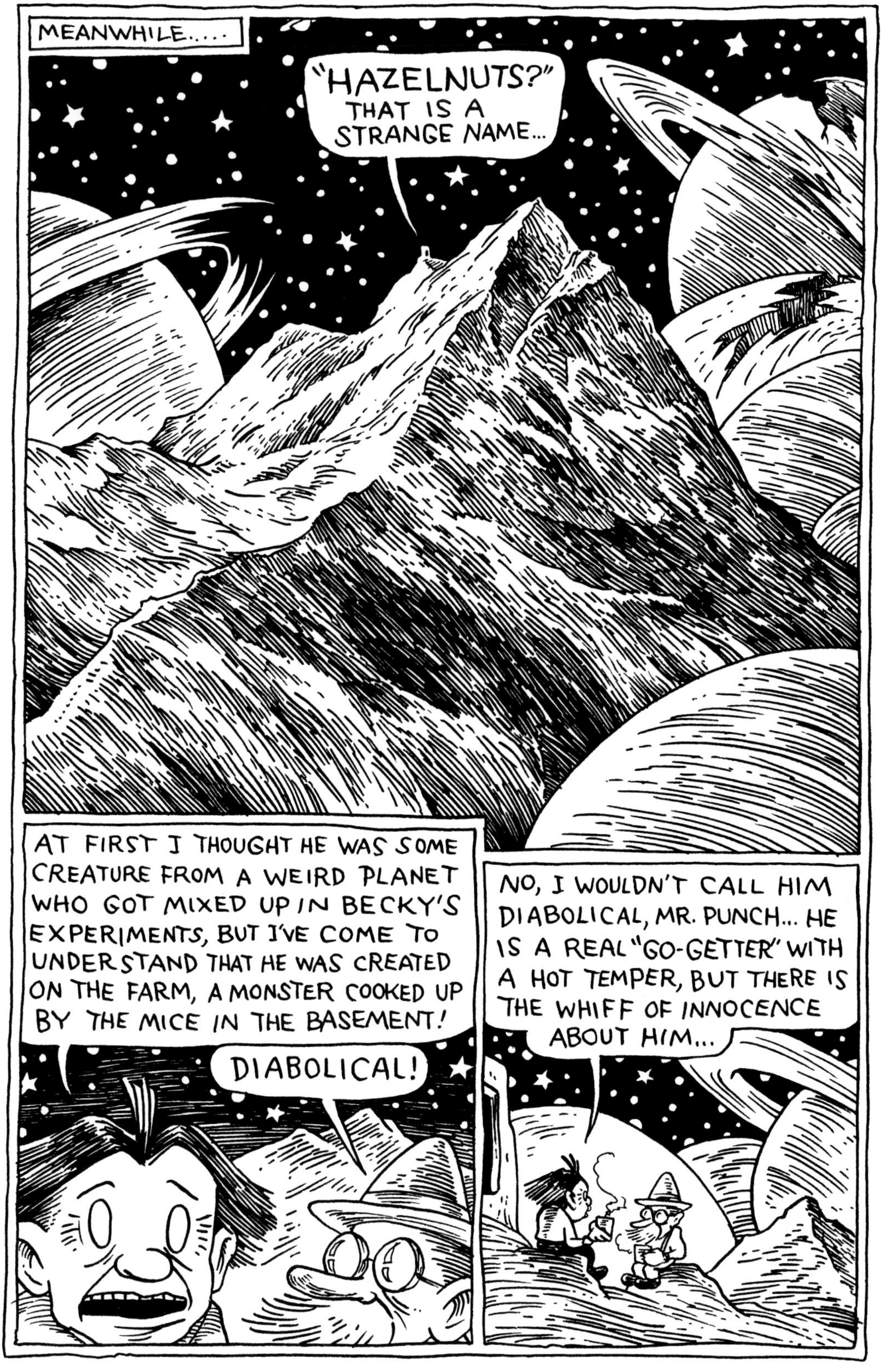
MEANWHILE.....
"HAZELNUTS?" THAT IS A STRANGE NAME...
AT FIRST I THOUGHT HE WAS SOME CREATURE FROM A WEIRD PLANET WHO GOT MIXED UP IN BECKY'S EXPERIMENTS, BUT I'VE COME TO UNDERSTAND THAT HE WAS CREATED ON THE FARM, A MONSTER COOKED UP BY THE MICE IN THE BASEMENT!
DIABOLICAL!
NO, I WOULDN'T CALL HIM DIABOLICAL, MR. PUNCH... HE IS A REAL "GO-GETTER" WITH A HOT TEMPER, BUT THERE IS THE WHIFF OF INNOCENCE ABOUT HIM...

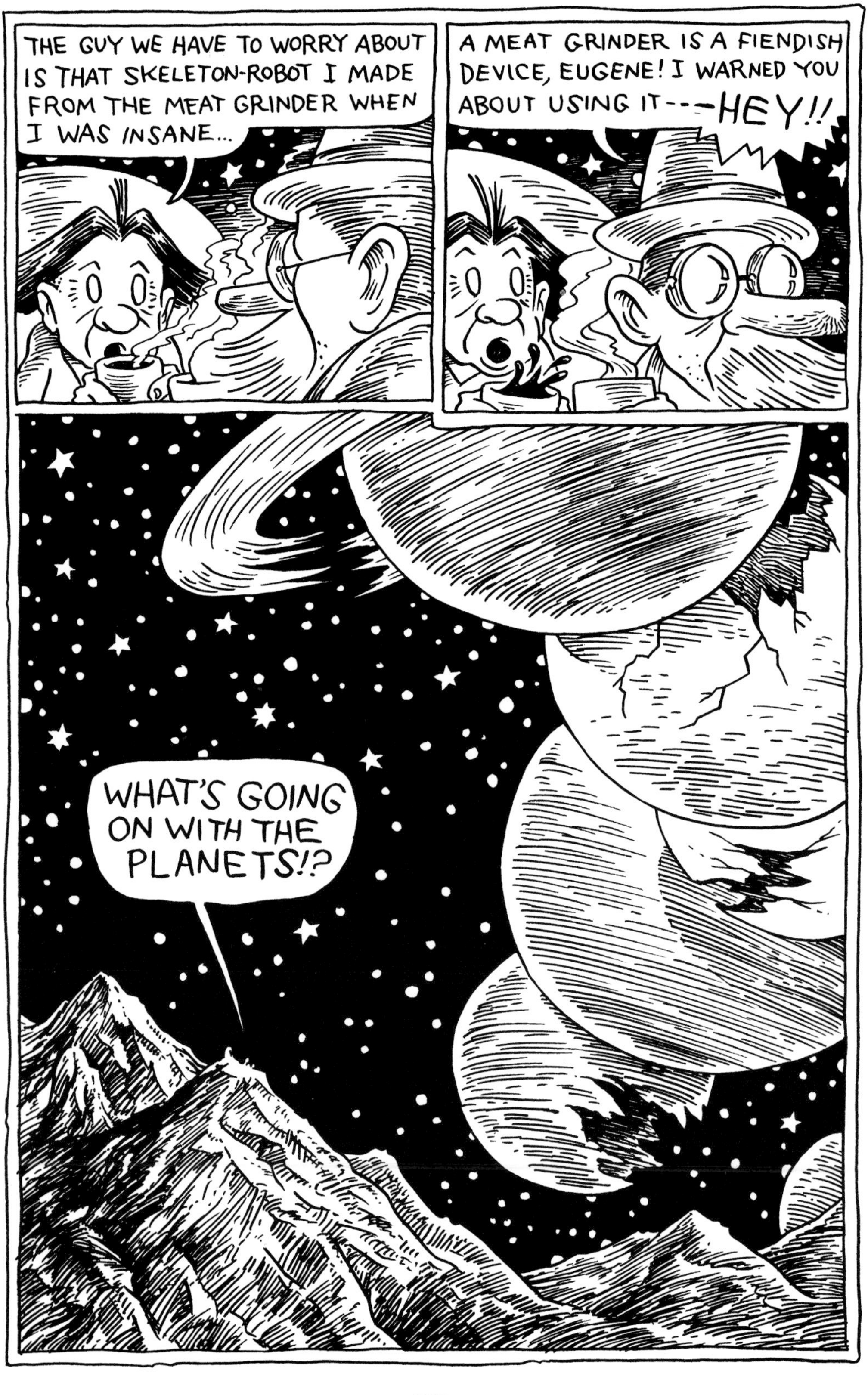
THE GUY WE HAVE TO WORRY ABOUT IS THAT SKELETON-ROBOT I MADE FROM THE MEAT GRINDER WHEN I WAS INSANE...
A MEAT GRINDER IS A FIENDISH DEVICE, EUGENE! I WARNED YOU ABOUT USING IT---HEY!!
WHAT'S GOING ON WITH THE PLANETS!?

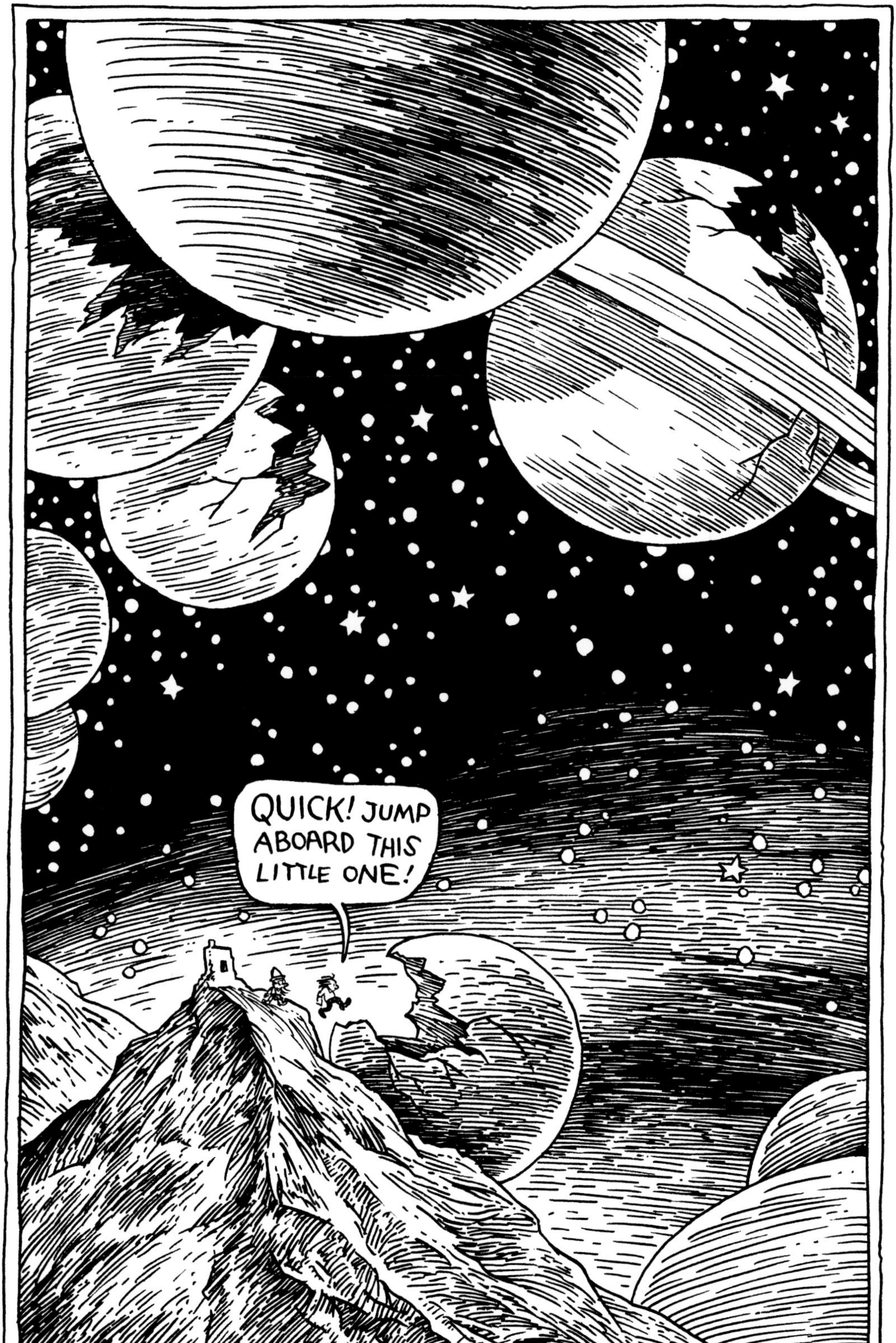
QUICK! JUMP ABOARD THIS LITTLE ONE!

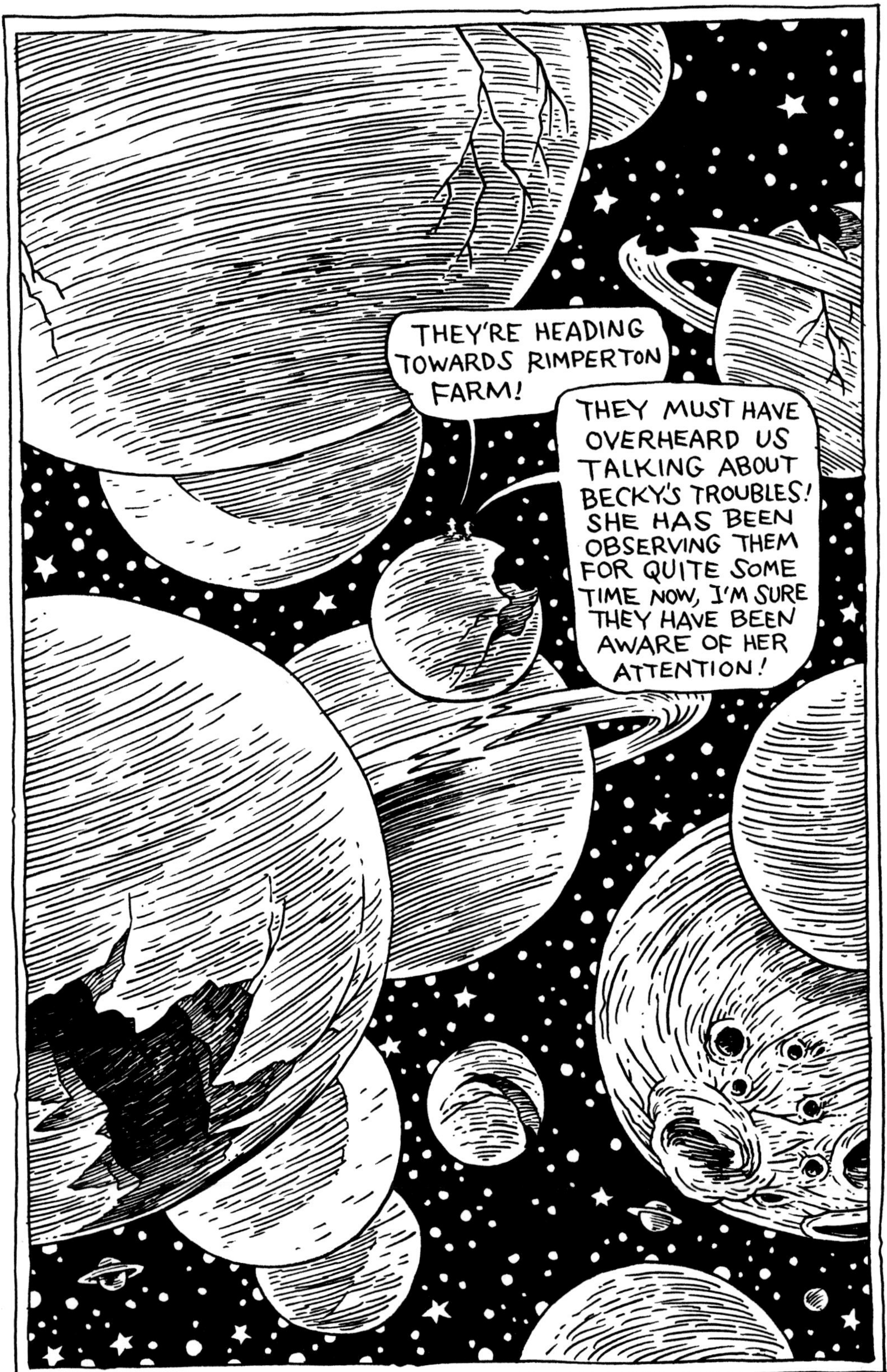
THEY'RE HEADING TOWARDS RIMPERTON FARM!
THEY MUST HAVE OVERHEARD US TALKING ABOUT BECKY'S TROUBLES! SHE HAS BEEN OBSERVING THEM FOR QUITE SOME TIME NOW, I'M SURE THEY HAVE BEEN AWARE OF HER ATTENTION!

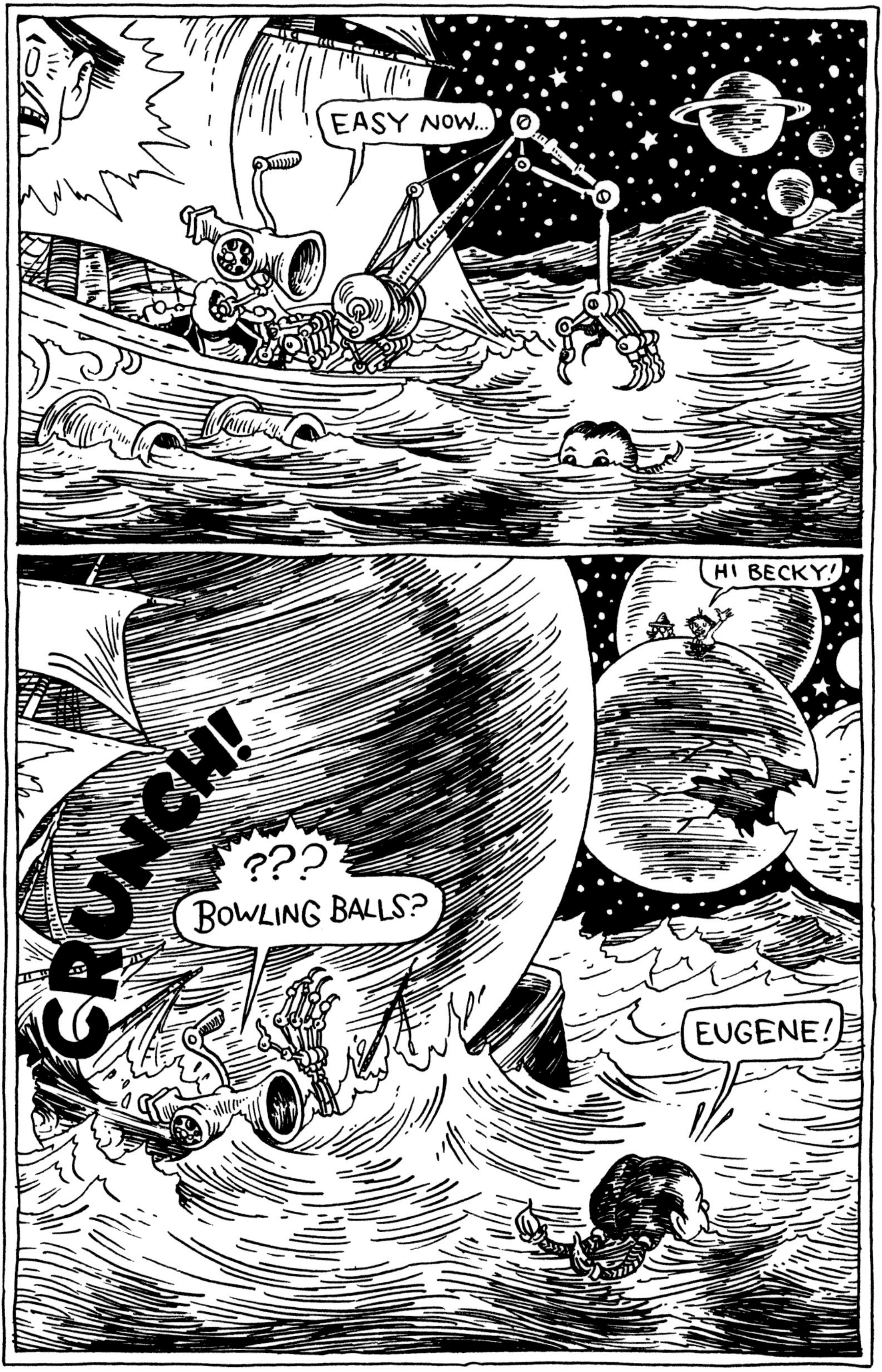
EASY NOW...
HI BECKY!
CRUNCH!
???
BOWLING BALLS?
EUGENE!

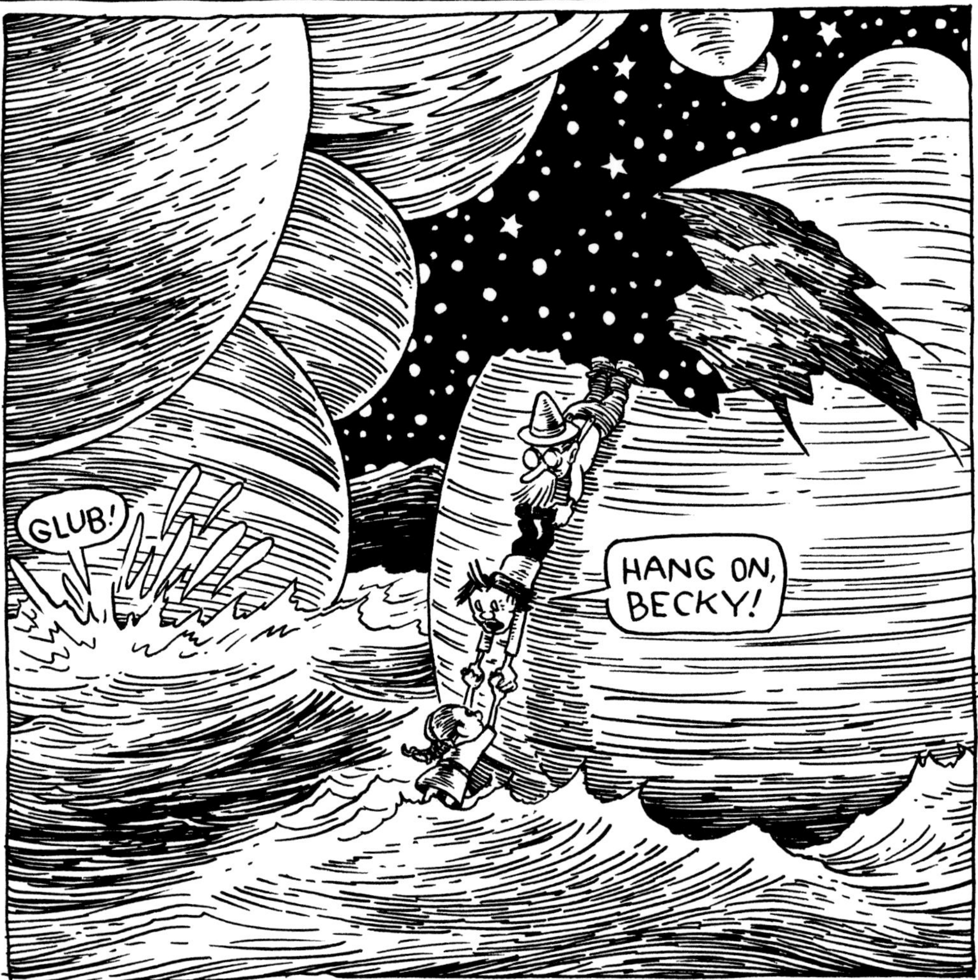
GLUB!
HANG ON, BECKY!

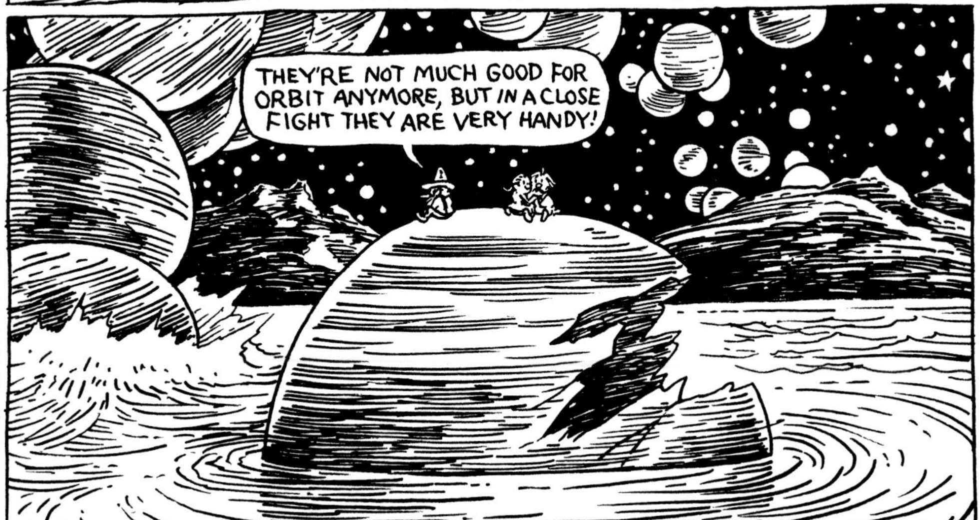
THEY'RE NOT MUCH GOOD FOR ORBIT ANYMORE, BUT IN A CLOSE FIGHT THEY ARE VERY HANDY!

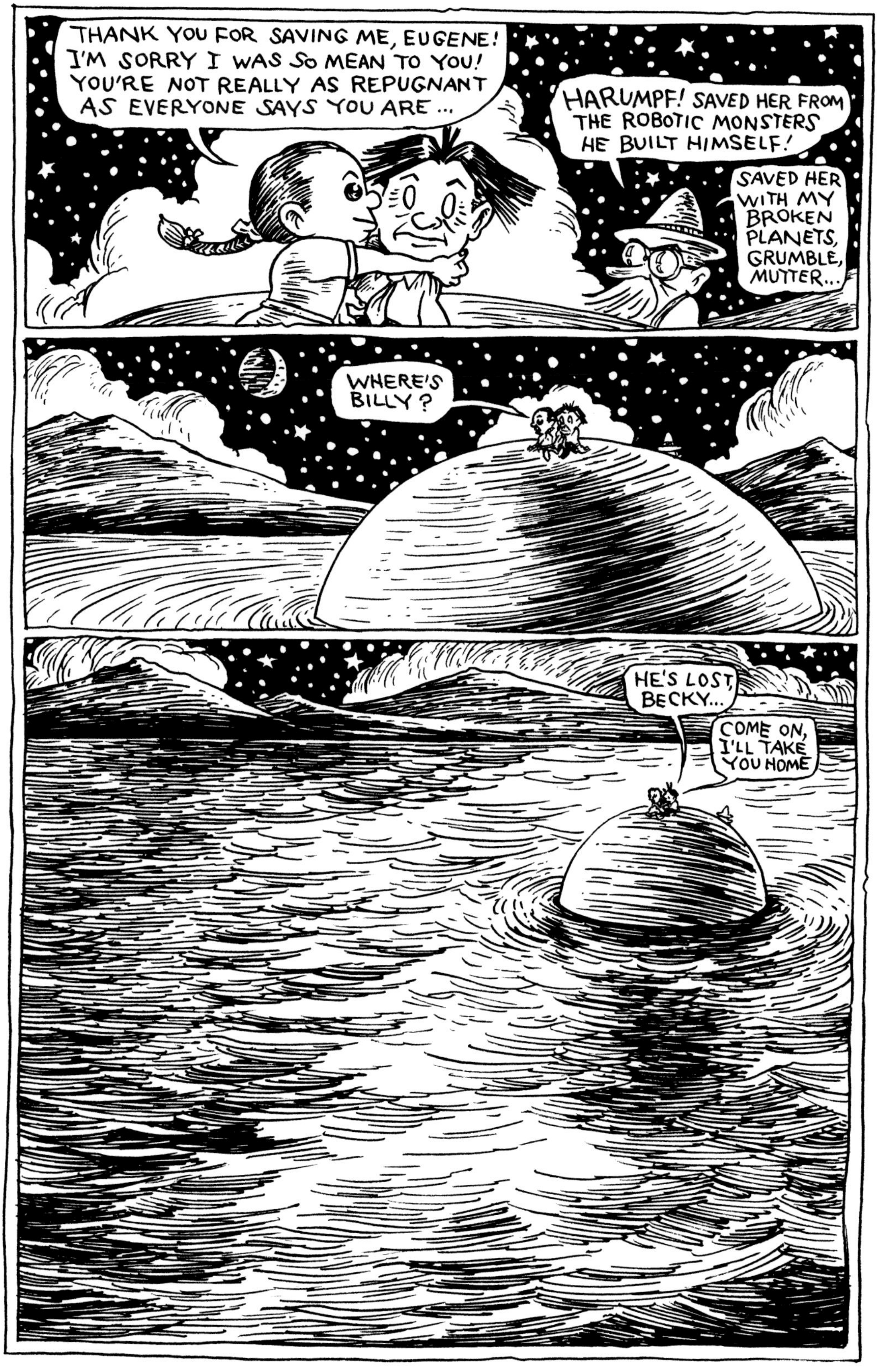
THANK YOU FOR SAVING ME, EUGENE! I'M SORRY I WAS SO MEAN TO YOU! YOU'RE NOT REALLY AS REPUGNANT AS EVERYONE SAYS YOU ARE ...
HARUMPF! SAVED HER FROM THE ROBOTIC MONSTERS HE BUILT HIMSELF!
SAVED HER WITH MY BROKEN PLANETS, GRUMBLE, MUTTER...
WHERE'S BILLY?
HE'S LOST, BECKY...
COME ON, I'LL TAKE YOU HOME

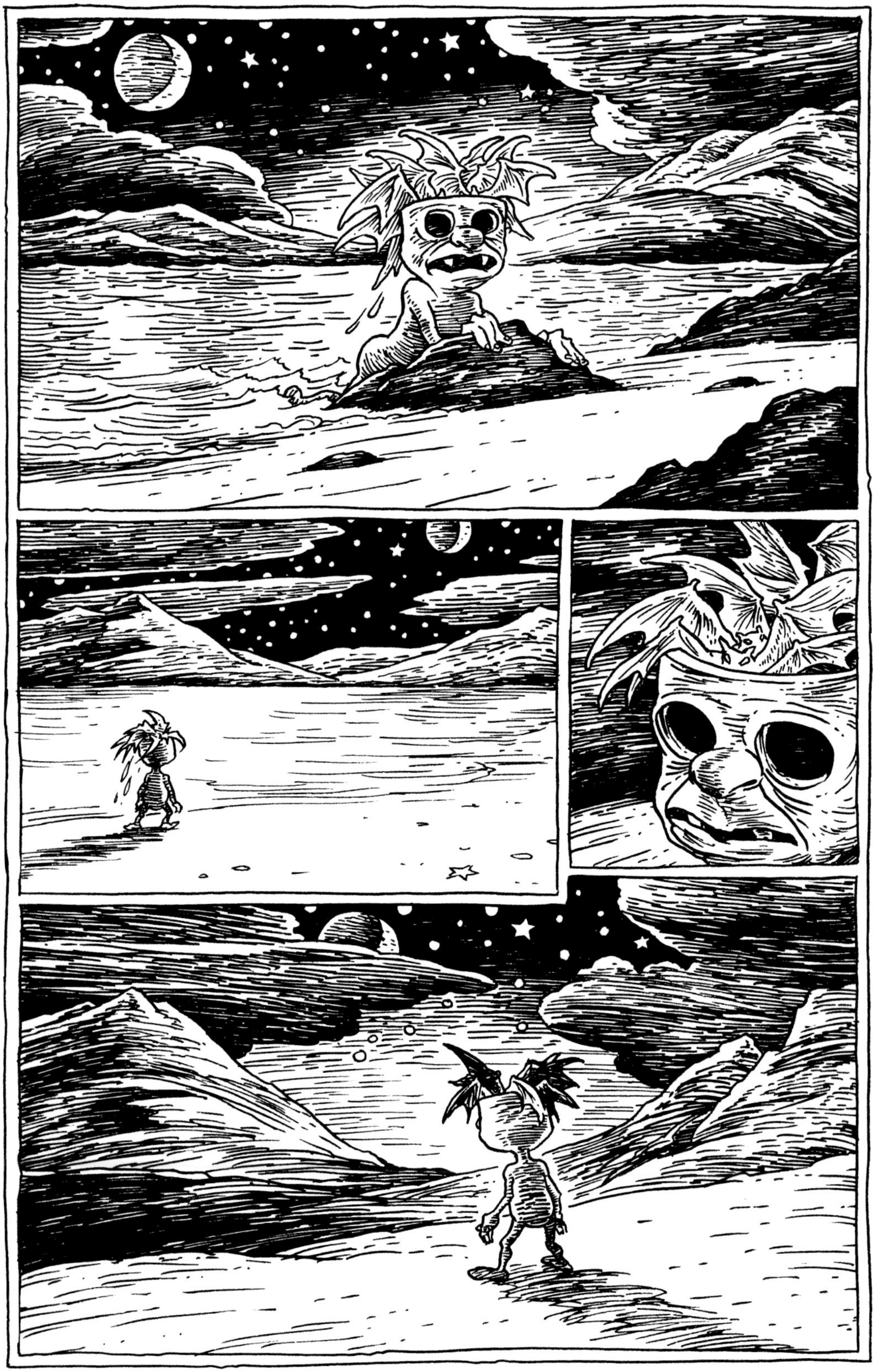

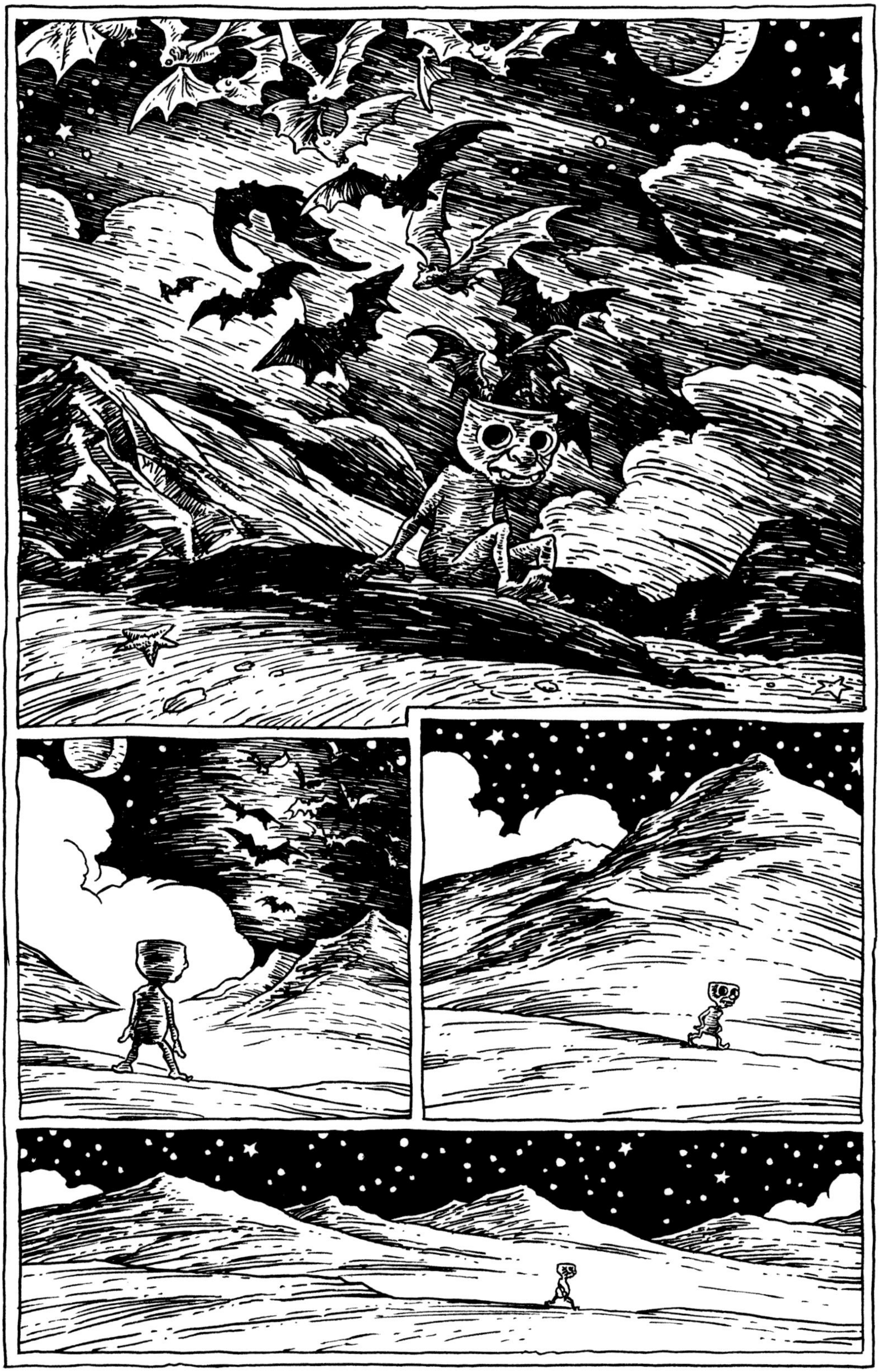

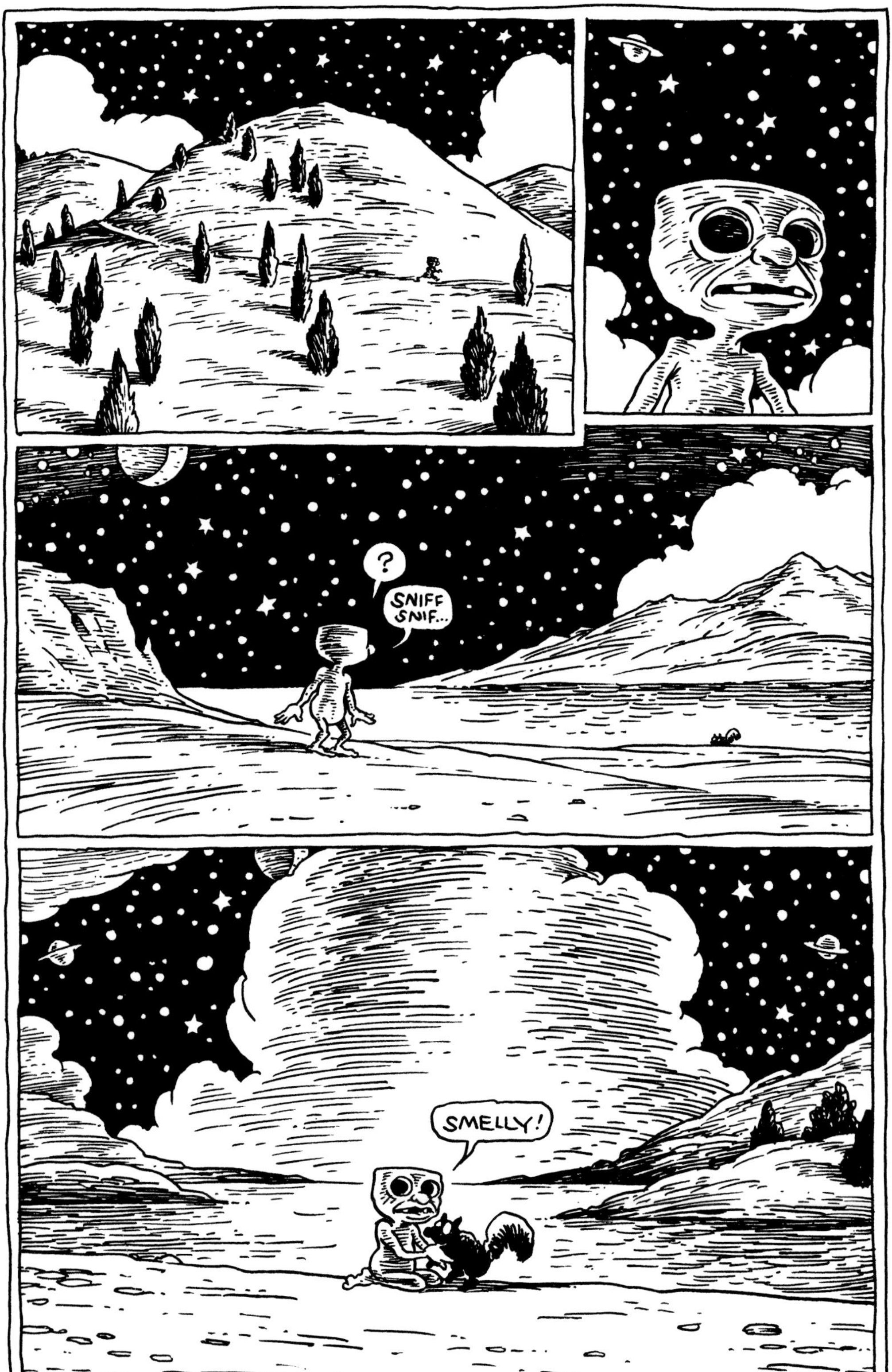
?
SNIFF SNIF...
SMELLY!

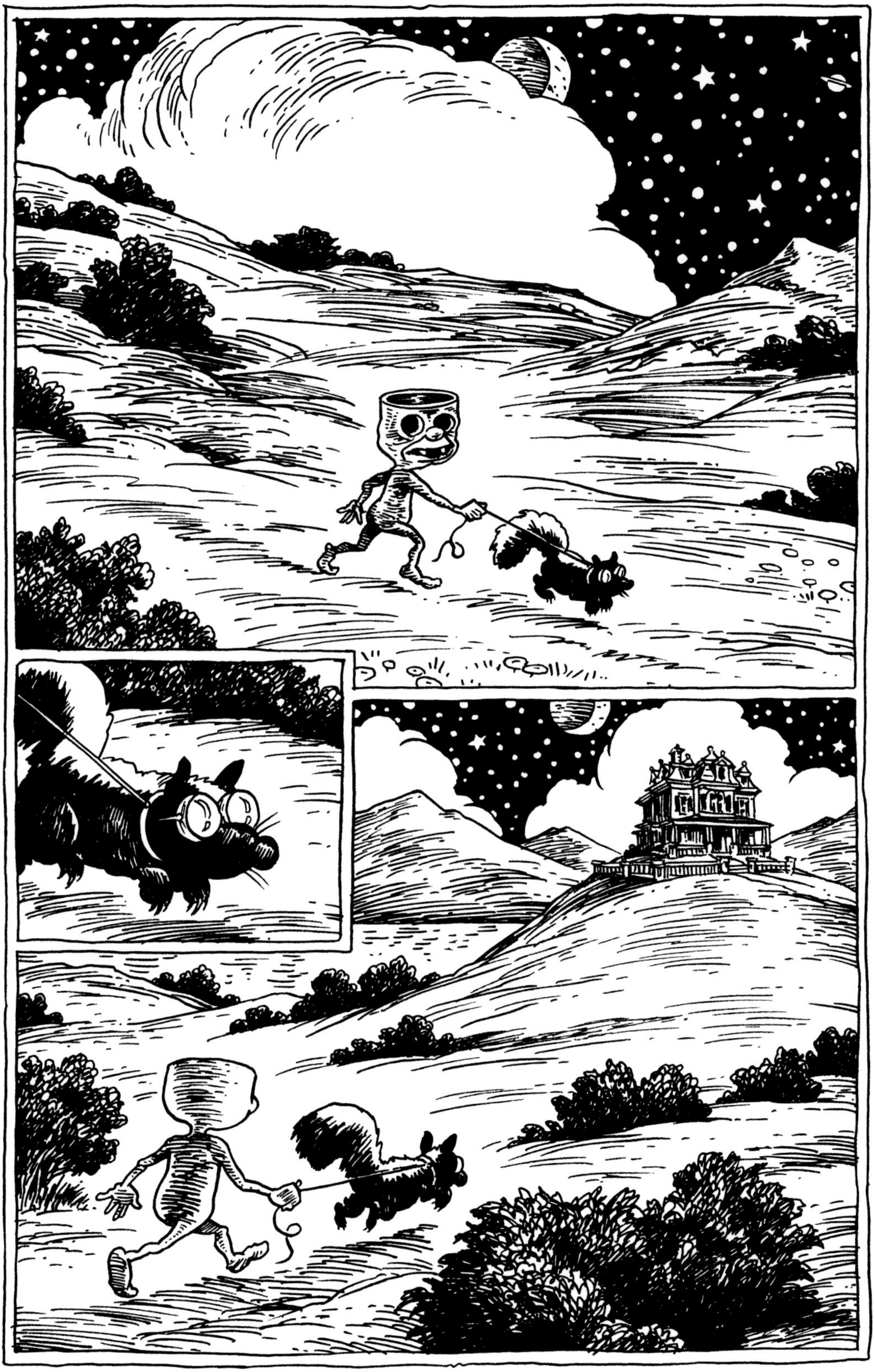

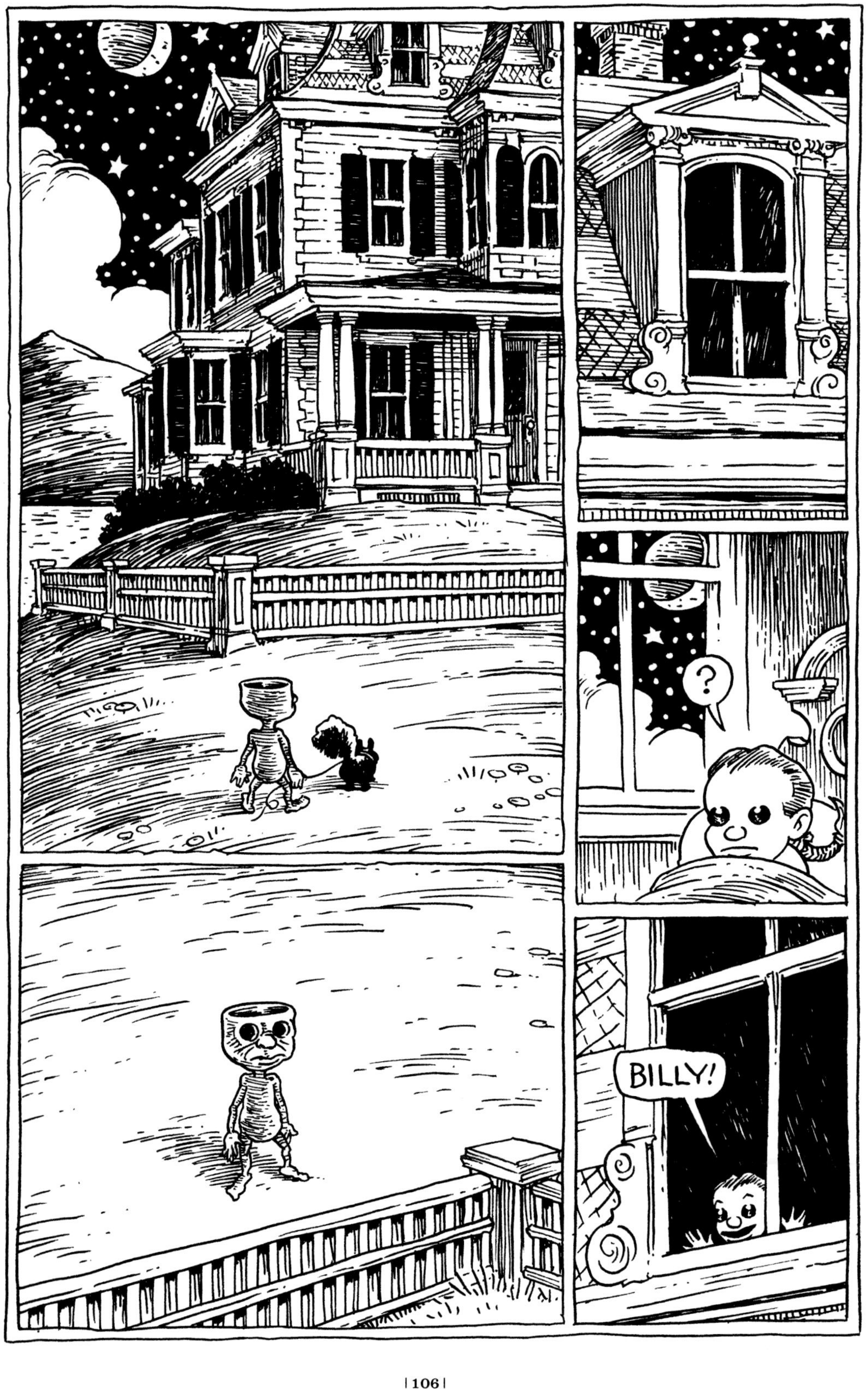
?
BILLY!

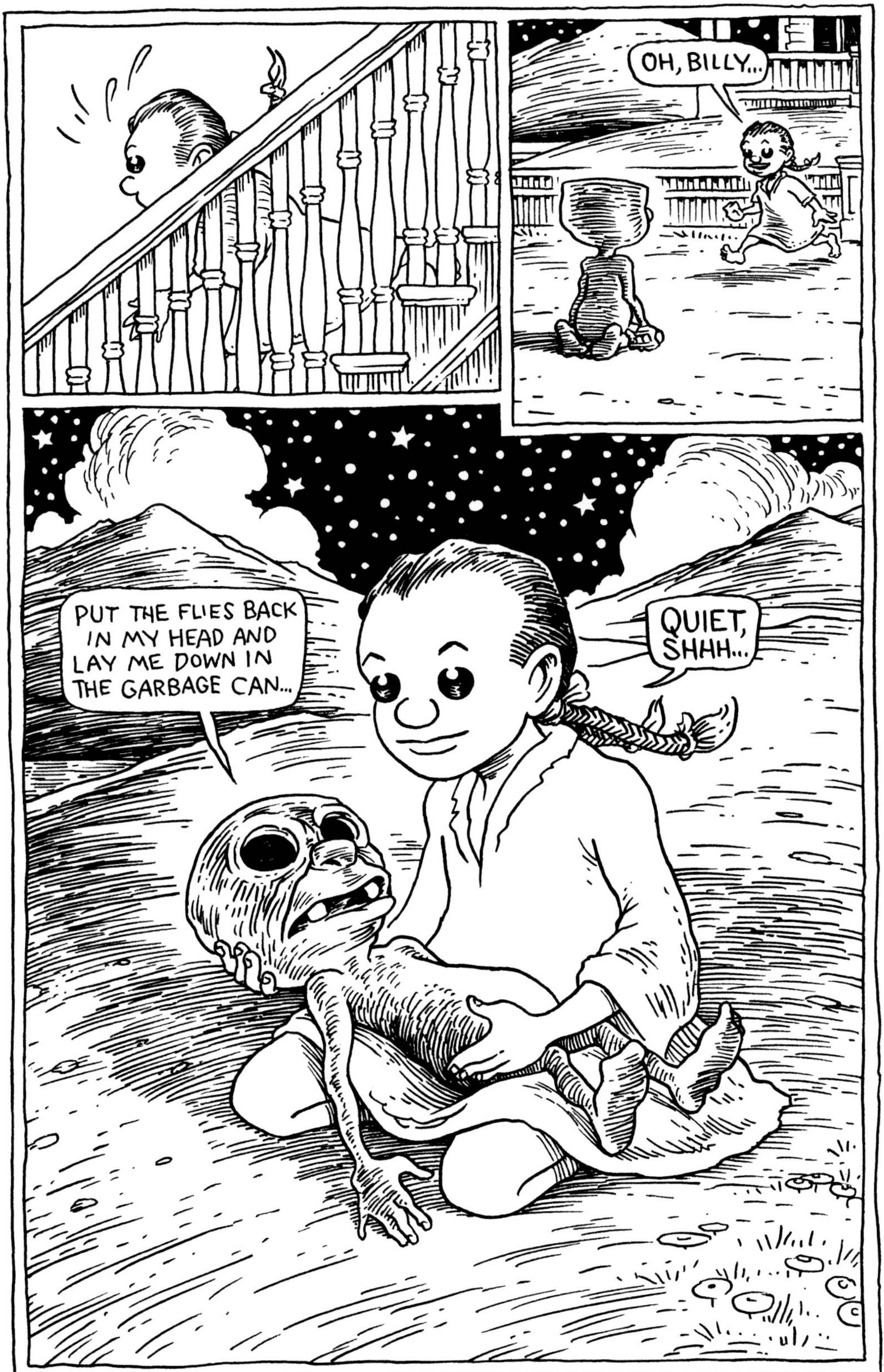
OH, BILLY...
PUT THE FLIES BACK IN MY HEAD AND LAY ME DOWN IN THE GARBAGE CAN...
QUIET, SHHH...

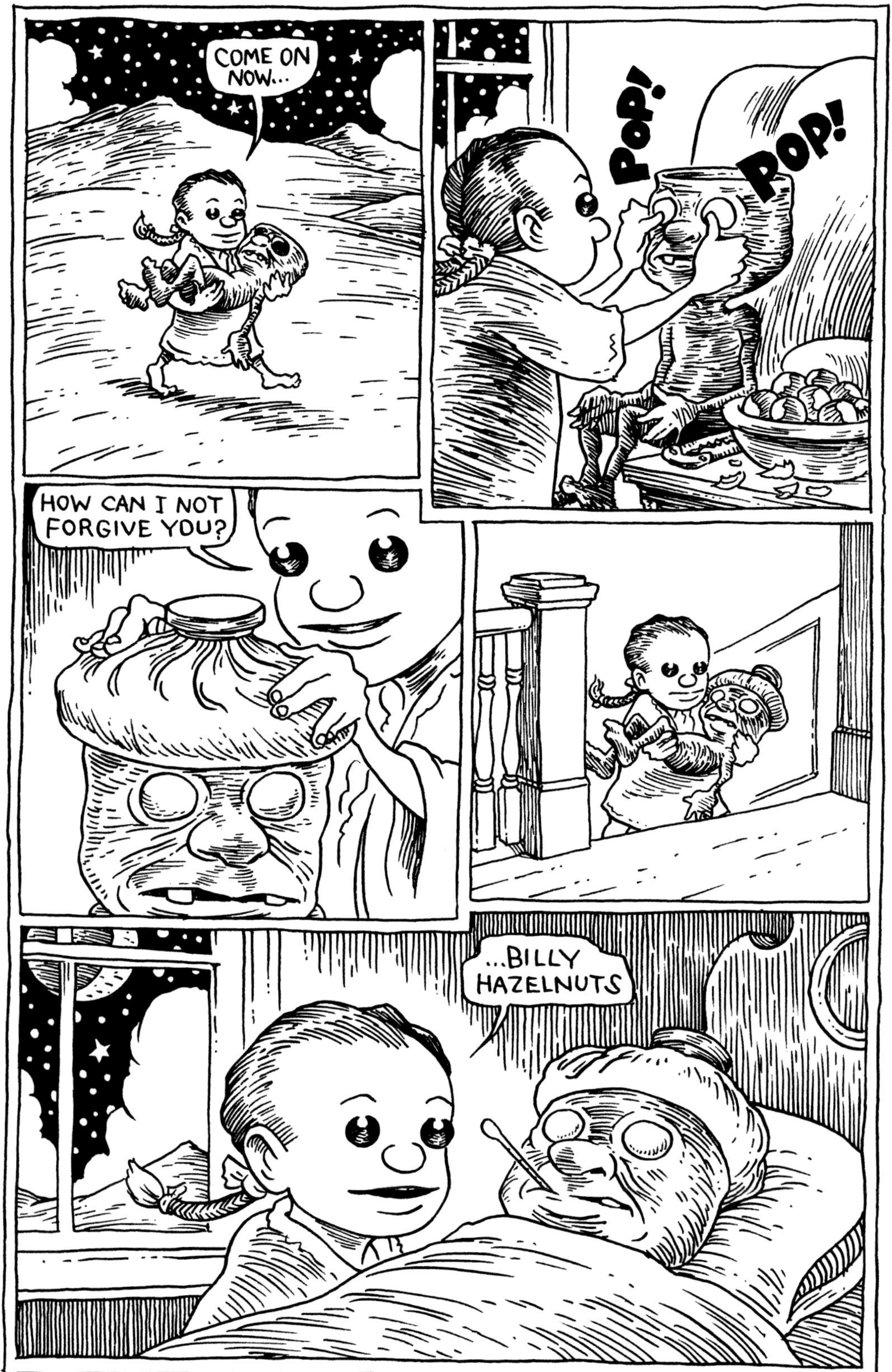
COME ON NOW...
POP!
POP!
HOW CAN I NOT FORGIVE YOU?
...BILLY HAZELNUTS

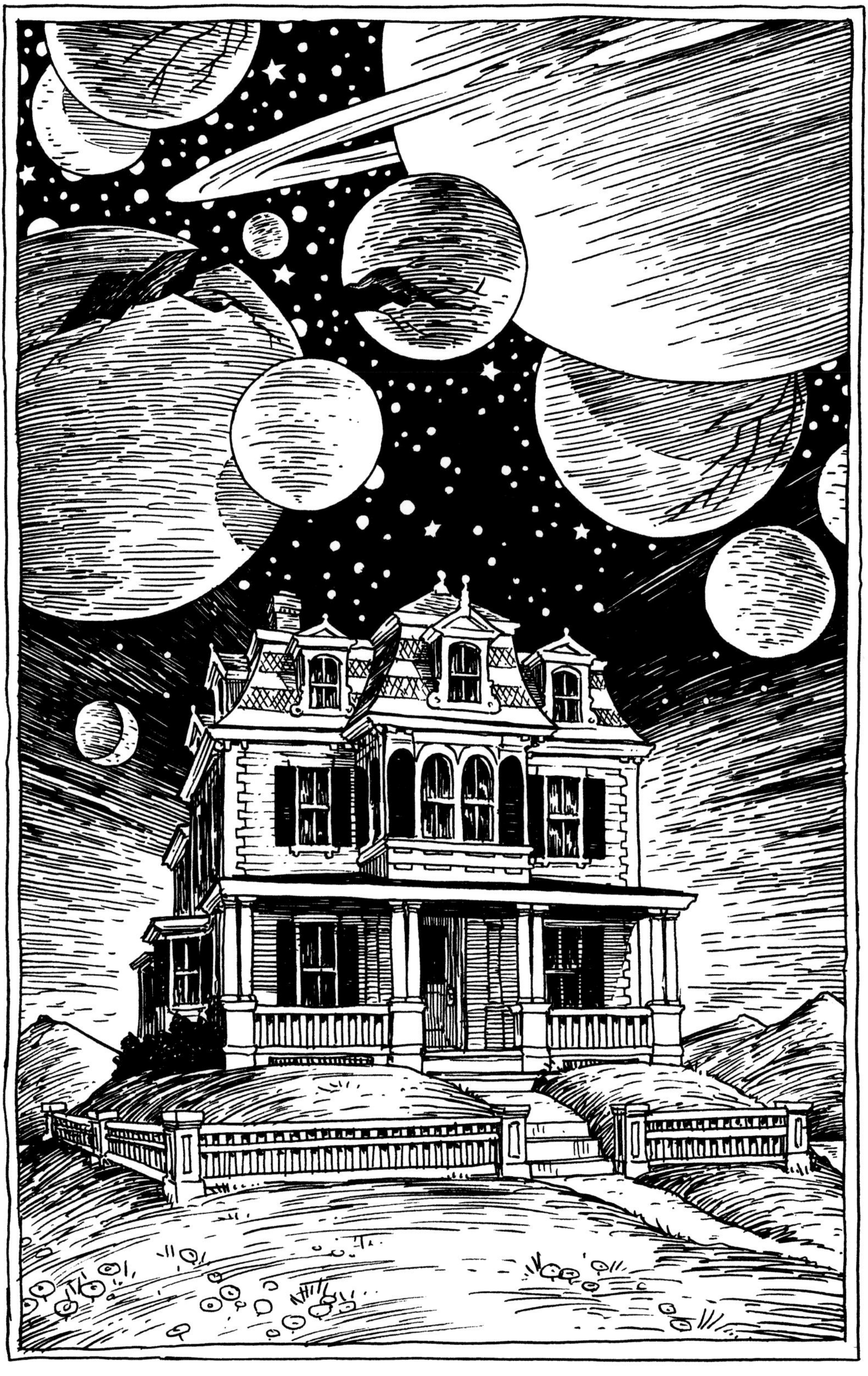

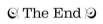 The End